MW01193953

i

Hope on
Distant Shores

*How Awakened Men Can Escape
the Anglosphere's Toxic Women,
Sexual False Consciousness and
Institutional Misandry*

Dr Rookh Kshatriya

Contents

Foreword

When I started my 'Anglobitch' blog ten years ago, it was my intention to create waves and cast shadows across the Internet. I knew my key insight – that Anglo-American culture's mistrust of male sexual freedom had created an especially misandrist, belligerent form of feminism – was entirely correct, and needed disseminating. Far from being 'revolutionary', as conservative Men's Rights Activists believe, Anglo-American feminism springs right from the frigid heart of Anglo-American civilization. This explains the unstinting support feminism receives from the state in all Anglo-Saxon countries, and why all attempts to resist it have proved so utterly futile. There never was a 'golden age' of gender relations in the Anglosphere; the puritanical Anglo-Saxon cultural bloc has been pedestalizing women and vilifying men for centuries.

When I began my blog, it was always my hope that thinking men in the different Anglo-Saxon nations would interpret my core concepts in their own way, and that other writers would develop them in new and interesting directions. Now, this dream has come to pass. As seeds are scattered by the wind to birth new forests, new scholars and writers have begun to develop a coherent online movement derived from my ideas.

Foremost among these is the New Modern Man, an American blogger who has thrown off the misandrist shackles of American society for a new life in the Caribbean. Since most of my readers are based in North America, the national specificity of the NMM's articles will be close to their hearts. He moves beyond my own strictly theoretical approach, offering life-coaching for Anglo males who really want that new life of true sexual freedom abroad. Yes, we all know the Anglosphere sucks for men but what do we do about it?

My first book 'Havok' (2009) focused on the condition of gender-relations in the contemporary Anglosphere. My conclusions – which have since taken root all over the English-speaking world, were that residual Puritanism has imbalanced gender-relations in favour of women, reducing Anglo-American males to disposable stooges, walking ATM machines and vilified deviants. Meanwhile the same secular Puritanism has, by sacralising sex as an elusive commodity, set Anglo-American women atop pedestals as exalted goddesses. Despite claiming to be a 'revolutionary' movement, Anglo-American feminism is in fact an extension – indeed, *amplification* of – existing values: Anglo feminism is sex-negative, misandrist and racist, just like Anglo-American society.

Further, feminism now serves as a smoke screen to disguise the real problems afflicting Anglo-American civilization – namely, socio-economic inequality, corrupt governance and racist policing. Thanks to feminism, rich hetero white girls like Emma Watson can proclaim themselves 'oppressed' and 'disenfranchised', making a mockery of valid protest movements such as Black Lives Matter. Additionally, the Anglo-feminist narrative which presents white women as oppressed outsiders also serves to mask white women's endemic racism and long-standing affiliation to the Anglo-American establishment. Not only is sex-negative Anglo feminism an exaggerated expression of Anglo-American values, it helps to *insulate* those values from positive reform.

In this view, conventional MRAs who invoke 'tradition' against Anglo-Saxon feminism are completely deluded: for Anglo feminism springs straight from the Anglosphere's repressive, puritan soul. Indeed, it will be noted that conservative MRAs have achieved precisely nothing in their 30-odd years of existence. Similarly, the MGTOW (Men Going Their Own Way) movement, which advises males to shun marriage, sex and relationships, is just as toothless, albeit for different reasons. First of these is the obvious fact that attractive women in the Anglosphere are happy to eliminate low-status MGTOW males from their lives; being practitioners of 'hyper-hypergamy', such girls are only interested in high status males anyway. Secondly, embracing monkish celibacy merely reflects the puritanical values which already permeate the Anglosphere. Similarly, the PUA or Pick-up Artist community are merely playing a game they can never win. The puritanical reality of the Anglosphere renders their various 'approach' techniques moribund at best and potentially dangerous for men in the #metoo era.

The movement that emerged from my first book is best called pan-Anglosphere Dissidence: the systematic rejection of repressive Anglo-American values. This rejection is associated with a yearning for the relative sexual freedom waiting outside the Anglosphere. Pan-Anglosphere dissidents view 'accepting' Anglo-American men as

2

deluded weaklings, pretending to enjoy high quality sex with multiple partners but usually miserable celibates. Pan-Anglosphere Dissidence is predictably strongest in the puritanical United States, with its entitled women, institutionalized misandry and fanatic aversion to prostitution. The US is also the global stronghold of sex-negative feminism.

This book builds on those insights, all of which are taken as given, eternal truths beyond doubt or question. It offers lifestyle guidance to the following groups:

- Men tired of entitled, selfish Anglo women
- Men wanting a better, more fulfilled life on foreign shores
- Men who do not want to 'adjust' to a culture which views them as third class citizens
- Men who do not wish to squander their hard-earned dollars on derisive strippers or punitive divorce settlements
- Men who want slim, warm, attractive women undamaged by sex-negative, misandrist Anglo feminism

Unlike my first book, Foreign Shores contains only a few references from 'canonical' historians, economists or philosophers. Like Saint Paul or the Buddha, I am fashioning something completely new and a completely new conceptual vocabulary is necessary to contain it. Instead, most of my references will be taken from the extensive correspondence to my blog which began in early 2018. These varied correspondents included practising attorneys, a former corrections officer and even a professor of law. Having no legal knowledge, I found this burgeoning commentary a genuine revelation. A theme that gradually emerged was the link between Anglo-Saxon common law and the punitive judgments handed out to men by Anglosphere courts and judges. However, there was also a lot of practical advice from very ordinary Anglo-American men who found love and happiness outside the Anglosphere. Here is a quote from Gearman, an American expatriate who demonstrates a perfect understanding of my arguments and their practical potential:

The difference on this site and with this thesis, is that Rookh and the commenters here actually provide a concrete solution that's practical and can be realized by men in the real world. Yes, a lot of MGTOW's will be fine with just celibacy and Internet porn, but many MGTOW's still want to have emotional and physical relationships with women, and to start families. It's just in the Anglosphere, for good reason, they see no solution. Rookh and the many informed expats here provide the solution—moving out of the Anglosphere—and ways to practically accomplish it (Appendix I4, p.261).

All the postings of these experienced and learned correspondents, some of them containing over twenty thousand words, are included in a remarkable series of appendices which will doubtless be cited and studied by awakened men for decades to come.

Rookh Kshatriya, 2019

Part One

Is the Anglosphere Really Puritanical?

The Repressive Backdrop to the Misandrist & Gynocratic Agendas across the Anglosphere

1.0 Introduction

The Calvinist puritan spirit which infected the Anglo-Saxon world in the Sixteenth and Seventeenth centuries has defined the Anglosphere nations ever since. This is especially true of the United States, which was actually founded by English puritans (namely the Pilgrim Fathers). Although its original religious inspiration has withered, Anglo Puritanism has become a secular entity which exalts women as passive 'owners' of sex while vilifying men for being active sexual beings. Anglo feminism has craftily retained this puritanical agenda while discarding the theology which spawned it. While Anglo popular culture has honed a gestural celebration of sex, this rarely extends to the real world. By contrast, the idealization of a mythical 'sexless' childhood found in Disney movies, the generic distrust of men in the 'conservative' Anglo media or the Anglosphere's sickly homosociality remain a potent aspect of Anglo-American experience. Only a few days ago a young white girl honoured my London Tube train with her hallowed presence. Perhaps seventeen, her demeanour of was one of utter arrogance and chilling coldness: the Anglobitch archetype made flesh before our very eyes.

The following essays in this section elaborate on this theme in various ways, demonstrating beyond doubt that the Anglosphere nations are indeed defined by Puritanism, albeit of a secular and gynocentric kind which sacralises women as sexual deities.

1.1 The Prostitution Ban

When writing a book like this, it makes sense to start with first principals. This is why I starting with the Anglo-American prostitution ban, the issue which touches every aspect of my thesis.

Anglo-Saxon countries are not the only ones with bans on prostitution; but their antagonism towards the oldest profession is extreme and definitive. Moreover, the contemporary Anglosphere is now largely secular, unlike most places with similar prostitution bans. Moreover, prostitution carries a strong informal stigma in the Anglosphere, as if it were on a level with paedophilia or bestiality.

This antagonism ultimately springs from the Anglosphere's puritanical legacy. Not only did this leave a distinctive stamp on Britain and the Commonwealth, the United States was actually founded by puritan fanatics. Hatred of physical pleasure and the sensual world persists in the Anglosphere because of this distinct heritage, although its religious component has long since vanished. Aversion to prostitution is the ultimate expression of this Calvinist fixation, and the secular Puritanism which is its contemporary manifestation.

And now it becomes plain why Anglo-American feminism – indeed, Anglo-American women – are so misandrist, sex-negative and hyper-hypergamous. Simply put, a repressed culture inevitably exalts them as 'owners' and 'dispensers' of sexual congress. It also explains the informal misandry of all the Anglosphere nations, since Puritanism reflexively stigmatizes male sexuality as predatory and debased. This also explains the close alignment between Anglo-American feminism and sex-negative temperance movements, especially those based in England and the United States.

Legalizing prostitution in any given society has a crucial effect on the female psyche, instantly dissolving the sexual arrogance and entitlement which defines Anglo-American women. Simply put, the pervasive knowledge that any man can buy a prostitute's time without legal repercussions, pound her body into submission without emotional obligation and leave without guilt quite simply terrifies them. Prostitution strips gender relations down to their bare essentials – a fee is paid by the male to sink his rigid penis up the female's vagina, and copulate with her until he ejaculates. Then he can leave without guilt or regret. If she falls pregnant and loses her sight to diabetes, so be it; he has not paid to pair bond with her, just to fuck her.

If every male were free to slake his sexual needs in this way, it would corrode the inherent status enjoyed by every female living in the repressive Anglosphere. Indeed, much of Anglo-American media culture – which one might compare to a pearl carefully cultivated to hide the grit of raw sex – would implode. Teen romances, anodyne pop music, the wedding fixation and Mills and Boon fantasies – the whole Anglo-American culture of romance would instantly collapse, crushed by the brutal reality of heterosexual gender relations. More important to women, the pedestals of existential and moral privilege they currently occupy would be snatched from under their feet. They would no longer be able to practice hyper-hypergamy, the exclusive pursuit of 'fantasy males' from film and fiction. The sexual manipulation of males via the costly rituals of romance would also be at an end.

The arguments wheeled out against prostitution invariably depend on spurious 'trafficking' data, or pertain to obscure third world countries. That such specious arguments are given airtime in the 'lamestream' media is best explained by the gynocentric and puritanical nature of the Anglosphere countries; simply put, women can do no wrong and must never be offended. For example, feminists invariably obsess over street prostitution when real research indicates it now represents only a tiny minority of paid sexual transactions. Moreover, extensive research by the British police demonstrates that 'trafficking' is largely a myth – most British prostitutes are native born and it appears that women who migrate to Britain to find work as prostitutes typically do so of their own volition (Davies, 2009).

Above all, its anti-prostitution fixation shows the true nature of Anglo-American feminism. It is the modern expression of traditional Anglo-Saxon prudery, not a repudiation of it. Most of its values would satisfy Victorian moralists or seventeenth century New Englanders, without any modification. Homosociality (obsessive gender segregation), racism, elitism and a zealous fixation on 'education' can all join repression in the factors uniting modern feminism with traditional Anglo-Saxon values. One of my correspondents, North Wind, writes:

Yes, there is a good deal of foolish PC, feminism and maddening short-sighted policy and culture infecting the non-Anglosphere nations of the West, too. But the vulture-like and predatory style of divorce, the rent seeking and extreme high risk to men's finances, well being and very freedom, is unique to the Anglosphere and especially the United States and Canada, where destitution and prison terms face even high-earning divorced men. There's a ton of good articles on why this is, and you've cited many of them. But the heart of it is the combination of legal precedent in Anglo common-law, plus lingering cultural precedents like Puritanism and the extreme cuck-ish nature of Anglo chivalry, have been absolutely toxic and suicidal for the Anglosphere when joined at the hip to feminism and cultural Marxism (Appendix A, p.220).

Another feminist motivation for the prostitution ban is the social exclusion of males of low sexual market value. By denying such males ready access to paid sexual encounters, feminists seek to eliminate these pariahs altogether. Again, such 'sexual fascism' can be traced to traditional Anglo-Saxon elitism and its reflexive animus against low status individuals. Since the Anglosphere is hyper-gynocentric, this animus is rarely directed against women; men invariably bear the brunt of it. The thought that low-SMV males might have normal human needs never troubles the feminist mind; such males are mere *untermenschen*, and do not deserve physical pleasure. Odd how the same feminists seldom rail against the womanizing nature of handsome male celebrities or 'chads' in general; sexual elitism is alive and well in the feminist enclave. Ultimately, this facet of feminist thought is driven by the hyper-hypergamy that prevails in repressive societies. By instinct, women despise low-status men, hardly considering them human; but the gynocentric Anglosphere has institutionalized this sexual fascism with its prostitution ban.

Apart from a few toleration zones in Britain and North America, the northern Anglosphere countries harbour deep hatred of paid sex acts. As we have seen, this not only expresses the Anglo world's secular

Puritanism: it also anchors these countries in gynocentric feminism while marginalizing the sexual needs of low status men. This has resulted in an explosion of male 'incels', sexually disenfranchised men with no stake in the world and nothing to lose. The Anglosphere future holds declining trust values, more crime and violence, more armed rampages – and of course, ever more coercion of male 'pathologies' using Internet watchlists, Prozac, Ritalin, 'education' and 'counselling'. And so the anti-male spiral will continue until all low status males are drugged, incarcerated or dead.

If I did not know better, I would say someone out there had it all planned.

1.2 The Wars on Pleasure

The pan-Anglosphere ban on prostitution is but part of a general war on pleasure. Anglo-American civilization seems to take issue with sensual self-fulfilment of every kind, as we shall see. This hostility encompasses simple pleasures such as nicotine, alcohol or coffee, and was often imposed on other cultures as part of the Anglo colonial project; as is well known, the English invasion of India involved the puritanical defacement of erotic statues and artworks in Hindu temples and other holy places. However, the rise of sex-negative misandrist feminism has seen a redoubled attempt by the Anglosphere authorities to extend its wars on pleasure into foreign lands.

In Part Two, we shall see how misandrist Anglo feminism seeks to remake traditional gender relations in traditional cultures via military intervention and cultural subversion. Although they are primarily directed against Anglo-American citizens, the wars on pleasure form a powerful adjunct to this cultural imperialism.

Sex tourism has become a recent target for the Anglo-feminist puritans, with 'Cuba Dave' Strecker being selected as their sacrificial lamb. Knowing the rapacious hypergamy of Anglo females meant no action for a humble carpenter like himself, Strecker preferred to roam the legal brothels of South America, banging warm and willing whores to his heart's content (Krumholtz, 2016). Surely a preferable lifestyle to the perma-celibacy he would have doubtless experienced in the States; also, whoring doubtless provided a better life for the girls than forced marriage to a local Pedro. And Strecker can't have done much harm to the South American economy, either.

But Cuba Dave's happy days came to an abrupt end in 2015 when a controversial Hillary Clinton-inspired 'anti-trafficking' law was brought into play. In no time Dave found himself serving a five-year prison term in a Costa Rican jail for 'promoting sex tourism' (posting a few pictures of nubile hookers on Facebook). Fortunately a local attorney took up his case free of charge and, the 'case' against him being the usual Anglo-feminist tissue of lies, he was acquitted in August 2017 (Rico, 2017).

Cuba Dave's case offers a robust answer to the feminist question: why won't MGTOWs or gender dissidents just 'go their own way'? Simple: because feminists won't let them. The Anglo-Feminist Matrix led by vicious harridans like Hillary Clinton and Emma Watson is on a global crusade to prevent men glimpsing – and experiencing – the sexual wonders of foreign lands. What they want is millions of sexually disenfranchised Anglo males begging pussy from insolent land whales and toiling for that dubious privilege. Or trapped in Sexual False Consciousness, pretending they are banging models every night. Like the Bounty's Captain Bligh, the Anglosphere elite want its 'crew' pulling ropes on a harsh, joyless ship, not enjoying soft kisses on tropic shores. In sum, the last thing they want is men 'going their own way'.

The Clinton Crusade has two prongs. First, it wants to stifle the sexual freedom non-Anglosphere nations enjoy, in order to keep Anglo-American men in repressed servitude. Second, it wants to hide misandrist agendas at home (male school failure, depression, suicide) by focusing on gender-relations in Mozambique, or some other irrelevant issue.

Why are they doing this? Simple: it suits their economic interests. Men toiling away on the economic plantation are, like slaves, lucrative assets; and if they are trapped in economic servitude by marriage, divorce or children, so much the better. Slave owners in the Antebellum South were not going to free their slaves without a fight, just as slave traders in the British Isles were never going to give up their vile trade without financial compensation. Similarly, the Anglosphere cannot afford to let guys like Cuba Dave flee the Anglo-American plantation for Latin America's boundless sexual freedom because his example would inspire too many men with dreams of escape. No: they had to make an example of him, not unlike a hobbled slave in antebellum Alabama.

So it is quite obvious that feminists and their apologists don't really want men enjoying true sexual freedom, and are taking decisive legal steps to prevent it. That makes sense: the last thing they want is Anglo-American men shunning entitled land whales (like themselves) for no-strings sex with nubile foreign women. While Anglo-American feminists are always prattling about separatism and 'freedom from the patriarchy', we invariably find them in houses and cities built by men, using electricity and water provided by men, and ranting against the patriarchy on electronic devices created and devised by men. What they clearly want is to retain those aspects of 'patriarchy' they approve of (male slavery, marriage, the Pedestal) while offloading the rest (responsibility, genuine equality and male sexual freedom).

As we know, the latent Puritanism that defines Anglo-Saxon culture often lapses into deluded fantasy – the infantile denial of reality itself. In turn, this tendency to fantasy leads to ridiculous and unworkable policies. We had a war on alcohol, we have ongoing wars on prostitution, sex tourism, fast food and drugs and, since July 2017, America has had a war on nicotine, too.

If tobacco manufacturers cannot supply the nicotine consumers want and crave, the Black Market will. Doubtless criminals of every stripe are itching for the Federal Drug Administration's proposed nicotine ban to begin. Tobacco will join drugs and prostitution as one of their big earners. And like 'cut' drugs and STD-raddled whores, their illicit cigarettes will doubtless be full of toxic impurities and infinitely worse than the high quality products presently furnished by the tobacco industry. Alternatively, people will just smoke more to get the hit they crave. But of course, facts cease to matter when the Anglo-American establishment is pursuing one of its virtue-signalling 'morality drives'.

As with other Anglo-American wars against the reality of human nature, the latest prohibitive initiatives are doomed to failure before they start. Instead of rationally accepting that people will always drink, smoke, use drugs and seek out recreational sex, the Anglo-Feminist elites assume human nature is perfectible (according to their warped standards). Unfortunately for them, human nature cannot be scoured of sensuality by white-light rhetoric; the human quest for sensual pleasure is inescapable. Yet the authorities never learn. The war on drugs is a total failure, as was Prohibition – yet still the Anglo-American Establishment refuses to leave its puritanical fantasies in the seventeenth century, where they belong. Instead they prefer to treat America's citizens like retarded seven-year olds, curtailing their right to choice and pleasure.

Ultimately, both Clinton's 'crusade' and the Federal Drug Administration's proposed nicotine ban reveal the Disneyland mentality of the Anglo-American Establishment – repressive, self-destructive and utterly out of touch with consensus reality. The most terrifying thing is how the post-feminist population of the United States have taken this pernicious assault lying down, without so much as a whimper. Back in the day, Americans reached for their muskets when freedom was threatened. That the FDA's proposals arose during a Republican administration only underscores the authoritarian depths to which America has fallen.

A term often used in this treatise is 'The Anglo-American Matrix.' Like the 'pill' terminology used so widely in the online male community or 'Manosphere', the term derives from the 1999 film of the same name. However, the term has more than superficial significance when applied to Anglo-American culture. In the film, The Matrix is not merely an artificial realm of self-delusion insulated from reality; it actively defends its own borders from within, quelling all potential for dissent or self-realisation among its exploited prisoners.

This is a perfect analogy for contemporary Anglo-American civilization. Not only does its veil reality beneath a cloud of media-generated delusion, it actively strives to suppress or distort the world beyond its confines: the non-Anglo West and the nations beyond. Anglosphere citizens are routinely told arrant mistruths about life outside the Anglsophere, partly out of reflexive habit but mainly to prevent mass defections among persecuted groups, such as divorced men. One of my anonymous correspondents describes this misinformation programme in detail:

One last point, don't listen to the morons who babble on about how "France is going majority Muslim!" These idiots are either deluded or full of shit, this kind of propaganda comes from the Gatestone Institute and other neocon rags trying to push the US into more wars in the Middle East, and they're terrified they'll lose their tax base for war if more Americans wise up and say adios to the Anglosphere and its bullshit. The France of 2018 doesn't give a shit about its former colonial empire, the immigrants now come from the old eastern bloc and ironically from North America while the Muslims are being shown the door. Macron's turned out to be a sly political fox, he pretended to be centrist but on culture and demographics he's more hard core conservative than Le Pen could have ever dreamed of being herself, and he's using clever measures to throw out the Muslims. For him it's more a matter of business and attracting tourists and workers to France, but whatever the reason, it works. Oh, and the taxes? I pay much less taxes in France than California or New York, both of which I used to work in. The numbskulls among the reflexive conservatives love to cite the claimed high taxes to Euro-bash. But when you put all the different American taxes on the ledger, including Medi/Soc Security, Americans pay more but get a lot less. There is no sensible reason not to come here, especially if you want to start a family, which we indeed still can and should (Appendix B, pp.226-227).

The Anglo-American Matrix presents its wars on pleasure as healthy, constructive and the only effective or rational option. Only since the rise of the Internet and popular international travel have its fictions been challenged and their folly exposed. Countries with progressive policies on drug addiction or prostitution such as Holland or Switzerland are prosperous and effective national entities, not crumbling dystopias. Despite costing billions of tax dollars, the American 'War on Drugs' has achieved nothing beyond the needless criminalisation of millions of young Americans who would otherwise have been contributing to the economy and society at large. The Anglo-American wars on pleasure are not only inane and ineffectual, they are incredibly costly.

Glimpses of more rational and effective policies than reflexive prohibition and persecution have begun to discredit the old Matrix narratives. Though these myths are still upheld in Anglo-American law, the media and among the socio-economic elites, they are largely dismissed and despised by most educated Anglosphere citizens. Because the Matrix is beginning to crumble, its wars against pleasure are becoming increasingly desperate and unregulated. Banning nicotine or imprisoning sex tourists are the frantic rear-guard action of a culture in its ideological death throes; and expect the Anglo-American Matrix to redouble its efforts as the rents in its fabric widen yet further.

1.3 The Religious Connection

As is generally known, my own contribution to gender-theory lies primarily in the cultural sphere. In sum, I do not consider feminism to be a 'revolutionary' theory, at all – rather, I have shown that most of the core feminist themes were already present in Anglo-Saxon culture long before 'feminism' ever existed. For example, feminist views on porn, prostitution and 'trafficking' resemble the views of Christian conservatives, not the progressive left. The residual puritan influence on Anglo-Saxon nations specifically explains why this is so. By keeping sex a scarce commodity, this latent Puritanism has given Anglo-American feminism a strong misandrist agenda and facilitated its expansion into every sphere of life.

One of my correspondents, Gearman, stresses how feminism in the non-Anglosphere West differs markedly and specifically from the Anglosphere variant:

As a contrast, look at the specifics everyone else is providing on why Anglosphere feminism in particular is toxic, and why it leads to SPECIFIC POLICIES that make families and normal interaction with females impossible in the Anglosphere. Divorce, for example: the permanent alimony, extreme excessive child support without caps (to fund the ex-wife's excesses not the kids), the stupid "spousal support to keep up previous lifestyle" standard, going to prison if you can't pay alimony or child support, the "deadbeat Dad" meme, Dads consistently losing custody, super-expensive divorces, and an insane high rate of divorce (more than half and rising of marriages). ALL THESE MISERIES ARE VIRTUALLY UNIQUE TO THE ANGLOSPHERE! That's what you don't get. Even though divorce happens in the non-Anglosphere West, it's much less common, it's far less expensive, it doesn't involve the financial wrecking ball of the Anglo West, joint-sharing custody, capped child support (a "playboy principle" that prevents a gold-digging ex-wife from any "profit" from divorce), no slagging on men after divorce, mediation, much more amicable. When divorce happens outside the Anglosphere, it's a minor blip rather than the complete devastation that couples in the Anglosphere routinely experience. And that's because the non-Anglo West has avoided the very division-promoting and hypocritical style of feminism of the Anglosphere (Appendix I1, p.247).

While it is fairly plain that Anglo-American feminism is driven by a kind of sex-negative misandry, a whole range of legal, economic and historical factors interact with it in order to achieve the deleterious effects Gearman describes. Indeed, this text was written to describe these factors in detail, expanding on the insights offered in my first book.

While I have revised my classic view that religion alone is the sole cause of sex-negative misandrist feminism and its unchallenged rise to become the Anglosphere's primary ideology, much of its form and most of its values still derive from a theological template. As we shall see in later sections, religious puritanism has been largely supplanted by a secular puritanism in the major Anglosphere countries; a variant stripped of all patriarchal virtues and even more hostile to men than its religious counterpart. However, the puritanical heritage retains a strong residual presence in the United States and among the Anglo-American elite generally. Its long-standing presence in the Anglosphere and deep alignment with Anglo-feminism explains the latter's puritanical values and reflexive acceptance by the parent culture.

Anglo-American puritanism originated in England during the sixteenth and seventeenth centuries, although its intellectual origins lay in continental Europe with theologians like John Calvin. English Puritans were radical Protestants who rejected the English state church as lacking biblical authority and infected with Roman Catholic values. 'Puritan' was in fact a pejorative term used by their various opponents; Puritans preferred to call themselves 'the Godly', seeing themselves as virtuous outcasts in a profane society. They would probably have remained a footnote in history, as they are in continental Europe, were it not for a strange historical accident. Because Puritans actually ruled England for over a decade, from 1649-1660, their influence on the English-speaking world was infinitely greater than in any other Protestant country.

While this might seem a short period a very long time ago in a country most of my readers find remote, its influence was profound and long-lasting. As I described in my first book, the English Puritans systematically smashed all artworks and objects of beauty as profane, closed down taverns and public meeting places, abolished prostitution and public sports and generally banished all forms of pleasure from the land. In just a few years England lost its rich heritage of medieval art and architecture, denuding English culture of visual beauty for centuries to come.

Although this period might seem obscure to Americans and other Anglosphere peoples, it must be remembered that the Pilgrim Fathers were English Puritans possessing the same austere values as these fanatical statue-smashers and pleasure-haters. Although America is now a nation of immigrants, the puritanical values of its founders still define the cultural, economic and political establishments. This is my argument, in essence: that far from being the 'revolutionary' movement it claims to be, Anglo-American feminism *embodies all the sex-negativity, misandry and joylessness of the parent culture.* Indeed, the unstinting support it receives from the establishment suggests not just an accidental alignment of values but rather more: *that Anglo-American feminism is just another wing of the Anglo-American establishment in terms of its ethnic and social composition, aims and ideology.*

After a century-long hiatus, the Puritan impulse returned with a vengeance in the Victorian era. Although its nexus was England, its influence echoed across the whole Anglosphere during the late nineteenth century. In many respects this second Puritan revolution is still with us, albeit in secularized form. Although the first Puritan wave was linked to Companionate Marriage, an early form of Anglo woman worship, this second wave coincided with the rise of bourgeois proto-feminism and permanently marked it with the long-standing Puritan themes of sex-negativity, hysteria, gynocentric elitism and racism. In almost all respects, modern Anglo feminists such as Catherine MacKinnon or Jodie Foster would fit quite easily into the crusading, sex-negative, white-bourgeois ranks of Victorian feminism. The only real difference is that most modern Anglo feminists have replaced overt Christian belief with various forms of cultural Marxism, though that has not changed their fundamental value system.

So where specifically is the puritan religious influence most evident in modern Anglo-American feminism?

As I noted in my first book Havok (2009), a puritanical fear of adult sexuality has long found cultural expression in the Anglo-American idealisation of childhood as a sexless utopia, from books like The Water Babies and Peter Pan to modern Disney films. More recently, Anglo-feminism has acquired a deranged interest in 'non-binary' gender identity and gender reassignment. Again, this specific fixation is best explained by the 'sexless' ideal extolled by puritanical Christianity; since male sexuality is especially repugnant to this perspective, eliminating it via gender-reassignment is the Anglo-feminist equivalent of 'banishing sin'.

Another strong link between Anglo feminism and Puritanical Christianity is a certain undercurrent of sexual hysteria. Because they strive to suppress (or even deny) natural feelings and instincts, Puritanical cultures are in a perpetual state of latent hysteria. Inevitably, this periodically bubbles to the surface in witch-hunts and other emotive displays. Both the Salem Witch Trials in seventeenth century Massachusetts and the #metoo madness of the twenty-first century are driven by the same sexual hysteria. Pursuing the analogy further, both Salem and #metoo revolve around the hare-brained testimonies of teenaged girls whose wild accusations are glibly accepted by the authorities without a shred of supporting evidence. Once the female finger of accusation is pointed, the 'offender' (guilty or not) is effectively ruined. And in both cases the state acquires both material and cultural capital through officiating over such travesties of justice. Here is one of my correspondents on what #metoo really means for Anglo-American men:

In specific policy which is what actually affects people in the real world, the Anglosphere is concretely far worse for men and families in general. More specifics, as the same goes for the metoo hysteria. Once again, look at where metoo has caught on, and become an ever more massive wrecking ball that's making it impossible for men and women to have normal relationships, posing concrete danger for men's livelihoods and making "sexual harassment" and "sexual misconduct" a weapon that can be used anywhere, at anytime, in any workplace or for any reason, with an accuser having total power to ruin an accused without any

evidence even for things that may (or may not) have happened decades ago (Appendix I2, p.253).

Like faith itself, neo-Puritan Anglo feminism is impervious to reason. However much rational evidence is martialled against its primary assumptions by the men's rights lobby, this is summarily dismissed in favour of the lame old narratives: that women are all oppressed in every sphere of life, that men are all advantaged in every sphere of life, that women are not shown preferential treatment before the law, that men are not held to higher standards in the workplace, that men do not kill themselves in far greater numbers than women or that there is no male empathy gap. In sum, the men's right lobby signally fails to grasp that that Anglo feminism has more in common with religious faith than a rational belief system.

The fact that feminism is surrounded by an aura of fanatic moral righteousness is also extremely interesting. Puritanical Protestantism also assumes this transcendent moral position. No prominent Anglo-American feminist displays any capacity for reflective self-awareness, never expresses regret for her beliefs, never recants or apologizes even when proven wrong.

Historically speaking, Anglo feminists have always been prominent in puritanical social agendas and crusades against alcohol, prostitution and encroaching non-puritanical nations like Imperial Germany. Whatever their revolutionary rhetoric, their views are essentially identical to the tyrants who ruled England in the seventeenth century. In fact, #metoo is just the same; a puritanical, hysteria-fuelled crusade aimed at life, happiness and normal gender-relations. While some of my correspondents stress the role of cultural Marxism and unresolved colonial tensions for the specifically adversarial nature of Anglo feminism, some of this also comes from the fanatic 'crusading' spirit of the feminists' Puritan forbears.

One of the most tragic things about Puritan values is their tendency to twist healthy natural drives into dark and perverted caricatures. Child abuse is rampant in the Anglosphere, and the recent feminist fixation on transsexualism has already been mentioned. Freud discredited the Anglo-puritan project by demonstrating that sexual drives are ineradicable and will only be sublimated if suppressed or denied. The overall impact of Anglo-feminist neo-puritan initiatives has been null or negative because they deny the reality of human nature. Here is Lawrence, one of my most voluminous correspondents:

I know a lot of you guys have talked about how the crazy Puritan tradition in the Anglosphere, or maybe the Victorian era, is responsible for making the Anglo version of feminism so toxic by making sex itself an item of scarcity that women gain power by making rare, and that pushes the societies to harmfully separate the genders from an early age so they don't understand each other. Now, I'll say I think there's something to this. Repressing male-female sexual interaction in the Victorian or Puritanical tradition does lead to a lot of societal perversions directly and indirectly. Directly, I feel like we saw this in the Victorian period, and today in Afghanistan with the sexually repressed Pashtun tribes that make young women unavailable for sex before marriage, resulting in men's schools and clubs plagued by homosexual weirdness. More importantly, I feel like this does contribute to the "men are evil" misandry of family courts and #metoo extremists since it paints any sexual association as evil, and since men in general are more associated with sexual interest towards women, it means that Anglo feminists frame their misandry with a lot of Puritanical shaming and disgust at sex itself (Appendix Q, p.303).

It seems the distinctive Puritan Christianity of the Anglosphere remains indeed a potent influence on modern Anglo-American feminism. However, behind Puritanism lies the conceptual loam of Judeo-Christianity itself. Could the ultimate origins of misandrist feminism be Christianity itself? After all, feminism flourishes above all in the Christian West, not in Muslim, Hindu or Buddhist lands.

Examination of Christianity's turbulent history strongly supports this view. Its cringing emotionalism has always appealed to the passive female mind. Many of Jesus' followers were, supposedly, women. Even today, women greatly outnumber men in Protestant Christian congregations. The earliest Christian martyrs were whimpering, asexual masochists. Indeed, the Roman Catholic Church seems fixated on murdering male sexuality as 'evil' and 'sinful'. Monks and priests are expected to repress all sexual self-expression, a course not only misandrist but deeply damaging to the individuals concerned.

Even more telling, scholars have raised valid questions about the sexual orientation of Jesus, St Paul and other important Christians. An impartial observer would have to say that their frantic asexuality quite possibly concealed carnal drives of the most disordered kind. Indeed, a huge proportion of modern Christian clergy are homosexuals or paedophiles, especially those within the Catholic Church and the Evangelical movement.

At a more general level, Christianity has little to offer men beyond submission, passivity and sexual repression. It is also noteworthy that the United States is both the most feminist and the most overtly Christian nation in the western world. The limp resistance offered by Western men to feminism owes much to Christianity. While Muslim women who defy male authority are scarred with acid, lashed or beheaded, Anglo-American men 'turn the other cheek' even while their rights, assets and lives are stripped from them. Despite what Anglo-American conservatives believe, Christianity offers married men very little protection from divorce. One of my correspondents, Legal Eagle, writes:

If it wasn't clear already, pre-nups offer very limited protection that's all but useless amidst the full discretion of divorce court judges, esp. after kids are born but even before-- even my own ex-law firm partners virtually laugh when husbands request them now, they simply don't help. Not "marrying a good girl" or "marrying a Christian or religious girl". Here's a nasty stat for you: the biggest jump in divorce, esp. nasty expensive divorces, in past decade has been among Christian and esp. Mormon women (!). Not marrying a foreign woman in the US-- once under US law, she'll have the same power to ruin you as an American woman, and fall under the same poisonous "deadbeat man" Anglosphere cultural influences that push other "nice women of good character" to divorce in Anglo countries (Appendix J2, p.270).

Some critics will point out that Medieval Catholic Christianity successfully repelled successive Islamic invasions and clearly embodied many martial virtues. However, the Roman Catholic Christianity of the Middle Ages was a complex syncretic belief-system incorporating Europe's rich classical heritage and pagan warrior traditions, such as those of the Romans and Vikings (Davis-Hanson, 2001). These potent non-Christian factors sufficiently obviated the residual Christian element to make Catholic Europe an effective military power. In sum, Medieval Catholicism had little in common with modern Protestant Christianity, which has thoroughly purged these martial traditions in favour of 'true' Christianity.

As an atheist, I do not hold Hindu or Muslim beliefs any 'higher' than Christian ones. However, it seems self-evident that Western Christianity shows a deep historical tendency to pedestalise women and exalt passive, distinctively 'feminine' values. In particular, it holds misandrist (and entirely fanciful) notions about the dynamic, life-enhancing force that is male sexuality. Certainly, no healthy male could long endure the asexual/celibate 'ideal' extolled by Christianity. Indeed, the Roman Catholic Church has much in common with feminism in its hatred of male sexuality and preoccupation with asexual gender-relations. It could even be said that Anglo feminism is a form of secular Neo-Christianity. For all their faults, at least Judaism and Islam deal with men as men, the true sign of a 'masculine' faith. As always in the Anglosphere, the gulf between feminist 'revolution' and 'traditional' western values is disquietingly small.

1.4 Secular Puritanism

An objection often raised against my thesis is this: if religious Puritanism is the source of all the iniquities we discuss, why have things seemingly gotten so much worse for men since the decline of religion? If puritanical religion were the sole culprit, surely institutionalized misandry would have withered with its decline?

During the pre-secular era, widespread sex-negative misandry was at least understandable. For example, George Orwell's Down and Out in Paris and London (1933) or Keep the Aspidistra Flying (1936) are full of bleak references to female hypergamy and its intimate association with religious repression. Similarly, the disastrous and failed policy of Prohibition in the Twenties demonstrated the enormous political power of puritan opinion in the United States. However, the US still has some of the most punitive laws against prostitution and drugs in the western world. Such puritanical repression is much harder to explain in a secular society where religion is relatively weak and marginalised.

I would argue that the real culprit is a distinct shift from religious Puritanism to secular Puritanism that occurred in most Anglosphere countries during the late twentieth century. And the secular Puritanism that now prevails is far worse for men than its old, religious counterpart, while retaining many of its worst themes. This is because women have dethroned divinity as the presiding ideal of Anglo society; in sum, they are worshipped as deities in the absence of God. Impressing women to gain their sexual favours, once seen as a biological necessity, is now paraded as the loftiest goal men can aspire to; yet the puritanical heritage of the Anglo countries ensures sex remains a scarce commodity. Little wonder, then, that female arrogance and entitlement have reached radioactive levels. Meanwhile, men across the Anglosphere have been reduced to beasts of burden fit only to serve and honour women as disposable serfs. One of my correspondents writes:

Our friends and colleagues who lost everything were typical of the hypocrisy that's infected all US family law. The men were "working too hard", you see, not enough time for the wife and kids even though the men's hard-earned paychecks were supporting these selfish bitches' ability to shop themselves silly and whine and moan in the first place! American and Anglo grown women with kids are still basically whiny little girls this way, they're never satisfied with their lot no matter how much their husbands slave away for them, even if they work 80 hour weeks in some struggling software company to give them a life of luxury. This is where the Anglosphere goes full stupid. Almost any other country would realize the wives complaints have no basis, that they're acting like spoiled brats and tell them to shove it. But US family courts thanks to feminism, the politically correct "mainstream media" and the collusion of moron white knight cucks, instead indulges this female infantilism from coddled, spoiled brat wives with no appreciation for things like hard work, sacrifice and patience (Appendix B, p.225).

The dramatic online explosion of manosphere blogs, websites and discussion groups represents a masculine backlash against this state of affairs. In their respective ways, all these movements are trying to remove the pedestals on which Anglo women now stand (MRAs and PUAs), simply avoid them (MGTOWs) or pursue non-Anglo women (pan-Anglosphere Dissidents). Under genuine religious Puritanism, men still enjoyed several benefits implicit in the Judeo-Christian religion: male employment was still valued and protected as a basic human right, men were still fashioned in God's image and men retained a strong voice over reproductive issues directly affecting them. With the rise of feminism and the emergence of secular Puritanism, those vital male benefits were instantly swept aside and a wave of masculine resistance was the inevitable result.

The pan-Anglosphere shift towards secular Puritanism has wrought deleterious effects beyond the narrow field of gender relations, however. Once, other Anglo-Saxon institutions were also infused with religious belief – commerce and temperance both arose from an implicitly spiritual consciousness, albeit puritanical and repressive. However, in the modern era these institutions persist only as hollow, secular shells bereft of spiritual purpose. Commerce has lapsed into mindless consumerism, the family into gynocentric dysfunction and temperance into a witch-hunt against sensual pleasure. In other words, the Anglosphere's key institutions persist only as malefic shells of their former selves.

This brings me to another important point. Part of the mass alienation which grips the Anglosphere nations, an alienation expressed as a widening gulf between the elites and the masses, is the insincerity underpinning elite discourse and governance. Although Anglo-American society is now effectively secular, the elite still persist in pretending we live in a pre-secular society. I call this 'The 1958 Thesis': a tendency among Anglo elites to exaggerate mass attachment to tradcon values when not one person in a hundred actually believes in them. Because of this, the Anglo-American world is now ruled by puritanical reflexes rather than meaningful ideals, creating an oppressive and alienating civilization. Above all, the Anglo-Saxon spirit of temperance has devolved into mindless hostility to freedom, pleasure and experiment – consider America's costly and pointless 'war' on drugs, resulting in the needless criminalization of millions of young people. Successive Governments give no rational explanation for pursuing this ridiculous policy, because none exists; habit, not reason is their guiding principle. The reader can doubtless think of many more examples, not least the American state's inane hostility to prostitution. For some vague and inchoate reason, the US authorities outside Nevada still see fit to stigmatize and criminalize a reasonable transaction between two consenting adults.

The foregoing discussion not only describes the contemporary Anglosphere, it illuminates it. The present condition of the Anglo-American world is secular Puritanism, a cultic ideology that worships women as the pinnacle and meaning of existence. Sometime during the mid-twentieth century, gynocentric woman-worship began to supplant religion as the primary motive force in Anglo-Saxon culture. This rapid secularisation process retained a puritanical ethos while transforming key Anglosphere institutions into grotesque, feminised caricatures maintained by sheer force of habit. Even Anglo-American foreign policy now follows the same gynocentric and puritanical trajectory, attempting to impose its warped misandrist values on unwilling nations and peoples around the world (see 'The Hillary Doctrine' by Hudson and Leidl, 2017).

The question arises: why does sex-negative puritanism persist even in the secular Anglosphere, where religion is a spent and marginalised force? Also, other protestant countries such as Holland, Sweden or Northern

Germany have no obvious puritan agenda, yet they too experienced a strong puritanical influence (though admittedly not as strong as England, which experienced two instances of puritanical dictatorship). One of my correspondents, an American expatriate calling himself Phil, describes the relative sexual freedom of the non-Anglo Protestant countries relative to the Anglosphere:

And what I said above, all the invigorating and healthy cultural elements of Belgium and Germany, and of France like the guys before pointing out? They apply to everywhere in Europe, at least aside from Britain. The Nordic countries and Holland really are awesome too, even though they have some of the stupid cultural flottsam from the Anglo countries they water ti (sic) way down and still have common sense, plus men and women are a whole lot more open and free around sexual matters, and they're just culturally stronger. Italy and the other Mediterranean countries are a whole lot like France, just with more distinctive cuisine and more sunshine, and improving economies to work in too. All good choices, you won't go wrong working and staying anywhere in the EU. Not hard, and it's well worth it! (Appendix E, p.238)

Religion alone cannot explain the deep and ongoing sex-negativity that defines Anglo-American culture. It might even be that religion follows some deeper strain of puritanical sex-negativity, rather than merely augmenting it. Although this work discusses the interaction of social, economic and cultural factors, might there be some innate foundation for the persistence of sex-negative values and female exaltation even in the secular Anglosphere? Aside from the usual cultural factors such as secular puritanism, residual misandry and malleable common law, are there any demographic/biological factors specific to Anglo-Caucasians which might be responsible for their mass promotion and acceptance of misandrist feminism?

One notable thing about white women in general - and Anglo-American women in particular - is that they mature very badly. Whatever charms Anglo women display last only from puberty to 26, while females of other races mature better and more evenly across the lifespan. East Asian women can be hot up to 40 or beyond but this is very rare among whites, especially Anglo whites, who typically look haggard by 30. Such an intense imbalance leads to a 'beauty shortage' in Anglo societies, with female beauty being incredibly rare. This imbalance inevitably leads to insane female entitlement during those prime years and contributes to the rampant woman worship which defines the Anglosphere relative to other cultures. The Dark Triad of female personality disorders - histrionic, narcissistic and borderline - runs rampant for exactly the same reason.

Since a young female with a normal body mass index is 'beautiful' in the arid Anglo-American context, she is essentially free to act as a goddess during her prime decade. In this view, baby murder, thug chasing, no-fault Divorce and other malefic behaviours are merely warped expressions of this deranged power. And all the feminist efforts to stop Anglo-American men contacting foreign women - VAWA and invented trafficking hysteria - are designed to preserve it.

But why has this female tendency worsened so much in recent years? And why has it been allowed to? Do other dynamics underpin this development? Changing demography probably plays a significant role. Because people live longer in modern times, five generations now coexist in the same moment. Since older females are unattractive to most males, there is a huge surfeit of thirsty men from all five generations lusting over one generation of women (women under 26, if that). This is why some young Anglo-American girls can make seven figure salaries displaying their body parts online. More, the whole technological thrust of modern society allows these women to exploit their sexual power over all sexually disenfranchised men, whom they can contact in an instant. A traditional prostitute was limited by proximity to a relatively small circle of males; not so the modern Anglobitch, whose charms are only a screen-tap away.

Another factor one might consider is the high 'power distance' or depth of inequality experienced in Anglo-American societies. The Anglosphere is a potent colonial bloc that still bestows considerable status on white Anglo-Saxons in a global context. Anglo media, culture and institutions remain the primary global exports, in ideological terms. The obvious international power of say, Victorian Britain or post-War America surely wrought some heightening effect on female hypergamy in those nations. After all, the 'hypergamy bar' is necessarily raised when a country is a great colonial hub with huge international influence and prestige; since the female frame of reference reflexively broadens and deepens in response. In this view, the Anglo female's misandrist hostility is an insane extension of natural hypergamous instincts: almost no male or his offspring is good enough for a female raised in a global superpower. Here is one of my anonymous correspondents on the wider social ramifications of this tendency:

Feminists in North America are now in the process of formally making sex equal rape, and the man has no defense. So I guess the fertility bearing rate of the Anglosphere is about to drop to 0.5. Oh, except for the Africans, Latino groups, native Americans and of course the Muslims, who ironically enough, actually will mass rape and then impose a real shari'a patriarchy on the stupid Anglobitches who no longer have the protection of the men or more rational women who've all left. North America is toast. Leave while you can (Appendix F, p.240).

This exalted form of Anglo hypergamy is best called 'hyper-hypergamy', female sexual elitism and selectivity carried beyond all rational measure. This is not exclusively associated with the Anglo West's colonial values. Britain and America have lower social mobility rates than other industrial societies, together with wider wealth and power divisions. This must also exert a strong impact on female hypergamy, with a much larger proportion of males being dismissed as potential mates than in progressive, egalitarian societies. It must be said that modern romantic life in the Anglosphere has become a form of misandrist eugenics, where women arbitrarily select which males get to breed on the basis of hyper-hypergamous criteria. This even applies to sperm donation, where donors have to pass the most stringent criteria related to intelligence, education, height and health. In sum, fat, ugly Anglo women riddled with personality disorders get to sit in genetic judgement on the gender that created and maintain civilization. Of course, mass abortion is an even more active and deadly expression of eugenic hyper-hypergamy, predictably falling heaviest on the offspring of low status males (which is almost all males in the Anglosphere). The British economist Gregory Clark has demonstrated that social mobility across the Anglosphere is achingly slow, with surnames from the Norman Conquest (over nine hundred years ago) still greatly over-represented among the British and other Anglosphere elites (Clark, 2015). People with names like

Osbourne, Lacey and Montgomery not only earn and own more, they even live longer. Like the international prestige of Anglo-Saxon countries, such inequality and social stagnation has bred a uniquely eugenic form of hypergamy among Anglo-American women, a programme sustained by Anglo-American law, politics and other institutions.

The extreme individualism of Caucasians relative to other races also contributes to the conflict-driven nature of misandrist feminism. In East Asian countries, the nail that sticks up is hammered down; in the West, it is coated in gold. This unchecked individualism is of course strongest in the Anglo-Saxon West, where almost everyone sees themselves as a 'brand' and billionaire celebrity in waiting while normal aspirations are scorned for cloudy visions of ideal love and self-aggrandisement. Obviously, Anglobitch selfishness exemplifies this agenda as do poor mothering skills, lifestyle abortions, no-fault divorce and offhand hatred of men. The obvious sense that Anglo women are more 'fucked up' than other women - even non Anglo white women - seems to partly derive from this innate and unregulated individualism.

Lastly, do Caucasian - and especially Anglo men - have an innate disposition to 'pedestalize' women and grant them far too much freedom? This argument has floated around the manosphere for some years, especially those regions with a high proportion of non-white commentators. Perhaps the West's 'beauty shortage' and the relatively brief flowering of Caucasian women has wrought some deep psychological effect on them, now embedded in their culture or biology at a primordial - even unshakeable - level. Ultimately, Caucasian men have allowed their females to wreck society with complete impunity and it would be churlish to blame women exclusively for this; since men are stronger and smarter than women, they are ultimately responsible. Despite the truth of my message, only a tiny handful of enlightened Caucasian men pay heed to it: the vast majority remain blue-pilled cucks and White Knights listening to saccharine Beatles records. What will it take to rouse them? Are they even capable of being roused?

Whether the distinctive non-cultural factors listed here have permanently altered Anglo women at a behavioural level, or merely artificially inflate universal female tendencies, is difficult to say. What is very clear is that they contribute to the misandrist, evil tendencies so prevalent among Anglo-American females, and explain their persistence in the face of social change.

Alt-right and conservative MRAs are quick to blame cultural outsiders for the demise of functional gender-relations in the Anglosphere. Many conservatives specifically blame the Jews; however, Jews were banished from England – then the sole Anglosphere country – by Edward I in 1290. They were only allowed to return in the mid-seventeenth century, long after Anglo puritanism had emerged. In fact, they were invited back by the Puritan dictator Oliver Cromwell in 1655, largely to reinvigorate the economy. These facts undercut the Alt-right belief that Jews are responsible for misandrist feminism or the values underlying it. Another widespread Protestant belief is that the Catholic counter-reformation subverted gender-relations in the Anglosphere. However, during the key years of Britain's global expansion – the late 16th and early seventeenth centuries – Roman Catholics were an oppressed and marginalized minority in Britain. They were not allowed to hold government positions or preach their religion in public. This anti-Catholic animus survived in England – and the Anglosphere in general – well into the twentieth century. As with the Jews, Roman Catholics simply lacked the power or presence to subvert anything at that time. Given these facts, it is clear that Anglo-Saxon culture itself –and its puritanical strains, in particular – is responsible for misandrist feminism in all its forms and manifestations. As we shall see, other distinctive Anglo-Saxon institutions such as common law have greatly assisted the expansion of misandrist feminism; but these too adhere exclusively to Anglo-Saxon culture.

Now, it may well be shown that subversive forces such as cultural Marxism deliberately widened pre-existing socio-cultural fissures during the late-twentieth century; however, the fissures were already present in the pan-Anglosphere cultural nexus. Moreover, the key puritanical Anglo memes coexist quite happily within the Anglo variant of cultural Marxism. For example, Marxist Anglo-feminists such as Catherine MacKinnon retain a puritanical loathing of heterosexual relations even while preaching the rhetorical virtues of Marxist 'equalism' from elite American universities. And although they are avowed atheists, they retain an avid attachment to the suppressive morals of seventeenth century religious fanatics. It is almost comical to Anglo conservatives and feminists bandying insults when both groups share a moral framework derived from precisely the same source: the drab meeting houses of sixteenth century England. It is also notable that Anglo feminists are happy to enjoy the residual benefits of colonial privilege as affluent white women, even when such benefits are explicitly repudiated by cultural Marxism. In short, Anglo feminists are adept at cherry-picking ideas from the 'orchard of ideologies', even when these ideas are growing on completely different trees. This intellectual dissimulation means they can always retain the sex-negative puritan meme, whatever other concepts they adopt: for puritanism is the very spine of Anglo-feminism.

1.5 The Work-Life Imbalance

Anglo American culture is obsessed with work, careers and accumulating wealth to the exclusion of all else. Its lack of self-awareness is absolute. The Anglo-American work-life imbalance has become chronically dysfunctional, resulting in broken families, unhappy children, tumbling birth-rates, mass alienation and premature death. Yet still the Anglosphere nations plough on, unable to restore any existential balance to this declining quality of life.

As ever, Anglo-American conservatives fail to see that this work-life imbalance is not some alien agenda foisted on the Anglosphere by subversive elements. Rather, it springs from the crabbed Puritanism at the heart of Anglo-American civilisation – like misandrist feminism, like #metoo, like paedophilia, like anti-male courts and the gynocentric media.

Of all the Anglosphere countries, the United States has pursued the puritan work ethic into a realm of dysfunctional imbalance. This is predictable, given that it was founded by puritan fanatics who frowned on leisure and happiness as sins. Various commentators have commented on the declining quality of life in the United States. While this primarily refers to gender-relations, it also embraces loneliness, social isolation and existential despair that increasingly govern American life. Steve Hoca (Hoca, 2017), Winston Wu (Wu, 2014; Wu and Stark, 2016) and Relampago Furioso (Furioso, 2018), all American citizens, all agree on this despite their other differences. Here is my correspondent Gearman on the chronic lifestyle imbalance which afflicts American life:

Bottom-line is, In practice, the non-Anglo West (that is the continent of Europe) plus Brazil, most of South America and the advanced countries of east Asia, all provide a reasonable compromise of conditions that make them not only livable but prosperous first world countries for Anglo men to become expats in, both modern but also without the toxic feminism and toxic, "at each other's throats all the time" culture of the Anglosphere and of North America in particular. It's specific policies, like rational divorce and marriage policies and lack of the #metoo hysteria, in the non-Anglo West, Brazil/South America and most of Asia that give proof of this. Like most of the other posters here I've worked all over the world (photography and mechanical engineering in my case, contracts wherever I'm needed), and we're posting here to share that perspective to help a lot of you guys, as we know you're fearful that you can never safely have loving relations with women. We're here to help you realize that there are great alternatives for us. It's just that they have to be pursued outside of the Anglosphere, and especially in the non-Anglo Western countries of the continent in Europe and in Brazil and the rest of South America (Appendix I4, pp.261-262).

In 2018, much was made of the fact that American life-expectancy had fallen for the first time in many decades. Much of this fall can be explained by opoid addiction and rising suicide rates among blue-collar whites. According to the US Centers for Disease Control National Center for Health Statistics, the suicide rate in 2016 reached its highest point in 50 years. Meanwhile, the drug overdose rate rose 9.6% in 2016 (O'Donnell, 2019).

Part of the mythology of the United States is that it transcends all other countries in terms of opportunity and quality of life. This narrative has so much traction because of the self-selected nature of its population, who are often descended from immigrants who left poor circumstances in their home countries. This feeds the American national myth that all other countries are primitive and poor, a myth compounded by the fact that so few Americans travel outside their own country. Of course, the mainstream media narrative focuses primarily on young, affluent and attractive people, presently a highly-skewed image of life in America to both its inhabitants and the world at large. These shimmering falsehoods inject the atomized populace with deluded assumptions about the average American's income, appearance, age and lifestyle, thereby compounding its alienation and self-loathing.

Many if not most of the Anglosphere's leading feminists are embodiments of work-life imbalance, as one would expect. Germaine Greer, Catherine Mackinnon and Jodie Foster are all ageing Anglohags without husbands or natural children, having sacrificed their prime productive years for the vapid chimera of a 'career' (a secondary consideration for any normally-adjusted woman). While they enjoy a certain status in the feminist community and society at large, as human females they are abject biological and emotional failures. In terms of work-life they have almost no life to speak of, deriving all sense of identity from their academic 'work' and their secondary roles as feminist commentators and celebrities.

Doubtless this explains their near-religious attachment to feminist beliefs. Since their identities derive exclusively from the cherry-picked intellectual junkyard that is Anglo-feminism, a coherent critical treatise such as this threatens their very identities, not just their beliefs. The refusal of Anglo-American feminists to debate their ideas outside the ivied walls of academic privilege or the cosy cocoons of the liberal media reflects a hysterical terror of psychic dissolution, not just the simple fear of defeat.

Because of its intrinsic imbalance, the Anglosphere warps female characteristics into dysfunctional and debased caricatures of themselves. Hypergamy becomes hyper-hypergamy, modesty becomes frigidity and ambition becomes reproductive sterility. Anorexia is another example of Anglo-puritanism wreaking havoc with the female mind. Predictably a condition associated with upper-middle class, white and highly educated teenage girls of Anglo-Saxon heritage, anorexia represents no more than a Calvinist loathing of the physical world taken to suicidal extremes. As usual, the condition springs from the anti-life fixations particular to traditional Anglo-Saxon culture. This is demonstrated by its intimate association with the culture-bearing Anglo elite, among whom the Calvinist values of striving, guilt and self-mastery remain strong.

In my first book, I invoked the philosophical ideas of the English artist, poet and mystic William Blake to cast some light on the difference. Profoundly alienated from the soulless commercialism of his era, he developed a spiritual system which shed much light on the modern Anglosphere. Blake believed that God was immanent in the world, albeit divided into four distinct manifestations: Luvah (heart), Urthona (loins), Vala (unity) and Urizen (reason). In his system, a spirit called Urizen governed the material world. Blake considered English culture to be imbalanced in favour or Urizen, to the exclusion of the other three manifestations and their presiding spirits (Rosso, 1994).

Although couched in mystic and poetic terms, Blake's analysis is just as valid today as when it was first created. The Anglosphere countries are still completely imbalanced in favour of materialism, consumption and repression while the emotional, sexual and spiritual aspects of life remain primitive and undeveloped. The Anglosphere – with its vapid consumerism, sexual false consciousness, inane cult of 'progress', soulless empiricism, homosociality, #metoo hysteria and hollow workaholism – is the ultimate embodiment of Blake's 'Urizenic' culture. Moreover, the imbalance also defines the Anglosphere's philosophical and intellectual heritage.

The Anglo-American empirical tradition, with its narrow fixation on symbolic and mathematical minutiae, is a more abstract expression of the Calvinist spirit. Philosophical movements like American pragmatism or British logical positivism are notable for denying the unity of human experience, instead focusing on sterile questions of meaning and utility. This tradition is directly responsible for the Anglosphere's obsession with material and financial quantification, an obsession which reduces human beings to factors in business equations and numbers on balance sheets. We might consider the Anglosphere's commitment to industrial-scale abortion as the eugenic expression of this quantification programme. Writing off millions of children surplus to economic requirements as 'human collateral' every year makes perfect sense to a culture which subordinates human life to numbers and profits. Indeed, Anglo-American empiricism is rapidly morphing into a 'machine culture' fixated on replacing human workers with androids and supplanting human government with artificial intelligence. These developments are entirely what we would expect from an imbalanced civilization ruled by reason, numbers and materialism. Blake depicted Isaac Newton as a man enslaved by the spirit of Urizen, fixated on the material world and its operating laws and blind to all else in human experience. Given the changes afoot, his famous painting remains a terrible warning to all Anglosphere citizens. At present, Anglo-feminists think that reproductive technology serves them and their agendas. And they are right, for sperm banks, contraceptives, abortion clinics and labour-saving devices have largely liberated them from reproductive or material dependence on men. However, once female reproductive capacity is obviated by machine culture the same feminists will find themselves just as disposable as the low-status males they despise.

But why is the Anglosphere (and the United States in particular) far more imbalanced than other Protestant societies? Holland, Germany, Switzerland, Denmark and the Scandinavian countries seem to have a far better work-life balance despite being protestant. Here is North Wind, one of my well-travelled correspondents:

Sweden stands out for this. Even with its own dumb forays into cultural Marxism, Sweden is one of the most pro-husband and pro-father countries in the Western world, with paternity leave, near forbidding of alimony in practice and none of this permanent spousal support BS like in the US. There's also capped child support, tradition on shared custody and a requirement that any women initiating divorce have to go out and earn a living. Yes Sweden has feminism, but in the absence of Anglo cuck chivalry and Puritanism, divorcing women don't get the "have your cake and eat it too" bullshit of the Anglosphere where they suddenly become needy dependents after divorce. In Sweden, the feminist credo of being an independent woman means what it sounds like, women after a divorce have to step up and work, without using the ex-husband as a meal-ticket. It's similar or even better in the rest of Scandinavia, the Catholic countries of the Mediterranean and South America, the German and centrally European countries and especially eastern Europe (Appendix A, p.221).

The answer, as usual, lies with the specific Anglo-American experience of Protestantism. Since puritan fanatics uniquely ruled the Anglosphere for long periods, their systematic removal of the visual and artistic heritage permanently deformed Pan-Anglosphere culture. Once it sets a nation's course, puritanism becomes an ineradicable force which can endure the decline of organised religion. And if it is implicated in cultural expansion, its impact will be greater still. In accordance with Joseph Unwin's theories of sexual sublimation (Unwin, 1934), the Anglosphere's creation was inescapably associated with sexual repression. For example, the Pilgrim Fathers were English Puritans with abnormally high levels of sexual restraint. When a nation is founded on repressed sexual energy, repression becomes synonymous with the culture itself. This is surely why workaholic puritanism remains so persistent in the United States and why the North American work-life imbalance is so acute. Yet while repression to linked to workaholic *activity*, it is not linked to cultural *creativity* in the way Unwin imagined. There has probably never been a more creative society than that of ancient Athens, which was notable for its sexual freedoms. The same is broadly true of Renaissance Italy. Puritan New Englanders might have worked hard but produced no advanced culture of lasting worth, in any sphere. Conflating toil with productivity is one of the crucial flaws in Anglo-American thought and behaviour; in truth, they are quite unrelated.

Jews are often blamed by Anglo-American conservatives for financial malpractice and the plutocratic nature of Anglo-American nations. However, the Anglosphere's distinctive financial instruments – namely, trusts – arose in medieval England, from which Jews had been banished in 1290. Thus the Anglosphere's financial dishonesty, dynastic wealth accumulation, unregulated business practices, corporate tax avoidance and well-attested international links with 'dirty money' have little to do with Jews, who certainly had no role in their creation. Like Roman Catholics, Jews simply lacked the power or presence to create such powerful institutions in an anti-Semitic country with a burgeoning global empire.

As usual, it will be seen that the problems of the Anglosphere arise squarely within the Anglosphere itself, however much conspiracy theorists protest to the contrary. In truth, British financial corruption is synonymous with its empire and is still nurtured via ambiguous relationships with its former territories (the Cayman Islands, British Virgin Islands and the Channel islands), all of which serve as tax havens and strongholds of financial malpractice (Shaxson, 2012). While Jews and Catholics might exploit these opportunities, they are an exclusively Anglo-Saxon creation. In sum, Anglo-American anti-Semitism should best be seen as a projection of its own acquisitive tendencies rather than a serious perspective. In fact, an interesting counter-theme among some of my correspondents (whom I suspect are Jews) is that Anglo common law is an alien imposition on their own society and culture, together with its puritanical pedestalisation of women. The distinctive 'anti-life' misanthropy and miserliness of the Anglosphere certainly owe nothing to Jewish religion or culture, which both celebrate life.

Ultimately, the sheer antiquity and integrity of the Anglosphere has no small role to play. The City of London, the world's major financial centre, was founded by the Romans in the first century. Not even the Norman Conquest in the eleventh century weakened its autonomy, since William the Conqueror was keen to maintain its good favour and even granted it a Royal Charter (the William Charter) guaranteeing its independence (a status it still enjoys). This ancient commercial nexus financed the English Age of Discovery, expanding the City's influence across the globe and securing the offshore centres of administration it still exploits today. In sum, the definitive orientation of Anglo-American culture has always been acquisitive rather than aesthetic, spiritual or experiential. This is not some recent external imposition but rather the culture's presiding ethos for almost two millennia.

This is not to decry wealth or its pursuit, since a reasonable amount of wealth is essential for aesthetic, spiritual or experiential achievement. However, the pursuit of wealth for its own sake represents only psychic impotence and imbalance, the core dysfunction at the root of contemporary Anglo-Saxon culture. By making marriage and family-formation impossibly dangerous for men through misandrist divorce laws, the Anglosphere has closed the link between wealth and the spiritual, aesthetic and experiential areas of life, thereby exalting the material world to the exclusion of all else. In terms of William Blake's analysis, the tyranny of Urizen is now absolute. Successful men in the Anglosphere are doomed to lives of sterile wealth accumulation, unable to direct their wealth into the soul-nurturing aspects of life and doomed to genetic extinction with their physical death.

Truly, the Anglosphere's work-life imbalance has turned it into one of the lower hells.

Part Two

Is Anglo-American Feminism Really that Different?

How the unique misandry of Anglo-American Feminism advances gynocratic agendas across the Anglosphere

2.0 Introduction

It is our contention that the feminism which has arisen in Anglo-Saxon countries has absorbed and integrated the surrounding culture's sex-negativity, homosociality and reality-aversion to produce an entity more focused on promoting sex-negative misandry than any kind of genuine equality. Consequently, Anglo feminism is uniquely hypocritical: while preaching the virtues of progress and equality, it retains a Victorian view of gender-relations in which all women are presumed to be stainless damsels and all men abusive brutes. This double-barrelled agenda has been remarkably successful at securing 'rights' for Anglo-American women while retaining their traditional privileges. Meanwhile, men in the Anglosphere now occupy the worst of all possible worlds – burdened with traditional obligations while viewed as deadbeats and alimony 'cash cows' by the pro-feminist divorce courts of the Anglo-Saxon world. Anglo-American feminism is thus unique in its adversarial attitude to gender-relations; and even more unique in its avowed misandry. Unlike the 'partnership' feminism of the non-Anglosphere West, Anglo feminism draws strength and vindication from the sex-negative and misandrist values of the surrounding culture. It also craftily exploits the residual colonial resentments which uniquely define the Anglosphere, despite Anglo women's historical complicity in the colonial project.

In many respects, misandrist Anglo-American feminism is the ideological expression of various psychological disorders. Psychologists claim that around 2% of the female population suffers from each of the 'Cluster B' psychiatric disorders (Narcissism, Borderline and Histrionic Personality Disorder). However, I would argue that far more Anglo-American women exhibit characteristics of all three – in fact, most women under 35 are either Borderline, Narcissistic, or Histrionic. Indeed, many simultaneously exhibit all three disorders in the cluster. Moreover, Anglo-American culture acts as an incubator for these personality disorders, which is why they are far more prevalent in Anglo-American women than women raised outside the Anglosphere.

In brief, most young Anglo women have unregulated emotions, act impulsively, are totally self-deluded and spend their prime years in abusive relationships with thugs, psychopaths and criminals. While they might not fit all the diagnostic criteria, it has to be conceded that many if not most young Anglo-American women show strong Borderline tendencies. And among lower class, uneducated young women such tendencies are so pronounced as to be normal.

Similarly, an obvious majority of Anglo-American girls display narcissistic tendencies. After all, hypergamous expectations of ideal relationships with wealthy celebrities, rampant entitlement issues, lack of empathy and general selfishness are quite normal among young Anglo females, especially those of the white middle class. Certainly, only a blind man raised in a bubble could think that these traits only characterize 2% of American women.

Again, the young Anglo female's romantic obsession with 'exciting' criminals and psychopaths, her endless need for 'drama' and social stimulation, her unending quest for dangerous and dysfunctional relationships - these are textbook traits of the Histrionic Personality Disorder, which is also massively underdiagnosed in Anglo-American women. A brief glance over the women's magazines on any Anglosphere newsrack suggests HPD is almost synonymous with Anglo females.

For psychologists to admit that huge numbers of Anglo women exhibit severe personality disorders would create a lot of 'waves' in society. In a puritanical culture that places women on pedestals, the idea that so many women are broken and dysfunctional is not admissible. After all, the aim of the Anglo-American authorities is to promote the delusion that the Anglosphere is incomparably superior to other cultural blocs, that life in the UK or the USA is some kind of Shangri La where everyone is happy and fulfilled. Admitting that Anglo culture incubates relatively high numbers of unstable, entitled women does not fit that agenda and is consequently suppressed. Yet if the mental health services were to actually acknowledge the problem, huge savings could be made on the pernicious welfare bills of all Anglo nations; after all, the costly Anglo-American underclass is largely the product of dysfunctional female mating choices and other Borderline traits.

Why do so many young Anglo-American females exhibit serious personality disorders? How has this appalling situation arisen and why is it not acknowledged and addressed? Here are my suggestions:

Princess Syndrome / Pedestalization – the Anglosphere, because of its puritanical heritage and tendency to sexual repression, has created a situation where women are set on pedestals from their earliest years. They can do virtually anything with complete impunity; make false sexual allegations, kill their own offspring, dismiss anti-feminist arguments without rational counter-claims, murder their husbands, drink drive, sexually abuse minors and deny fathers access to their children. Little wonder that so many Anglo-women are so narcissistic: the culture that surrounds them actively promotes such tendencies. Think of young Anglo girls' fixation on Disney Princesses and hypergamous fantasies of perfect relationships. If the Anglosphere were committed to genuine equality as opposed to promoting misandrist feminism, and women truly had responsibilities to go with their endless 'rights', one can be sure that the rampant narcissism and BPD that currently define Anglo-American women would immediately shrink to negligible levels.

Rampant Individualism – at a general level, the English speaking countries are defined by a potent individualism which, while it is the source of the Anglosphere's entrepreneurial strength, has contributed much to its collective pathologies. One recent study found that as many as 25% of American students exhibit narcissistic tendencies: tens of millions of people.

The Anglosphere Beauty Premium – because most Anglo women are obese and generally unattractive, any remotely attractive female grows up knowing hyper-entitlement in every sphere of life. At an anecdotal level, it is obvious that attractive Anglo girls are those most riddled with narcissism and BPD. Basically, any remotely-attractive Anglo female can get away with literally *anything* until the Wall hits them at 35. In a repressive, sickly culture that vilifies male sexuality and exalts all women, beautiful women are essentially goddesses who can do or say whatever they like. Consequently, mild genetic tendencies to narcissism or Borderline are massively amplified by Anglo culture; which is why virtually all beautiful Anglo females are selfish, cruel and evil. That said, even plain or ugly Anglo women often exhibit the same dark constellation of female personality disorders. One assumes this relates to the generic entitlement enjoyed by all young women in the Anglosphere. The obvious observation that BPD traits decline as women age strongly validates the Beauty Premium thesis; for once their beauty has faded, they can no longer act out their neuroses with total impunity. It really is as simple as that… cue witchcraft, wire-frame tampon sculptures and misandrist feminism. As we shall see in this section, the latter is little more than the Dark Triad of female personality disorders dignified with the term 'philosophy'.

For normal men, Anglo-Saxon culture is an inherently flawed creation. Everything about it from the ground up is designed to exalt women and denigrate men. There is nothing male-friendly in the existing Anglosphere; it has declared war on men politically, economically, conceptually and legally. There is nothing there of interest to men at all. The situation has deteriorated beyond tinkering with minutiae or putting the clock back – only complete rejection of pan-Anglosphere civilization and all its institutions, root and branch, can now serve the awakened man effectively. One of my Correspondents writes:

Anglo fools at one point thought their civilization was superior to the French, Germans, Spaniards, Italians and Portuguese. But now with all the Anglo men (and halfway reasonable women) realizing they can find a sane society only in places like France, Germany, Portugal, Italy, Spain and South America and Asia, the Anglosphere is going to see a massive, increasing exodus of millions of its people, leaving only the non-reproducing dregs behind. No sympathy from me, the Anglosphere has slit its own throat (Appendix D, p.233).

2.1 Post-Colonial Racism

Why has misandrist feminism been so successful in Anglophone countries? Too many anti-feminists rely on conspiracy theories to explain the rise of misandrist Anglo feminism. While there have certainly been a number of social, political and religious groups promoting feminist agendas, their writings would never have achieved mass or institutional support if such support did not already exist in the wider culture. The Frankfurt School and other pro-feminist intellectual movements can only flourish if the social soil is already receptive to their message. For example, the Frankfurt School only adopted an infiltration agenda when its calls for a proletarian revolution failed in affluent post-War North America. There is also the issue of institutional compliance. Some nations or cultural blocs have pre-existing institutions which are especially ripe for subversion. Similarly, existing historical memes or traditions can facilitate subversive agendas.

One distinctive pre-existing pro-feminist dynamic present in most Anglo-Saxon countries is the colonial legacy. Although it might seem strange to link this legacy to misandrist feminism, Anglo-American colonialism is responsible for the distinctive strain of racist puritanism which still mars gender-relations across the Anglosphere. In its turn, this repressive agenda ultimately derives from a pragmatic yet distinctive Anglo-Saxon obsession with limiting the reproductive fecundity of 'subject' races or classes coerced by their colonial project. It is no surprise that this obsession is strongest in the Anglo countries with a troubled colonial past built on slavery and genocide, such as Australia or the United States. After all, those nations had most to gain by regulating or limiting the reproductive fecundity of slaves and 'subject' races.

This realization came to me from free discussions with Hondo Solomon, an insightful black American writer who teaches the virtues of polygamy. In his view, the Anglo-Saxon obsession with imposing sexual repression on subject peoples is largely to keep their numbers low, thereby minimizing the threat of revolt. In addition, Hondo also claims that Anglo-puritan monogamy was also promoted to keep subject populations at a low genetic standard by deliberately preventing the natural proliferation of alpha genes for leadership and intelligence: a kind of soft dysgenics. Judging by the hunchbacked, autistic morons inhabiting British towns and cities, this policy has proved fairly effective in its original testing-ground. Hondo also claims that the American obsession with professional sports also derives from its colonial legacy – the obsessive measurement of physical attributes originating in the slave trade, wherein black slaves were sold and even bred on the basis of attributes like arm length and height.

If we focus on the sexual elements of Anglo-American colonialism we see a ubiquitous and concerted attempt to associate religious guilt with sex among subject populations. We also see a determined attempt to replace religions which celebrate reproductive fecundity (voodoo, Islam, Catholicism, Judaism and Hinduism) with guilt-laden Protestant Christianity and its sickly cult of reproductive sterility. Let us note that this insidious campaign is colour blind: it oppresses Highland Scots or the English lower classes as much as is does Black Americans, Aryan Hindus or Black Africans. Wherever he goes the patrician Anglo-American tries to impose his woman-worship, guilt and latent homosexuality with one goal in mind: to limit subject populations' numbers and genetic quality, thereby reducing the threat of revolt against his rule. Religion has no intrinsic value to the Anglo elite beyond its manipulative power as a tool of oppression. This is why patrician Anglo-Americans play 'fast and loose' with religious morality to support whatever agendas best preserve their power or enhance their profits.

Even though its original inspiration has long gone, the same repressive colonial spirit persists as a habitual residue in all Anglosphere countries. Moreover, it is one of the residual memes that has contributed most to the rapid rise of sex-negative misandrist feminism across the Anglosphere. As usual, Anglo-feminism draws strength and succour from the very forces it claims to oppose.

Anglo feminism has nurtured a racist seed since its very inception (Ware, 2015), so such an alignment should come as no surprise when we consider the colonial origins and uses of Anglo-American Puritanism. Lynchings and other Anglo-American race-crimes represented a working collusion between early feminists and imperialists, typically framed as a hysterical campaign to 'protect' exalted white women from the animal lusts of black slaves. This sexual Nazism still contaminates Anglo feminism, albeit at an unstated and subliminal level (consider feminist

Reclaim the Night marches through black areas, which covertly assume that all black men are rapists). Of course, inculcating the colonising race with puritanical values also serves the colonial enterprise by inhibiting interbreeding with subject peoples, with obvious benefits for the colonial project. It is far harder to maintain a colonial culture of exploitation when many of the exploited share genes from the colonising race. The 'Pretty White Girl Syndrome' which saturates the Anglo media is entirely dedicated to exalting white Anglo girls as unattainable deities beyond all reproach; surely another warped legacy of colonial Anglo-elitism.

In turn, Anglo feminists have an obsessive concern with policing (white) male sexuality. When we consider the colonial nature of most Anglo-Saxon countries, the motivations behind this fixation are obvious: simply put, colonising white women do not want their men 'straying' into liaisons with indigenous or non-white women. To some extent, these fears are entirely rational. A colonial nation is usually engaged in ongoing struggles with indigenous males, often resulting in extensive sexual opportunities with native women coerced and corralled for reasons of military expedience. For example, George Armstrong Custer fathered a child on a Native American woman captured during one his campaigns, a common practice among American frontier soldiers. Because such liaisons diminish their own sexual market value, Anglo women have always been keen opponents of ludic male sexuality. The same fanatical opposition to male sexual freedom can still be seen among modern Anglo feminists, a residual meme derived from the Anglosphere's distinct colonial heritage. Indeed, the rabid racism so common among early Anglo-American feminists shares the same source.

It is no longer enough to consider the Anglosphere's puritanical religious heritage the primary force underpinning the Anglo-feminist agenda. Other countries have a strong Protestant tradition (Holland, Germany, Denmark) yet still lack sex-negative feminism of the Anglosphere variety. Other factors must underlie misandrist Anglo-feminism in the modern secular context, sustaining its distinctive agenda. As we shall see, malleable common law is one of these; other prime candidates are genetics, empirical machine values, homosociality and class distinction.

However, the post-colonial dynamic serves and abets Anglo-American feminism in many important ways. Its legacy gives Anglo feminism its distinctive racist, misandrist and sex-negative character, especially in those countries where colonial oppression was strongest (Australia and the United States). A former corrections officer called Lawrence posted an extended essay on my blog in which he argued that Anglo feminism exploits the residual resistance of former subject races in post-colonial Anglo countries to lever outrageous and unwarranted privilege for entitled white women:

Still, I think there's something else at work in the Anglosphere which has to do with Anglosphere history. Most countries in the Anglosphere were settled by invading British colonists who pushed out the natives and took slaves. That's the history of North America in essence. But this all changed in a nasty and bloody way for the Anglosphere that was very different from Latin America, where there wasn't the history of open and hateful group conflict like there was in America's civil war in later history. It just seems like the lines are more blurred in Latin American countries. So North America, in particular, has had this nasty history of rival ethnic and racial groups, displacing the natives and fighting bloody wars against each other, and never came to an understanding about it. And then cultural Marxism came, whipping up and playing on these conflicts as a wedge against the West, and it found its most fertile ground in the Anglosphere. The malicious Anglo feminists of US divorce courts and #metoo seem to borrow a lot of that group warfare language, and maybe that combined with the Puritanism has made the Anglo strain very ugly and hostile (Appendix Q, p.304).

While these pithy observations are obviously valid, the strange irony is that the same Anglo feminists who appropriated the oppositional rhetoric arising from the colonial struggle were intrinsically affiliated to the colonising race and shared most of its values (racism, puritanism and elitism). This partly explains the absurd hypocrisy of Anglo-American feminists: white, upper-middle class Anglo-Saxons at Ivy League colleges considering themselves 'downtrodden' and 'oppressed' is not only ridiculous, it rightly offends those genuinely living on the wrong side of the Anglo colonial project.

Lawrence's observation about the Anglo nations never reaching true self-awareness or 'understanding' about their colonial past is also telling. The John Ford western The Searchers (1956) captures this post-colonial confusion perfectly, with its racist protagonist and troubling ambivalence over race mixing and white female sexuality. The film presents no resolution to these issues, reflecting the ongoing refusal of the Anglosphere nations to acknowledge their complicity in an oppressive colonial project replete with historical crimes and their troubling legacy.

Indeed, it could be argued that Anglo-American colonial eugenics remains an ongoing programme. In their documentary on the current gender imbalance afflicting many Asian countries, Christ and Dorholt argue that the 'one child' policy pursued in Korea, China and India during the 1960s and 1970s essentially served an American racist and eugenic agenda (Christ and Dorholt, 2019). The UN Population Fund was backed by the Ford and Rockefeller Foundations and other American think tanks, with the US providing 40% of its funding. Through this body, the US (together with Sweden, Switzerland and the UK) made India, China and other developing countries enforce strict population controls in return for international aid - a policy which only ended in the 1990s. While this programme was presented to developing nations as essential to raise their living standards, its backers were avowed eugenicists who feared the world risked being 'swamped' by non-whites unless drastic measures were taken. Given the Anglosphere's scurrilous colonial transgressions, the obsessive Anglo-American fixation on Nazi war crimes in books, documentaries and films can best be seen as an ideological smoke screen to hide its own misdeeds.

2.2 Sex Negativity

The dysfunctional state of modern North America seemingly embodies all the worst qualities of Anglo-Saxon culture: usury, legalism, hypocrisy, misandry, socialism, repression and rampant gynocentricism. While Canadian and American men consider their lot unique and unprecedented, their benighted region is in fact extremely reminiscent of the English Commonwealth (1649-60), which was in many respects a template for the future United States. This period in English history saw puritans under Oliver Cromwell take full charge of government and impose savage repression on the British people for over a decade. All objects of beauty were systematically smashed, free speech punished, taverns and innocent pastimes outlawed while dour cruelty came to dominate law and punishment. In sum, the Commonwealth embodied all the cold, frigid inhumanity of the Anglo-Saxon soul. As I have written elsewhere, this period left a permanent mark on the English national character – and by extension, the whole Anglo-American world.

Although the terrible state of modern North America is unendurable for men, it does serve a positive instructional purpose. Because it is so close to the English Commonwealth in values and outcomes, it allows us to trace the true origins of modern Anglo feminism, misandry and usury to their true source.

To begin with, modern North America's ongoing sexual witch hunt is really a puritanical war against physical pleasure itself: it is not 'revolutionary' at all, just a feminized restatement of traditional Anglo values. The real motivation behind such 'abuse' claims is reflexive hatred of male virility and indeed, sex itself; in short, the erotophobia of Cromwell's Commonwealth. After all, as Matt Damon opined, the accusations lack any notion of moral proportion; a slap on the ass or an unwanted verbal proposition is arbitrarily conflated with full-on rape, as though they were legally or morally commensurate misdemeanours. All sexual manifestations are equally heinous to the modern Anglo-feminist mind, just as they were to the Commonwealth puritans.

Closely allied to this systematic war on pleasure is a deep Anglo tendency to hysterical herd conformity. This moral socialism tries to drag everyone down to the lowest common psycho-sexual denominator:

50

a hypocritical, repressed, embittered Anglo shit-heel. In sum, North America's cultural Marxism is really the same old 'Commonwealth' moral equalism in modern guise. Because of it, the Anglo masses will follow whatever they believe to be the 'dominant ideology' like a horse with blinders – even if that ideology works against them and their own interests. For example, some of the most fanatical modern sexual witch hunters are men who work in the entertainment industries. On course, this lemming-like hysteria is closely linked to and fed by sexual repression: hystericus means 'womb' in Latin, and the repressive Anglosphere is uniquely renowned for its 'moral crusades'. The Puritan witch trials in seventeenth century England and America are eerily similar in tone to their modern sexual counterparts: teenage girls making wild accusations are lionized by the authorities; the accused are duly removed and punished without a shred of evidence; and in a few years people will be scratching their heads and wondering what it was all about. But forever fixated on reflexive repression, the Anglo nations never, ever learn… Go figure.

As Lord Protector of England, Cromwell restored usury for the first time in centuries; he was the true architect of modern North American debt slavery. In truth, the definitive Anglo-Saxon obsession with material wealth while neglecting all else begins at this time in English history. And now, trans-generational social dysfunction is so rampant across the Anglosphere that its criminally-acquired wealth is largely wasted on costly public crime and welfare programmes. Moreover, trillions of dollars in unsecured debt generated by women pursuing useless college degrees have permanently wrecked the North American economies. Again, go figure.

As the English Commonwealth had no real ruler, just a Lord Protector (the tyrant Cromwell), so America lacks any coherent leadership. Despite his dynamic rhetoric and intentions, Trump is a toothless force who has been completely nullified by the Marxist Deep State. Whatever the expressed wishes of the American people, they might as well have Hillary for President. A rudderless nation with no confident pilot is a ship adrift on stormy seas, at risk from every peril. Without a properly-defined psycho-social template emanating from a tried and trusted leader, no nation can hope to thrive.

Both the English Commonwealth and modern Anglo-America are defined by a futile hatred of reality itself. The Commonwealth was obsessed by banning pleasure in all its forms, whether visual, physical or sexual. Unfortunately for them, pleasure has too deep a root in the human genotype to ever be arbitrarily abolished in this manner. Meanwhile, the 'progressive' wing in modern Anglo America tries to deny the brute fact of human gender differences while promoting the LBGTXYZ fiction than anyone can self-identify as anything - even inanimate objects. Aside from being obviously insane, these attitudes repudiate the classical Greek roots of western civilization. Just imagine applying such absolute semiotic relativism to activities beyond politics and society. What if scientists or engineers decided tin was iron, and iron was mercury? In a few days, half the population would be buried under rubble. Yet the Anglo 'progressive' brigade demand that such arbitrary values prevail in social and sexual affairs. Although pleasure-repression and gender denial seem very different, their underlying motivation remains identical: deluded puritanical rage against reality itself. In sum, Anglo-American 'progressives' embody the same puritanical values they claim to challenge; and the same can be said for Anglo feminists.

Of course, there is one important difference between the Cromwell's English Commonwealth and modern North America. The Commonwealth was a true patriarchy, not a gynocracy like modern Anglo-America. But if we replace Cromwell's dusty Old Testament God with Anglo women – America's new deities – the two regimes are essentially identical in their goals, aims and methods.

2.3 The College Obsession

Our age is defined by the decline of retail stores and shopping malls in the US. Once-thriving malls are now derelict shells and only food stores look set to survive. Exactly the same phenomenon has beset Britain in recent years: C&A, Woolworths, BHS, Comet, Blockbuster and Phones4U have all 'gone West' since the Millennium. And other retailers have had to write-off hundreds of stores just to survive. The manosphere's plausible argument is that women – society's inveterate shoppers – now lack the disposable wealth to indulge their dubious passion. The jobs they hold are generally not very remunerative; and men are no longer prepared to support their profligate ways.

This incisive analysis is also supported by the figures on female debt. Most debtors are women, by a considerable margin; and much of their debt arises from paying expensive college fees for worthless qualifications in the arts and humanities:

Women are now the majority on college campuses across the United States—representing 56% of all students enrolled as of fall 2016. And according to a new report, they're also shouldering the lion's share of the nation's student debt problem.

A report by the American Association of University Women (AAUW) found that on average, women hold $833 billion—or almost two-thirds—of the country's $1.3-trillion student debt, compared to the $477 billion that men hold.

Overall, after completing a bachelor's degree, women's average accrued student debt is about $1,500 greater than men's. African American women take on more student debt than any other group of women, with an average of $30,000 (Farber, 2017).

In the UK, most college loans are never repaid and 48% of graduates get jobs they could have had after leaving high school (Wilson, 2017). In sum, the majority of students pursue higher education out of snobbery (it is still mistakenly considered 'middle class'), outmoded parental expectations and the (largely false) promise of hedonistic excess.

Reality soon bites, however. Newly armed with irrelevant qualifications, the average college graduate quickly learns that a line of computer code outweighs a million lines of poetry. Now, culture is a wonderful thing and yes, it should be studied and transmitted to succeeding generations. But do we really need half the population studying it? Times were when the humanities were hardcore disciplines requiring mastery of ancient languages and intimate knowledge of the great canonical works of western civilization. Since the Sixties counter-culture infiltrated academia, those days are long gone; any clown can do Cultural Studies.

In many ways, the problem arises from a long-standing mismatch between reality and expectation. The western worldview is still rooted in the post-War era, an age of unprecedented prosperity and opportunity. In those days, going to college automatically made someone 'middle class' for life. Even blue collar workers could buy their own house, run a car and sent two kids to college. Although that era ended in 1974, it continues to define the West's general outlook – a legacy worldview, if you will. Most middle aged people still assume that a college degree in any subject from any institution will confer privileged status on their offspring. Indeed, the whole 'happy families' narrative to which Tradcon politicians cling is also a legacy of those times. These mistaken beliefs are incredibly stubborn and persistent, something only fully apparent to someone from a non-western cultural heritage.

And in many ways the misty-eyed nostalgia for those golden years is understandable: they were times of unprecedented opportunity for ordinary Americans. However, this nostalgia has become problematic now the West faces tough competition from regions armed with higher IQs and the Confucian work ethic. Moreover, Anglosphere nations are so maladjusted to existing conditions that young people can longer expect rational guidance from their elders. This especially true for young men, whose parents told them 'the right girl' would happen along if they conformed to societal expectations; or that looks and money 'don't matter' (for fuck's sake). Indeed, the Manosphere in all its digital, misogynistic glory arose to fill this 'advice gap' that yawns like a crevasse in the lives of younger men.

But the post-War legacy hobbles women, too. Armed with pointless degrees in finger painting and womyn's studies, they waste their prime years riding the thug carousel (or snarled in sterile hyper-hypergamy) and shuffling papers for a pittance. When the Wall approaches, they hastily revert to the post-War narrative: surely Prince Beta will ride up on his white charger, write off her debts and save her ageing ass with a wave of his credit card?

Not really. Thanks to the Manosphere, even the dumbest Beta knows the score. Besides, with sex tourism booming in South America, Slavic Europe and the Far East, he needs dusty white tail like he needs a kick in the nuts. And so our crusty Anglobitch stumbles towards middle age, accruing ever more debt, her SMV sinking with each passing year. We know where this ends: a broken-down cat lady abusing opiates on Welfare, renting her rancid ass out to gammas for the price of her next fix. The economic repercussions will be seismic in the decades to come.

I don't claim to be an economist but even I can see that if a huge proportion of women take out huge loans they can never repay, someone somewhere must be getting shafted. Limiting college access to STEM students would probably go some way to fixing things. However, that would greatly reduce female enrolment rates – complete anathema in the gynocentric Anglosphere. In any case, American women must believe they are 'middle class' – a superior caste – for the post-feminist narrative to work. Even if this 'status' is illusionary, the illusion has to be sustained to keep females 'onside'; an absolute imperative in our gynocentric civilization.

Ultimately, it is hard not to link the rise of Anglo-American feminism to the Anglosphere's economic woes. Permitting trillions of dollars of unsecured debt so that mediocre Anglo princesses can feel successful, superior and 'middle class' is irrational in the twenty-first century. Palliating women in this way began in the prosperous post-War era, and doubtless hastened its end. Essentially, women are clowns; and building societies around their infantile whims is a recipe for disaster. By nature, women are not productive; they cannot create, build or innovate. Though many of them study the arts and humanities, their contributions to these fields is zero. Jurisprudence, the only 'serious' field where they outnumber men, predictably requires no imagination. However, law does allow women to indulge their atavistic yearnings for social destruction and systemized misandry, abetted by the Pharisaic Anglo-American obsession with punitive legalism.

2.4 Homosociality

Debra Ollivier's *What French Women Know* (2009) offers some interesting insights on the Anglobitch phenomenon. The author is an Anglo-American expat female who married and settled in France.

This has given her an unusual cross-cultural perspective. However, her most interesting insight into the Anglobitch phenomenon involves her analysis of Anglo-American feminism's 'homosociality': a deep-embedded puritanical tendency for the sexes to be segregated from earliest childhood, leaving little room for mutual understanding and ultimately leading to an implicitly misandrist form of feminism.

Recollecting her own youth and childhood in the United States (presumably in some bourgeois enclave), the author cites many examples of homosociality working to deform Anglo-American gender-relations:

One tribute to French feminism is that the "stereophonic richness of the exchange between the sexes" still flourishes in its own way two centuries after de Stael put her own brand of feminist iconoclasm on the map. Personally, I'd never given much thought to "stereophonic richness" while growing up in the States except when fiddling with the woofer on a car radio, though even in the playgrounds of my youth and during some of feminism's brightest moments, I could recall the enduring seeds of "homosociality" in the way boys and girls were often segregated. (The day we were ushered into the school auditorium with the solemnity of a slightly alarming liturgical rite to watch gender-specific sex education films comes immediately to mind) (Ollivier, 2009: pp.44-45).

Awareness of homosociality and its potential problems in fact enjoys a long and illustrious history in the francophone world. Many French writers - or expatriate Anglo-Americans viewing the Anglosphere from afar - have long made pithy comments on the effects of Anglo-American puritanism. The rather one-dimensional, blinkered nature of Anglo women is one particularly well-worn topic. Of course, the Anglobitch Thesis maintains that Anglo feminism has always been an *expression* of Anglo values, not any kind of revolt against them.

One terrible by-product of unchecked homosociality is whole nations of women who hate and resent men, fuelled by sexual paranoia and disquiet. Phil, one of my correspondents, describes twenty-first century North America in some detail:

Americans nowsadays are tight, anxious, looking over their shoulders, #metoo and the media lynch mob has everything to do with it. Men in America, and it seems like about everywhere in Anglosphere, can't date for fear of having any slight misconstruance or bad communication aired out as dirty laundry on Fabricatebook- oh, I mean "Facebook" or Twitter or the extreme feminist blogs the next day. Even normal women are constantly under pressure from their "feminist sisters" to "you go girl" and find any reason they can to make the men around them miserable. Both men and women in America are miserable at the work place, can't even look at each other without the spectre of harassment coming up. What's worse, the feminist radicals at Vox, Bustle, TheVerge, Ohnotheydidn't, Vulture and the shrill echo-chambers of the FBverse and Twitterverse are fanning the flames, to encourage women in North America to "name and shame" every single man they've had the slightest unpleasant encounter with over the past 2 decades, and any going forward. Sadly it seems like this is spreading to everywhere in the Anglosphere (Appendix E, p.235).

By contrast, gender relations in the non-Anglo West reflect its relative lack of Anglo gender-paranoia:

As smart as you guys observations have been, I'm not even sure your observant words capture how beyond miserable the US and Anglo world is compared to not only Europe's mainland but also Russia, Brazil, Argentina, Chile, and most of East and Southeast Asia. I've seen it every time I return to the US, but now more than ever before, the contrast is extreme, the metoo mess is directly impacting completely normal, nice and good people in the worst possible way. In Belgium where I now work, and this goes equally for Germany where I was posted at 3 years ago, the

58

culture is a world away from the non stop gloom of the US where I grew up. And the picture y'all posted at the top is so on-target! In Germany and Belgium you run into hot girls like that all the time, fit and trim, wearing thong bikinis out in public, strong and confident women but also sweet and sexy, genuine and happy to interact with men. Not to mention more true blondes than anywhere in the US but they're also intelligent enough to have a real conversation with. People are ambitious and motivated and they do work hard to advance their careers, but men and women know how to eat, dance, enjoy other's company. Oh, and to have sex like normal human beings. Belgian and German girls love for men to hit on them, yes they want you to take care of yourself, stay neat and in shape, be ambitious and have at least some game, and eventually you gotta pick up some of the language(s) (French and/or Flemish in Belgium depending, obviously German in Germany or east Belgium). But they don't expect you to read their minds and they don't call out harassment for flirting even at the workplace, heck If there's a hot girl on your project team both the men and the women in the office will be puzzled if you don't ask her out at least once. The pretty femmes even in the small towns in Wallonia (south part of Belgium where I am now), or western Germany (Nordrhein Westfalen for any y'all traveling this way), will just casually stroll out in a little string bikini onto the side streets on a warm Saturday, far from the beach, just for the sake of being sexy, nobody bats eyelashes (Appendix E, p.234).

Another correspondent called Ripper contrasts the sensuous grace and 'common sense' of French women with the shrill hysteria of their American counterparts:

Give me France any day with the majesty and nuance of a superhot bikini model like Laetitia Casta speaking out against the stupidity of this "movement", joined by her graceful, elegant sisters like Catherine Deneuve and the thousands of other French women who've called bullshit. Let's not just talk about this here to our own choir, let's get onto other forums, Reddit and the chans, write letters to the editor or even newspaper and magazine articles- if you want to have a halfway normal love and working life these days, and real relationships as humans have had for millennia, you need to get out of the Anglosphere. There is no other way. This goes both for men and for the remaining sensible women in the Anglophere. Leave it. This is our era's "Go West, young man". We have to leave the civilizational shithole of the Anglosphere, there is no other way anymore (Appendix D, p.232).

After these exhortations for men to flee the Anglosphere, Ripper links Anglo homosociality to the Anglosphere's generic anti-life agenda:

To you American c***s and Anglosphere losers in general, the French are showing us what real women, with class and confidence, have understood for eons courtship, love and mating are a dance, a delicate and often misunderstood dance of seduction, and any civilization depends on it for its own survival. The puritanical and Victorian fainting couch f---witness of the Anglosphere was a poison pill for the civilization for the beginning, that seems to have been activated into a death blow for the Anglo world when added to fourth wave feminism, neo-Leftism and the corporate "throw 'em under the bus" attitude of US and Anglosphere "money above people" corporations (Appendix D, p.233).

Since female identity is by nature empty and formless, developmental isolation among other females creates a 'Hall of Mirrors' where no coherent personality can ever form. Without a defined personality to guide female emotions, they grow unchecked like plants in a hothouse. This explains not only the astronomical levels of BPD and HPD among Anglo females, it explains their generic proneness to hysteria and irrationalism. Despite often being 'highly educated', almost no Anglo female can explore a rational conversation on any serious topic for more than three minutes without lapsing into giggles or unchecked sentiment. This one-dimensional dullness of character is largely the product of homosociality, and is rare in the non-Anglosphere West.

While homosociality is a discrete entity, it obviously springs from a puritanical, anti-life fixation distinct to the Anglosphere. Since this Puritanism seems to define the Anglo-American world, it is inevitable that homosociality will also continue to define it. Although constriction of healthy gender-relations is grievous enough, homosociality also feeds and incubates the Dark Triad of personality disorders which define Anglo women (see section 2.1). In particular, the Borderline and Histrionic personality disorders engulf the female the female mind when it develops in gendered isolation, although narcissism is also nurtured by it. This is because homosociality incubates a generic female sense of aloofness and superiority over men as a class. Moreover, homosociality creates a heightened impression of sexual scarcity in any given society. Inevitably, female narcissism is strongest when sexual scarcity prevails – hence the feminist desire to abolish prostitution and criminalize all heterosexual expressions and manifestations, even while extolling deviant sexualities of every kind. The ultimate expression of female homosociality is hyper-hypergamy: this is the final form of female narcissism, wherein women consider themselves too good for any man. Hyper-hypergamy is in fact very common among educated Anglo-American women, and largely explains the reproductive sterility of the educated classes in the Anglosphere. Hyper-hypergamous Anglo women have moved beyond relational interaction with men into a new psychic realm of narcissistic homosociality that is unique in the world's history. The Anglosphere's caste-like social structure, historical racism and neurotic infantilism all contribute to this condition, combining with homosociality and Puritanism to produce women who view all reproductive matters with hysterical revulsion.

In sum, homosociality is a hugely overlooked but highly significant feature of Anglo-American existence; one which militates strongly against male fulfilment in every sphere of romantic life.

2.5 Misandry

As has been well-established, the Anglosphere harbours deep tendency to Puritanism. The Anglo-American obsession with policing public sexuality for 'the public good' owes much to this unstated agenda, as does the long-standing (and bogus) Anglo assumption of moral superiority over other cultures. Of course, Anglo-American feminism has co-opted these agendas, as well as the Puritanism underlying them. It will be noted that Anglo feminists presume the right to ban paid sex work or regulate sex tourism without a moment's thought, as if this were morally right by definition.

However, Anglo feminism also has a strong misandrist cast distinct from other forms of feminism. Again, this hatred owes much to prevailing Anglo-Saxon values, although it has amplified their misandrist elements a thousandfold. This misandry uniquely defines the Anglo brand of feminism, and explains its adversarial, rapacious and destructive nature.

Since male sexuality is by definition active, potent and vigorous, it automatically offends the infantile morality of the Anglosphere. In a normal, life-affirming culture, potency and vigour are positive qualities. In a denatured culture which has severed all links to the primal wells of life and joy, these virtues acquire sinister associations. Little wonder then that the Anglosphere now tacitly views men as unwelcome interlopers, party crashers and defective females.

However, Anglo feminism has taken the deep-rooted Anglo-Saxon distrust of male sexuality and twisted it into a creed of hatred. Since the Anglosphere is by definition a matriarchy, feminism has effectively remoulded mainstream Anglo culture into a 'girls only' playpen from which men are systematically excluded (despite having to maintain and even defend it). Consider male exclusion from higher education, the burgeoning rates of male suicide and depression, the instant institutional acceptance of 'metoo' hysteria and now calls to imprison all male incels – all products of post-feminist feedback, yet all ultimately rooted in misandrist Puritanism.

And this is the point of this chapter: to explain the unique misandry of Anglo-American feminism. Because Puritanism raises the scarcity value of sex, automatically placing women on exalted pedestals, they will always be drawn to it. However, since misandrist Puritanism is already deep-rooted in Anglo-Saxon culture, it has spawned a form of feminism which is openly adversarial towards men and seeks to ostracise them from society at large. The pre-feminist culture of the Anglosphere, with its infantile homosociality, sexual repression, crabbed legalism, latent homosexuality and sickly cult of woman worship was the perfect soil for these developments. Anglo feminism is not a 'revolutionary' entity at all; it merely represents a more extreme variant of the source culture, with heightened misandry and repression. One might even call it a caricature of Anglo-American culture.

One of my learned correspondents, Gearman, describes this hypocrisy at length:

What Rookh and everyone else is making clear here, it's not feminism alone that's so damaging and wrecking to the lives and livelihoods of modern men, and to women and families, but the combination of a particular type of feminism—the adversarial driven "us against them" third and fourth-wave of the Anglo world— combined with Anglo Puritanism, cultural Marxism, the common law tradition (which makes divorce and the "metoo" witch hunt profitable to the extremists pushing it), the cuck chivalry white knights who enable "have your cake and eat it too" hypocrisy of Anglo feminists (claim to be strong and independent but need permanent alimony after a divorce) and the crony corporate capitalism of the Anglo world which sees politically incorrect men as easy targets to vulture off of. All of these things are unique to the Anglosphere, and they're what makes Anglosphere feminism uniquely toxic (Appendix I1, pp.248-249).

Gearman moves on to analyze how the Anglosphere reflexively demonizes male sexuality, and has even transformed it into a tool to pauperize men:

In specific policy which is what actually affects people in the real world, the Anglosphere is concretely far worse for men and families in general. More specifics, as the same goes for the metoo hysteria. Once again, look at where metoo has caught on, and become an ever more massive wrecking ball that's making it impossible for men and women to have normal relationships, posing concrete danger for men's livelihoods and making "sexual harassment" and "sexual misconduct" a weapon that can be used anywhere, at anytime, in any workplace or for any reason, with an accuser having total power to ruin an accused without any evidence even for things that may (or may not) have happened decades ago (Appendix I2, p.253).

While acknowledging that western (and even non-western) countries outside the Anglosphere have well-developed forms of feminism, Gearman makes a compelling case that the Anglo-American brand of feminism is uniquely misandrist, gynocentric and sex-negative:

And as a result of the way information spreads, and modern living standards have evolved, yes all of the countries in the non-Anglo West, South America, Russia and eastern Asia are going to have some degree of feminism in them and women wanting to be somewhat independent. But that in itself doesn't make them bad places, in fact if it encourages women to be truly independent and not try to leech off husbands during marriage or after a divorce, it boosts the living stands of men and fathers, and makes it safer and a more encouraging environment to start families. This is the "Sweden type paradox" a lot of expats are bringing up, even though feminism is strong up in the Nordics, it's not the toxic Anglosphere type up there because it's not hypocritical. Women who claim independence actually have to be that way, so there's no alimony, limited sort of child support and cultures that are quite favorable to fathers, paternity leave, and men's and father's rights. I also know plenty of Anglo men who've moved to Scandinavia for their jobs or to marry local girls there, and they're all very happy. Even the divorcees have emerged with no trouble at all, they're still able to raise their kids and start new families (Appendix I2, p.254).

Read the things that Roosh Valizadeh posts up or the forum commenters are posting up on Rooshv forums or Return of Kings, or at Chateau Heartiste. It's not some nebulous "Western feminist culture" that's the problem for men in English-speaking countries. It's that the Anglosphere, and specifically the Anglosphere, has made it far too dangerous even for normies—perfectly normal men who want to be husbands and fathers—to marry, have kids or even enter into normal dating relationships with women. The cost-benefit calculation shows it's far, far too dangerous to consider marriage or childbearing when you have a greater than even chance of winding up in poverty or even prison from marriage or having a kid in the Anglosphere, or losing your hard won career, earnings, reputation and savings from sexual harassment hysteria, even from casual dating or work interactions, that's only going to get even worse and more oppressive in the next few years. That's because of specific marriage, divorce and harassment policies particular to the Anglosphere and Israel, and those are a direct result of the unique toxic feminism combined with Puritanism, cultural Marxism, opponent-driven court system and common law that's unique to the Anglosphere and Israel (Appendix I4, pp.260-261).

Another of my learned and interesting correspondents, a former corrections officer called 'Lawrence', invokes the Anglosphere's rapacious and profiteering legalism to explain much of the blatant misandry in Anglo feminism. In simple terms, it *pays* lawyers, the legal system and the State in general to maximize misandry:

The MGTOW's are correct in the corruption they've identified in the divorce court system, but even most of them don't see the horrible path this corrupt system eventually leads to. However, it is something you see as a prison guard with your jail cells filled with men who committed no crime, confined there because US, Canadian and British family courts have imposed impossible financial demands on them, literally making them slaves for the prison-industrial complex to profit off of. This is one of the ugliest sides of the society wide disaster that the Anglobitch culture has given rise to, and Rookh was well ahead of his time in putting many of the threads together. In my former line of work, I saw the horrible, kafka-esque end result of Anglo misandry and feminazi feminism: total impoverishing, a jail cell, literal slavery, even for wealthy and highly skilled men. In fact, ESPECIALLY for wealthy and highly skilled Anglo men, who are this corrupt machine's favorite targets in America and the Anglosphere (Appendix Q, p.285).

Exactly so. Law is a business and, like all businesses, its aim is to maximize profits. What better way to do this than by targeting the most affluent and successful men? There is little point in targeting tramps on Welfare living in the projects: they have few (if any) resources to extract. Affluent, successful men are quite another matter:

The catch of it is, to make money from a slave economy, you need lots and lots of slaves, and you don't want them to be too violent or dangerous either. But then how do you get normal, law-abiding men (and also many women) into the heavily profitable US prison slave system, when jail is only supposed to be for criminals or bad guys? The answer, you simply fill up the prisons with people, mainly men and preferably white men, who aren't actually criminals, but who can be tossed into jail for victimless "crimes" like drug possession. And for simply doing the thing that humans are biologically programmed for—having relationships with women and fathering children. So how to drive these decent law-abiding men into the slave plantations of US prisons? Simple. Create a vicious, misandrist culture in the USA, and the Anglosphere more generally where men and particularly white men are vilified, demonized and turned into objects of hatred and scorn, encourage women at every opportunity to divorce men and "sock it to 'em" in divorce court, and now with #metoo, encourage women all over the workplace, bars, gyms, wherever to start a massive witch hunt against men for simple flirtation or even looking at them, while lobbying to make the vaguely defined "sexual misconduct" charge (that is, it's whatever a feminazi decides it is) into a punishable offense. And there you have it, millions of American men and other Anglosphere men ripe for confinement in the lucrative slave complexes of the Anglosphere, which we call penitentiaries (Appendix Q, p.288).

When I first began writing about misandrist Anglo feminism, my perspective was largely cultural, psychological and interpersonal. I focused on how the latent Puritanism of Anglo-Saxon civilization tended to produce women with a pronounced sense of entitlement, unchecked arrogance and bland, one-dimensional personalities. While all these traits are bad enough, the Anglobitch Thesis has grown into something altogether far more lofty and serious: a complete socio-economic and legal critique of the Anglosphere. I do not claim any legal or economic expertise; however, several practitioners in these fields have left me extensive correspondence showing that economics and law in the Anglosphere are uniquely susceptible to manipulation by misandrist feminism. However, the Anglosphere's cloying Puritanism ultimately underpins these factors, as Lawrence makes clear:

As reminder I'm in France now, have been for years, and as a Web designer who's often called on to help with the software used for prison intakes and legal briefings for law enforcement personnel, I also get a lot of international contract experience. I don't want to claim the non-Anglo world is a paradise, yes we do have dumb, shrill and annoying feminists here too. But there really is a huge difference away from the Anglosphere because the feminists have nowhere the level of the power or cultural approval they do in the Anglosphere, and in France and throughout Europe, are shunned and ridiculed by even the mainstream media and society. The misandry is combatted in a lot of surprising ways, the safety nets are open to men as well as women here, the "sock it to him" attitude of the USA is throttled, people are cooler with nudity and sexuality so harassment isn't an issue (Appendix Q, p.295).
.

Another expatriate correspondent called Brock also stresses the importance of national 'background' culture in shaping individual feminist traditions. Because Anglo-American culture is inherently misandrist, so is the feminism it creates:

Some anon commenters say feminism is a problem outside the Anglosphere, but it really isn't, the "feminism" in the Anglosphere is more like "feminazism", it's malicious, scornful, hate-filled, nasty, ugly and harsh. In Europe, Asia, the non-Anglo Americas, what passes for "feminism" is a whole different animal. It's not zero-sum or hate-filed or shrill like you see in the US. It's just more about spreading more opportunities (Appendix P, pp.280-281).

Of course it is! A fact I recognized decades ago. There is simply no equivalent of sex-negative fanatics such as Catherine McKinnon in Sweden, Norway or any other non-Anglosphere country. Similarly, law and economics outside the Anglosphere do not cohere with feminism to make unreasonable demands of divorced husbands and throw men in jail. As we shall see, the uniquely malleable nature of Anglo common law makes this institutional misandry possible; and legal research is the most tantalizing future direction for the Thesis.

As an addendum to this discussion of Anglo feminist misandry, it is interesting to note that Anglo feminists especially loathe men who threaten to co-opt their hallowed status as 'Anglosphere Angels'. This extends to male transsexuals, whom one might assume would be natural feminist allies.

The twenty-first century Anglosphere's obsession with transsexuals (especially male transsexuals) is curious. Everywhere one looks, transsexual rights are in the spotlight. Their right to use public washrooms formed a prominent plank of Hillary Clinton's failed Presidential election campaign, while the UK's progressive media obsesses over this marginal issue. I doubt that transsexuals of any kind constitute much more than 0.01% of the Anglo-American population; but listening to the mainstream media, one would think around half were considering 'transition'. But as always in the Anglosphere, nothing is ever what it seems. While 'trans rights' seem naturally affiliated to progressive political agendas, they are in some respects the ultimate expression of traditional Anglo-American misandry. After all, what could be more misandrist than transforming men into women?

Far from threatening the establishment, male transsexuals are in fact the Anglo matriarchy's ultimate stooges. Transexuality is not even a sexual orientation - it is a revolt against nature itself. The same hatred of biological reality also defines Anglo feminism, which views sexual intercourse as 'rape' and pregnancy as 'slavery'. In fact, they are no such thing. Placental mammals reproduce by the male injecting sperm into the female's body; the growing young are nurtured in the womb until the female gives birth to them. Only a sick and deluded mind fuelled by a terrible rage against reality would label these biological facts 'crimes of oppression', as Anglo feminists seek to do. As usual, whenever they attempt to 'stick it to the man' the feminazis invariably regurgitate the same old puritanical, anti-life themes of traditional Anglo culture.

Similarly, while their 'trans' protégés consider themselves 'gender revolutionaries' they are in truth cheerleaders for the Anglosphere's institutional misandry. After all, male transsexuals are the ideal of any matriarchy: men who want to be women. No wonder the pan-Anglosphere political and legal authorities are clamouring to rubber stamp 'trans rights' legislation. In some respects Anglo transsexuals are like Diaspora Jews: people prepared to subsist in a hostile environment at literally any cost. Transsexuals in Anglo nations have effectively foresworn their very identity as men, or as natural human beings; they have internalized Anglo misandry so completely that they prefer to become sterile women than exist as men.

Of course, the privileged status afforded Anglo women also factors into this decision. It is interesting how some of the male incel community are opting to 'transition' into transsexuals. Faced with the choice of a sexless, low-status male life and a sterile, high-status female life, many men will opt for the latter. Even as sterile pseudo-women, they automatically acquire a 'victimhood Karma' which is never extended to male incels (who are merely derided as disposable scum). And the system ultimately benefits, since angry sexless males are painlessly removed from the social equation. Is it purely coincidental that 'trans' agendas began to be pushed across the Anglosphere in the wake of various incel massacres?

However, sensing these incel pseudo-women co-opting their pedestals, Anglo feminists increasingly view their new 'sisters' with growing distrust and hatred. The repulsive Australian femihag Germaine Greer is one of these, having written several polemics against male transsexuals. This eruption of loathing is interesting, in that it highlights the utter hypocrisy and intellectual vacuity of Anglo feminists. While they reflexively condemn the very idea of innate human difference in every other sphere, they revert to neo-fascist biological arguments when their own unique gender-status is threatened.

Ultimately, for all their self-loathing, male transsexuals will never find the acceptance they crave from women or Anglo-American society at large. They have no reproductive potential or status – the master key to female privilege in the repressive Anglosphere.

Part Three

Is Anglo-American Law Really that Different?

The unique role of Common Law in advancing gynocratic agendas across the Anglosphere

3.0 Introduction

When I began writing Distant Shores, I never expected to produce a whole section on Anglo-American legalism. However, a post highlighting the feminist domination of top American law schools in early 2018 generated an avalanche of knowledgeable comments by readers with genuine understanding of the legal system, including practising attorneys and even a professor of law. All of these comments, some of them containing over twenty thousand words, are included in a remarkable series of appendices at the back of this book. This invaluable resource will doubtless be cited centuries from now, by scholars and informed laymen alike.

Having no real legal expertise or knowledge, I found this burgeoning commentary a genuine revelation. A theme that gradually emerged in the developing commentary was the distinction between Anglo-Saxon common law and the civil law which still dominates most countries outside the Anglosphere. The commentators concluded that common law is more open to manipulation than civil law due to its greater interpretative flexibility, a fact which allows feminists to mould society without recourse to normal democratic processes.

This section is therefore the most original and important in the whole book; and probably the most important thing I have ever written, in any sphere. It was constructed on the shoulders of giants, whose original words are recorded in the extensive appendices. In a wholly original work such as this, there are few 'official' authorities to cite; there is simply no academic or conceptual precedent for these seismic ideas. Given this restriction, a revolutionary post-Internet thinker can only look to commentary inspired by his own project to sustain his perspective.

Fortunately, the legal commentary on my blog is almost a book in its own right: the work of experienced legal experts and practitioners, not just educated laypeople (although these also made an impressive contribution). Therefore I ploughed this new furrow with strong horses and a sturdy plough. And there is little doubt that the tiny seed I planted with someday sprout into a mighty tree, one that will overshadow all future discussion of law, divorce and gender relations in the English-speaking world.

Before me, there was nothing. Yes, there were MRAs like Warren Farrell pointing out contradictions in the feminist narrative. But no one had recognized that Anglo-American culture already contained a plethora of deep-rooted misandrist memes, making it especially susceptible to the depredations of misandrist feminism. That is my unique contribution to the manosphere and 'Red Pill' thought in general (derived from seminal movie The Matrix (1999), the Red Pill represents bitter enlightenment as opposed to comforting Blue Pill self-delusion). And because my perspective is as valid as it is original, it has grown to influence all rational discussion of western gender-relations.

American expatriation seminars now even use my writings as motivational tools for men who want to escape misandrist America. One of my expatriate correspondents writes:

One thing I haven't mentioned yet, is that my wife is actually American herself, and she moved to France with me. There have been a number of expat conferences in the US recently drawing American expats in, across the world, to spread their wisdom to other Americans thinking about expatriating. (A lot of people at my conference are aware of Rookh's site, so I'd say there are at least thousands of men lurking specifically to find about expatriating from the misandrist mess the US and Canada have become) (Appendix Q, p.309).

So it was fascinating to visit an old friend recently, to keep him abreast of my career. We used to be neighbours – our back gardens adjoined. In England, gardens can inspire the most profound discussions. Furthest from the dwelling, where flowers, trees and bushes grow wild, where forgotten treasures rust in padlocked sheds and garages, the mind is often at its most liberated. We often met in this horticultural hinterland to discuss the most obscure matters across our shared fence. Some of these discussions inspired me to create the now-famous Anglobitch Thesis, wonder of the manosphere. In those days we yearned to identify some concrete factor that would explain the unique iniquity of Anglo-American feminism. When I described the Anglosphere's fixation on common law, and how rabid feminists use this to manipulate Anglo society, he had a Eureka! moment: literally shouting aloud with pure delight.

In a sense, a blog is also an unkempt garden, albeit a digital one. Ideas grow wild, like weeds. Comments arrive from around the world, like wind-blown seeds which the gardener can nurture into bushes and trees, as mood and inspiration take him. So it was with comments from North Wind, Lawrence, Brock and many others; their contributions were pruned into a magnificent tree, the common law theory of Anglo-American feminism.

3.1 Paper Chase

Despite the American state's unstinting legal support for false sexual abuse claims and misandrist divorce settlements, very few manosphere writers discuss the strong links between law and Anglo-American feminism. This is a startling omission, when one considers how many prominent feminists are lawyers, legal academics or politicians with legal backgrounds.

In fact, it must be said that law contains the intellectual 'cream' of the Anglo-feminist movement. Of course, the subaltern wing of academic feminism resides in the social 'sciences', with its non-patriarchal mathematics and other specious nonsense. The manosphere expends much (digital) ink discussing these poltroons, largely ignoring the legal wing of academic feminism. This is a pity, because the legal profession contains the best feminist minds; it is also the strongest feminist link to official institutions, the conduit through which feminism is imposed on the wider society.

Men always enquire, 'How did this come about?' whenever some misandrist agenda is arbitrarily applied to schools, public washrooms or sentencing procedures. More often than not, the answer is feminist legalism acting directly on 'official' institutions without reference to electoral processes.

Manosphere scholars seldom address feminist legalism for several reasons. First and most important, law is an obscure field full of specialist jargon. Second, manopshere scholars prefer easy conceptual victories against the (much weaker) arts-humanities wing of academic feminism. Third, the anti-Marxist fixation of the traditionalist manosphere blinds it to the intimate links between Anglo-American feminism and 'traditional' Anglo-Saxon culture. In this case the link is obvious, since 'rule of law' defines Anglo civilization. Indeed, law 'rules' Anglo-American society in a very literal way: think how many prominent Anglosphere politicians have a legal education or worked in the legal profession. In Continental Europe, a far higher proportion of politicians are scientists and economists (Angela Merkel is a scientist, for example).

Feminist legalism should therefore not surprise us, since the Anglosphere is defined by its legalism. The US is legalistic above all other nations; it has countless branches of law, all ever-growing like a vast tree. To pursue a biological analogy, if Anglo-American societies are the phenotype, law is their genotype; that is, they are regulated by pharisaic legalism above any other structural principle. Indeed, it might be said that the Anglosphere *is* law, in essence. Not only does Anglo-American feminism derive its legalistic character from this fact, it also derives much of its power from it. Curious, then, that the manosphere remains blind to feminist legalism and its power to engineer dramatic social change. One of my learned correspondents, an attorney called Legal Eagle, describes the situation for Anglo-American men:

That's it, the one reason above all why, as this Blog correctly makes clear, the Anglosphere is fundamentally more dangerous than the non-Anglosphere to basic rights especially for men, families and rational women. The state and a wife or ex-wife in the Anglosphere, or even a meddling busybody bureaucrat, has enormous and essentially unlimited power to drain and enslave a man financially. This is why you have to ditch the Anglosphere and set up elsewhere, and this is one area where the MGTOW's are exactly right Simply dating, associating with women and marrying in the Anglosphere literally and tangibly-- not in some abstract way-- expose even a highly skilled, wealthy, upper class men to real risk of improverishment, public humiliation and severe downward mobility in Anglosphere countries (Appendix J2, p.268).

Some admiration is called for: dissident males in the Anglosphere raise a lot of rhetorical dust, while their feminist counterparts infiltrate the cultural genotype – namely, the legal system – and proceed to systematically fashion society in their own image. Equally important is their domination of legal education, since it will shape the next generation of lawyers, judges and judgements. Unlike the social 'sciences', law is one of the oldest and most prestigious of the university subjects: all elite universities have law departments and these attract high-status students who will become active members of the future ruling elite.

Hillary Clinton, Elizabeth Warren, Cherie Blair and a host of other political feminists all trained at elite law schools. In sum, feminism has been wise to infiltrate Anglo-American jurisprudence, for whoever controls law has the true keys to power. Feminist sociology might be the yeast, but feminist jurisprudence is the finished loaf.

My research for this book unveiled a veritable hornet's nest of feminist jurisprudence. Nearly every major law school in the Anglosphere has powerful feminist representatives, as we can see from the 'Feminist Law Professors' website (http://www.feministlawprofessors.com).

It is no surprise that the site unambiguously links law to social engineering. Since no one really understands law except for specialist experts, it is perfect for the underhand manipulation of society in this way. Even more disturbing is the close link between law and politics, a seamless association in the Anglosphere. The contemporary Manosphere talks a lot about America's lapse into a police state: Feminist Law Professors is where that process really begins. The following passage gives some idea of the kind of articles posted there:

The U.S. Feminist Judgments Project seeks contributors of judicial opinions rewritten to reflect a feminist perspective, and commentaries on the cases and rewritten opinions, for an edited book collection tentatively titled Feminist Judgments: Rewritten Torts Opinions. *This edited volume is part of a collaborative project among law professors and others to rewrite, from a feminist perspective, key judicial decisions in the United States. The initial volume,* Feminist Judgments: Rewritten Opinions of the United States Supreme Court, *edited by Kathryn M. Stanchi, Linda L. Berger, and Bridget J. Crawford, was published in 2016 by Cambridge University Press. Subsequent volumes in the series will focus on different areas of law and will be under review by Cambridge* (Crawford, 2017).

It is easy to see what these legal activists are doing: rewriting legal precedents in order to create a corpus of pseudo-precedent for future judgements. In so doing, the future will be theirs (for as long as this dysfunctional civilization lasts).

The Anglo-feminist domination of the legal profession is of seismic significance, when one considers the vast power of jurisprudence in the Anglosphere (not to mention its deep historical links to politics and social administration). Conversely, masculinist activism in the English-speaking world lacks any legal wing, let alone an organized one. Instead, it assumes being 'right' will automatically confer 'victory' over feminist lawyers and politicians; sublimely missing the point that law, not truth, is the key to the Anglosphere.

Perhaps the fact that most male rights activists are engineers and tradesmen explains their political impotence; after all, engineers and tradesmen do not create/interpret laws or become politicians. To be blunt, Anglo-feminists are winning all the battles because they fight on the right battlefield, namely the legal one. Unless the Anglo men's movement adjust to this reality, they will always be marginalised and powerless.

Unless they leave the Anglo-American Matrix, of course.

3.2 Institutional Backing

All the major institutions of the Anglosphere are encoded with puritanical repression, which in turn nurtures misandrist Anglo-American feminism. But other countries and cultural blocs have a similar repressive heritage, yet do not suffer equivalent levels of institutional misandry. Similarly, feminists have infiltrated the legal systems of many other countries; but nowhere else are divorced fathers (and men in general) persecuted to the same degree as they are in the Anglosphere.

Is there some deep structural distinction between the Anglosphere which makes it especially pliant to misandrist feminism?

In a word, yes. One of the key institutional differences is the prevalence of common law in the Anglosphere countries. The countries of continental Europe and many other regions have only civil law, with no common law component to their legal system. But what is common law and how does it strengthen the arm of misandrist Anglo feminism?

In brief, civil law is a scientific instrument designed to deal with any situation the legal profession might encounter. It is therefore not amenable to casual manipulation or reinterpretation; it is fixed and inviolable, almost a sacred entity. By contrast, Anglo-Saxon common law is an ongoing corpus of precedents, judgements and cases which grows and adapts in a fluid, ad hoc manner. Because of its imprecise nature, Anglo-American judges have far more personal leeway when judging a case than their non-Anglosphere counterparts. And this leeway means a common law legal system is far more open to manipulation by pressure groups, trial lawyers and other arbitrary forces in the wider culture. Since misandrist feminism now rules the Anglosphere, we can see how Anglo-American law – the cultural genotype – has been exploited to alter the cultural phenotype, resulting in ever more oppression for Anglo-American men.

In short, common law is the primary channel through which Anglo feminists have shaped society to their will. Anglo feminism is in itself more vehement and misandrist than other varieties; but without its common law leverage it would remain relatively toothless and marginalized. With it, its force is almost limitless. This partly explains why the best feminist minds (as such) are inexorably drawn to law as an occupation; they rightly see Anglo common law as the societal 'schwerpunkt' through which they can realize their dreams and visions.

All the major universities in the Anglophone world contain prestigious law schools which in turn house militant feminist pressure groups. These groups often take existing cases and redefine them in feminist terms: in short, they specialize in manipulating Anglo-Saxon common law to advance their anti-male agendas. Since law affects all societal institutions – indeed, institutions are largely composed of laws – controlling common law gives these feminist academics the necessary leverage to shape society without reference to normal democratic processes. This is why Anglo-American society has transformed so dramatically in the past thirty years, without the populace explicitly voting for any such changes.

For example, Yale University possesses one of the world's most prestigious law schools and is an ancient stronghold of America's WASP (White Anglo-Saxon Protestant) elite. The Yale University Law School link to the 'Yale Journal of Law & Feminism' demonstrates the close - indeed, intimate - association between Anglo feminism and the American legal establishment:

The Yale Journal of Law and Feminism is committed to publishing scholarship on gender, sexuality, and the law, especially insofar as the law structures, affects, or ignores the experiences of women and other marginalized peoples. We encourage the submission of articles, essays, and reviews concerning these intersections of law and feminism. As we promote feminist principles to our readers, we also practice those principles ourselves.

The logo, created by Jacqueline Coy Charlesworth in three variations depicting women of different ethnicities, was chosen to illustrate the front cover of the Yale Journal of Law and Feminism (Yale University, 2019).

My more cynical interpretation considers the multi-ethnic logo to be an ideological smoke screen designed to hide WASP women's complicity in historical crimes like the slave trade; and to foster a fake association between women with radically different backgrounds, life-chances and interests. However, the gushing spiel continues:

Justicia--our icon of justice. She sits or stands above courthouses or in courtrooms, supposedly overseeing and inspiring choices between right and wrong...

It may be true, as many have observed, that the blindfold ensures Justice's impartiality towards those with more power and influence than she. But at the same time, the blindfold ensures Justice's impartiality towards those with less power than she, those who are, in some sense, disadvantaged. Unable to see whatever systemic disadvantages this latter group faces, unable to see her own membership in such a group and thereby possibly understand the nature of their plight, Justice can make her decisions based only on a limited set of facts before her. . . (Yale University, 2019).

Yes, the facts of the case; facts denuded of any other factor – in other words, impartial civil law. But feminist jurisprudence wants other dynamics (such as gender or race) to cloud the facts of the case. In sum, they want non-legal factors such as gender taken into account, factors which an ideologically impartial system of civil law would automatically dismiss. And the Anglo-American common law legal system *is especially vulnerable to feminist agendas for this very reason.*

The foregoing discussion explains why Anglo-American feminism enjoys unstinting support from major societal institutions in the Anglosphere. Of course, the Anglo-Saxon puritanical heritage plays a major part in this; for Anglo feminism is not a 'revolutionary' movement at all, as conservative MRAs often claim. To the contrary, it shares most of the same goals as the WASP establishment (for example, the legal suppression of male heterosexual choice and freedom). And let us not forget that the vast majority of Anglo feminists are themselves upper middle-class WASPs, their 'oppression' being largely imagined and rhetorical. However, the boundless institutional support they enjoy is greatly abetted by their unique control of common law, blind spot of Anglo-American jurisprudence. Since law defines all societal institutions, whoever controls the law ultimately controls society.

The most baffling thing about feminist legalists is why they still pretend that women are legally oppressed, when every impartial study proves that women enjoy enormous privilege in the Anglo-American legal system. In reality, feminism has already won the battle for the Anglosphere: its indirect but total control of Anglo-American common law has allowed it to redefine the social order with the full backing of the state and its various institutions. One has to have a certain admiration for the whole design; after all, they have won and we have lost. All that now remains for Anglo-American men is alienation and social exclusion, with expatriation the sole avenue of escape from divorce courts, penury and imprisonment.

3.3 The Killer Difference

Since I embarked on this great work, I have searched for a definitive mechanism to explain the Anglosphere's unique institutional misandry. In early 2018 various commentators began to post commentary essays on my blog, each more extensive than the last. Ever quick to capitalise on such resources, and in any case impressed by the sheer quality and insight, I gathered these comments into extensive posts replete with images. This was a wise move, because these posts inspired more commentary which I subsequently transformed into posts. I was lucky, in that this procedure seemed to coincide with various expatriation conferences being held in the US at the time.

From this broadening path of insight and discussion, a novel theme began to emerge: that the common law system which defines the Anglosphere is especially susceptible to feminist manipulation. I am in no sense a legal professional and had never considered this avenue before. I had merely assumed that misandrist divorce courts reflected the Anglosphere's puritanical, sex-negative animus against males in general.

Ranger, an ex-military man, described the appalling treatment typically dished out by American Divorce courts to decent and hard-working American men:

Some of my fellow grunts went back to the States and got married. Total mistake, total misery. Their wives slept around while they were deployed. All the frickin' time. Then they filed for divorce. And the wives got everything from a man who served his country getting shot at. She got the house. The car. The dog. She got his savings. A chunk of his pension. Alimony. Child support often more than the poor guy was making after returning to the home front, because divorce court judges are c*nts in the extreme and like you all said, can impute any BS amount to what the guy "should" be earning. And the worst? The man-hating she-beast feminists, joined by mangina and white knight assholes, cheer the gold-digging Anglobitches on in the USA for wrecking good men like this (Appendix O, p.277).

Billy, a cheerful character with great practical experience of life in America and beyond, was insistent that the same appalling results are not readily obtained by women divorcing men in Scandinavia:

But yeah I knew some American guys who got hitched with some hot blonde Viking girls in Norway and Sweden, got rich, then some of them split up. But they kept the money they made, their houses, car, shared raising the kids. The wives never got alimony, they don't do child support it's just they both continue to raise the kids as they would otherwise cause they share the raising. But no jail, no community property, you keep what you earn, and the ex-wife, she earns her own money, up there the ladies demand it of themselves even beyond the law itself. If these guys had got divorced in America, they'd lose their shirt cause the exes could take everything. But not Norway and Sweden, not Europe (Appendix N, p.276).

This testimony is especially interesting, since Anglo-American tradcons always insist that Scandinavian countries (especially Sweden) are even more misandrist than Anglosphere ones. However, Billy and others with actual experience of Scandinavian and European life were insistent this was not so. However, those with extensive experience of the Anglo-American divorce industry were full of nightmare anecdotes. The following case is related by Lawrence, a former corrections officer who encountered many divorced men in the American prison system:

The very worst case I saw as a prison guard was a surgeon, yes an American surgeon who was one of the most respectable guys I ever met, hard working, worked until 2 a.m. 6 days a week to save people's lives. With all the work hours, his wife got "lonely" and started sleeping around, eventually having 2 kids that weren't even his as he found out later. And then she filed for divorce so she could take the surgeon's money, blow it on cocaine and stupid luxuries for herself without doing any work herself (that's the real destination where the "child support" money goes) and sleep around with her favorite Chad of the week, all on her hard working surgeon ex-husband's money. She won an insanely high judgment in a US family court, millions of dollars in child support and "alimony" that the poor surgeon would have to pay. Since by the court's judgment, "she should be entitled to maintain the same standard of living after the divorce", even though this greedy gold-digging Anglobitch is the one who filed for the divorce to steal from her hard-working husband who was actually saving people's lives.

After a few years of doing this, and losing his house and his nice car, the poor surgeon threw out his back while helping a patient onto an operating table. He had to cut down his hours as a surgeon, and went to the divorce court asking for a reduction in the support demands, and ask that his lazy, spoiled brat bitch ex-wife get a damn job herself. But the court refused using the same delusion filled imputation bullshit they pull on other ex-husbands, claiming he could somehow make millions of extra dollars using his surgical wizard skills somehow. Which he couldn't do in reality with his injured back, something the family court judge couldn't or wouldn't even try to understand. So then now the alimony and child support were demanding 120% of his income. You see, the family court system will never let you off the treadmill once they target you, especially if you earn a lot of money. Eventually he drained his savings and retirement, couldn't make the payments at all—and he wound up in the prison where I was a corrections officer (Appendix Q, pp.292-293).

What is especially interesting about this case is that it encapsulates one of my major themes: a double standard distinct to the Anglosphere, wherein female freedom coexists with a kind of Victorian chivalry which simultaneously regards women as flawless beings on pedestals. Anglo-American women seem to have wrangled a perfect deal, wherein they are free to act like whimsical children while still enjoying the status of autonomous adults. Still, the precise mechanism for these perfidious outcomes remained a mystery until an engineer calling himself Gearman mentioned common law, a factor I had never considered before:

What Rookh and everyone else is making clear here, it's not feminism alone that's so damaging and wrecking to the lives and livelihoods of modern men, and to women and families, but the combination of a particular type of feminism—the adversarial driven "us against them" third and fourth-wave of the Anglo world— combined with Anglo Puritanism, cultural Marxism, the common law tradition (which makes divorce and the "metoo" witch hunt profitable to the extremists pushing it), the cuck chivalry white knights who enable "have your cake and eat it too" hypocrisy of Anglo feminists (claim to be strong and independent but need permanent alimony after a divorce) and the crony corporate capitalism of the Anglo world which sees politically incorrect men as easy targets to vulture off of. All of these things are unique to the Anglosphere, and they're what makes Anglosphere feminism uniquely toxic (Appendix I1, p.246).

After which an Attorney called Legal Eagle elaborated on common law at some length, opening a veritable flood gate of learned discussion:

The family law policies in the Anglosphere really have become THAT dangerous and perverse, and now with the #metoo hysterics and media push, it's only going to get even worse for men, families and reasonable women in the Anglosphere. I think other posts here have covered why, but if they haven't, here's the tl-dr: it's due to the particularities of Anglo common law (which is we learn from Day One in law school, is a whole different animal from civil statutory law), stare decisis and political/administrative inertia in Anglo legal tradition (feminists claiming female independence while clinging to "helpless wife" assumptions used to justify long term alimony), the oppositional essence of US law, media and culture (Appendix J2, pp.269-270).

The corrections officer Lawrence subsequently identified the precise mechanism for the misandrist nature of Anglo-American law. Since common law is based on socio-political currents as much as legal precedent, it has become uniquely susceptible to manipulation by the misandrist feminism which defines the Anglosphere and its cultural institutions. Since non-Anglosphere countries rely more on a civil law tradition, they are relatively inoculated from adversarial misandrist feminism (which is in any case a far weaker force in non-Anglo world):

The lesson to draw here is that it's the "playing with fire" basis of Anglo common law that makes this possible in the Anglosphere, as I'll explain, civil law countries reign in judges and don't let them do this. The essence of common law in practical sense, is that the law is based not just on prior court precedent but also— and this is the main point—on "broad political currents" in society that the court supposedly interprets. Despite the US Constitution, which is essentially statutory law, the common law, which predates the Constitution itself, means family court judges in the US and general Anglosphere can "go with the PC cultural flow" which family courts in France, Germany, Norway, Brazil, Chile and the non-Anglosphere in general cannot do. And when rampant misandry and "sock it to 'em"—even against a lifesaving surgeon whose gold-digging wife had 2 kids with other men—is the cultural current, US and Anglosphere judges have latitude to "go with it" and formalize the misandry in their decisions (Appendix Q, pp.296-297).

The discussion reached its zenith when a disillusioned law professor left an extended essay, which can be read in full in Appendix S. Here is its introduction:

Thank you, Mr. Kshatriya, in your Blog posts last month for a quality discussion of the real world distinctions between the common law of the Anglo-Saxon world and the civil law of mainland Europe, Latin America and Asia. As a law professor and father of a divorcee, and teacher of dozens of lawyers who have gone on to wear the judge's robe, I can speak to the topic of the Anglo common-law perversions of family law and the consequent need to expatriate, from professional and personal experience,

Several of my own students, current and modern directed me to the discussion of this topic on your Blog, and I have read with quite some interest how it has developed. From one of my student's remarks on recent Blog entries here, it appears you are writing a more detail-rich book on this highly relevant topic, and I thus seek to provide more rigorous information that corroborates and expands upon what you and your bloggers, apparently many attorneys themselves, have expressed.

To give a summary up-front what I will elaborate below, you are correct in that the divorce law and general family law picture in the US and Anglo world more broadly has become perilously distorted and corrupted by extreme ideology, to the point that marriage and family formation in the Anglo world in general, and America in particular, entail horrific financial and social risks that make them unviable options for any spouse with a good career, assets, children or indeed anything to lose. Family courts now are indeed quite "misandrist" and deleterious to men, and in particular to white (Caucasian) and Asian men as your Bloggers have noticed, due to something called "conflict theory" which I will explain below. But they are also quite harmful to family-oriented and professional women, and families above all, as I will also address.

I will detail why this is below, but to express it in outline form, it results from a dreadful combination of five factors which you have variously covered in previous Blog posts and comments, and which I will lay out rigorously here:

1: Anglo-Saxon (Anglo-Norman) common law and specifically, the fundamentally altered form of common law that has become dominant since the start of the 20th century due to critical philosophic and theoretic changes to its central elements, from prominent mostly American jurists in the century.
2: Conflict theory, the theoretic foundation of what you all generally recognize as political correctness, cultural marxism, critical theory and other modern sociologic thought systems that

base themselves in an ideology hostile to the West and its traditionally dominant cultural and ethnic groups.

3: Shameless predatory profiteering and rent seeker behavior grossly corrupting the US/Anglo divorce and family courts, a manner of crony capitalistic perversion that has also become perversely wedded to the cultural marxist side of things and drives many of its distorting extremes.

4: Absolute failure of the legal education system, particularly for future judges, to convey the realities of income instability and "breadwinning" in the modern economy compared to the 1970's, a criticism that many of us in law school faculties have launched to reform curricula, to no avail.

5: The broader unique cultural milieu of the Anglo world which leaves it vulnerable to strange puritanic excesses and public shaming tendencies, thus "metoo" in its extreme forms. This appears to be a topic you have already covered in more detail (Appendix S, pp.316-317).

For me, the issue is not common law itself as such; but rather, its susceptibility to external manipulation. When Anglo-American culture was less overtly misandrist, not just prior to 'metoo' but before the advent of bourgeois Anglo-feminism in the late 1950s, there was simply much less cultural poison to corrupt common law and its judicial interpretation. Of course there was the Anglosphere's inane puritanism but this was to a great extent negated by a less hysterical *zeitgeist* and the more patriarchal nature of the surrounding culture. Women were pedestalised but not armed with rights and entitlements, nor had militant Anglo feminists infiltrated the legal system at every level. As many correspondents have pointed out, the unresolved historical and ethnic conflicts latent in colonial Anglo culture were swiftly appropriated by militant feminism despite it being a white, bourgeois and objectively racist movement.

Aside from changing socio-cultural values, the Law Professor suggests that recent scholarship has reinterpreted common law in various ways which grant judges rather more 'leeway' when passing sentence, especially in financial matters. In real terms, this judicial freedom has meant that the external culture has never been more powerful in pressurizing judgement to deliver misandrist conclusions in the divorce courts:

On this point, I also wanted to make a clarification regarding some confusion my students have brought up on this topic. Any L1 student starting up at a law school learns early about the principle of stare decisis, Latin for "let the decision stand", and thus some of my students have been confused by the very accurate points you and your contributors have been making even before my elaboration above. How can judges in the United States, Canada, Britain and other nations classed as "Anglo" have so much power to make arbitrary decisions, or incorporate radical Anglo-American feminist theories (which are indeed thoroughly misandrist by contrast to the rest of the West), when stare decisis supposedly requires them to follow precedent? Doesn't stare decisis mean they should follow older and long-established customs, including prior judges' rulings, that are less misandrist?

The answer is no, and Mr. Kshatriya and his contributors are indeed right that judges in divorce courts have rather excessive powers particularly in the realms of monetary imputation and purview of a spouse's finances, and that alimony and child support payments can and regularly are harshly assessed. The answer to this confusion is that the common law since the 20th century has been quite different to what it was before. Most of you (referring to my law school students) have, or soon will encounter the treatises of critical 20th-c jurists such as Frankfurter, Holmes, Brandeis, Dworkin, Fuller, Wechsler and Bickel. In a gradual process of great significance, these legal scholars (several of them Supreme Court justices) re-interpreted the very concept of common law, to make it more flexible and responsive to modern scholarship. Since then, stare decisis and precedent don't mean what they did in the 18th or 19th centuries. Although prior case law remains greatly important in guiding future decisions, the evolution of these scholars' ideas in practice has meant that judges today have a lot of latitude in setting precedent based on prevailing social theories. Their ideas became so influential that they've now come to dominate the concept of common law across the English-speaking world, not just in the United States.

I don't in any form want to blame these scholars for the latter day corruption of common law, as they did not have the modern madness of American family courts in mind, and at least in the medium-term, their thoughts on the common law did help to make it more responsive to the fluid challenges of contract law and technological advance (Appendix S, pp.328-329).

In sum, Anglo common law was uniquely susceptible to infiltration by misandrist, conflict-driven feminism and so it quickly became the primary weapon for enforcing its sex-negative and misandrist agendas. In the United States, this seems specifically true of Divorce Law which has become the primary weapon for stripping men of their assets and livelihoods, transferring their wealth to the state and neutralising them in the North American Prison-Industrial complex. It is inviting to think that civil law's robust insularity has inoculated the civil law nations of mainland Europe and beyond from these misandrist currents, even where they exist. It is interesting that militant misandrist feminists are given swift custodial punishment in civil law nations like Russia, for example, not lionized as in Britain or the United States.

By maintaining closer ties to the wisest legal minds of the ages, civil law avoids the pitfalls inevitably associated with superficial trends and passing social fashions. The best institutions are maintained, effective social values endure and the mass alienation of whole genders and social classes is avoided. At the time of writing, the core Anglosphere nations are both experiencing an unprecedented cultural crisis. Britain and America are becoming less politically stable and predictable, with Brexit and the election of President Trump indicating mass discontent within Anglo-American civilisation. For me, mass male alienation is at the root of this destabilization process. Nations or regions with large proportions of alienated single men are demonstrably more volatile, blighted by low trust values and political instability. As is usual, mainstream commentators simply find the crumbling situation mysterious, assuming that all men are broadly committed to the social order when nothing could be further from the truth. Not only are men as a group increasingly alienated, the affluent middle class are entirely disenchanted with the Anglosphere and its misandrist legalism. This is because they have most to lose and, as many of my correspondents relate, are increasingly aware of what marriage within the Anglosphere can cost them.

3.4 Anglo-American Pharisaic Legalism

In one obvious respect, the contemporary Anglosphere resembles Old Testament Israel, in that it exalts lawyers above all other professions. This legalistic fixation explains why so many politicians and other top decision-makers were trained as lawyers, seldom scientists or economists. What underpins this legal hegemony is surely the fact that Anglo-Saxon countries are defined by common law legal systems which permit Judges and other legal professionals far more interpretative autonomy, bestowing almost godlike power on them. By contrast, Judges and lawyers outside the Anglosphere have a largely reactive role with very limited interpretative autonomy. Indeed, it might be said they are more like legal scientists applying a complex body of research to specific cases.

Aside from the obvious status common law bestows on legal professionals, it automatically binds them to politics as unelected shapers of policy. This partly explains why so many prominent politicians in the Anglo-American world are former lawyers; a common law legal system is a natural training ground for politics. It is also notable that many female politicians trained as lawyers, including Hillary Clinton and Margaret Thatcher.

The unique power bestowed on legal practitioners by Anglo-American common law makes law a natural career choice for those who wish to change society directly, without recourse to normal democratic processes. In short, legal professionals occupy a similar role to the Pharisees in ancient Israel, an unelected ruling class. It therefore makes obvious strategic sense for those with marginalized agendas (such as third wave feminists) to join the legal profession. Certainly the best feminism minds now gravitate to law rather than the social sciences, and all the top university law schools in the Anglosphere now have feminist divisions.

Like the ancient Pharisees, modern feminist legalists also exploit the fact that law is seen as an arcane and impenetrable body of knowledge that most people cannot understand. Moreover, the malleable and interpretative nature of common law assumes a high degree of 'cultural capital' on the part of legal practitioners; that is, understanding and accepting 'elite' values on a range of issues, including gender identity and multi-culturalism as well as feminism. This has produced an autocratic legal elite in the Anglosphere nations, one which is incredibly difficult for laypeople (or even their elected representatives) to question or challenge. The result is a misandrist legal system which does not reflect practical wisdom or the popular will but rather the idiomatic values of an upper-middle class, privately tutored, college-educated WASP elite with undue attachment to secular Puritanism in all its forms.

Little wonder, then, that the jails in English-speaking countries are filled with non-whites, males and the urban poor. Even less wonder that the legal system exhibits an arcane (some would say insane) obsession with #metoo fantasies, glass ceilings and transexual washrooms. Anglo-American jurisprudence has in fact been completely subverted by feminists and now stands at the absolute forefront of male oppression across the Anglosphere. Both omnipotent and almost autonomous, the Anglo-American legal system was the ideal target for feminist infiltration. It now stands as their greatest success, and reflects their puritanical, elitist and misandrist fixations in their entirety. Feminist jurisprudence now signs off all law in the Anglo-American world, and – backed by a host of bureaucratic toadies (not to mention the state-sponsored terrorists called police) – can destroy good men with complete impunity.

While the Anglosphere has lapsed into a legalistic matriarchy run by female Pharisees, the rest of the world is still protected by its civil law traditions. Consequently, divorce outside the Anglosphere is not a misandrist catastrophe which sees men cast into prison for failing to pay exorbitant maintenance to their former wives. Of course, the flexible nature of Anglo common law means that the definition of male malfeasance expands like a tumour, together with the repertoire of punishments available to Anglo-American judges and lawyers. The palmy, avaricious nature of Anglo jurisprudence also fuels this legalistic expansionism, since more divorces mean more money for greedy divorce lawyers. This is also true of unreasonable settlements and the inevitable payment defaults associated with them. In the last analysis, it pays Anglo jurisprudence to expand the grounds for divorce, separate solvent fathers from their children and hand over parenting to spendthrift former wives. With typical Anglo avarice and short-sightedness they fail to see that

94

middle class, solvent families are finite in number; and that every divorce, however profitable in the short term, reduces future profits for the divorce industry.

By contrast, the fixed and inviolable nature of civil law puts a brake on this legal expansionism and the profits that drive it, resulting not only in fewer divorces but more equitable results when divorce does occur. This is why the mass imprisonment of divorced husbands that plagues the United States could never happen in a civil law country. And of course, the wider social benefits of stable, solvent families define most of the civil law countries: low crime rates, low levels of imprisonment, lower rates of physical and mental illness, high trust values, rational voting, a large middle class and a relatively small underclass.

None of these varied and far-reaching benefits characterize the Anglo-Saxon nations, which have the worst divorce outcomes in the industrialized world. But of course, the Anglosphere knows best.

3.5. Divorce and Fathers' Rights

The foregoing discussions demonstrate that Feminist legalism has subverted common law as it subverted religious Puritanism. Partly because religion is now defunct in the West, Feminists have targeted law as the weak point of the Anglosphere. By a process of cultural selection the best feminist minds have gravitated to it; today, all top law schools have feminist divisions whose mission is to subvert society by manipulating the common law. And so successful has this programme been that law is now the primary tool of feminist social control across the Anglosphere.

This has led to a widening gulf between common and civil morality. By this, I mean a growing distrust between what people instinctively believe to be just, and the justice most men actually receive. This is especially true of the divorce courts, wherein judgements and settlements are routinely handed out to divorced fathers which leave the general public astonished at their cruel stupidity.

The insular nature of the legal profession means that divorce judgements are driven by narrow ideological convictions rather than practical considerations. As I am not a legal expert, this section opens the floor to my many correspondents who have direct personal experience of Anglo-American law, either as legal professionals, academics or corrections officers. These correspondents gave many examples of self-employed and even professional men being imprisoned for failing to pay child support payments after a temporary change in their financial fortunes. Clearly, Judges fail to understand that businesses can have bad years as well as good ones; they have little grasp of economic reality outside the legal profession. This socio-economic insularity, coupled with ideological convictions arising in the hermetic world of academia has shaped an Anglo-American judiciary intent on punishing divorced fathers on the most fanciful pretexts.

Moreover, my correspondents suggested that the residual misandry arising from the Anglosphere's secular Puritanism inspired the harshness of these decisions. Legal Eagle writes:

I'm an attorney specializing in family law, now working overseas myself with a basis to make the comparison, and this is really all you need to know about the real-life decisions you'll have to make in the Anglosphere versus outside of it:

Marriage and having kids are now fundamentally non-viable options in the Anglosphere because of one specific quirk above all in the way the Anglosphere handles divorce: You literally become a slave to the state upon marriage or having a kid in the Anglosphere because at that point, the state has the power to extract your assets without limit in the event of divorce, separation or abuse allegations. Again; ALL of your assets, your savings, earnings, even your work potential, before or after marriage, can be seized from you after you marry or have a child in the Anglosphere, because the US court and civil system gives women and family courts absolute discretion over all your assets and even future earning potential, WITHOUT LIMIT (Appendix J2, p.267).

Legal Eagle dismisses the notion that there is some safe way to navigate the inherent misandry of Anglo-American legalism:

And just to throw cold water on any assumptions that "there still must be a way to safely date and marry in the Anglosphere", I'm sorry, but there isn't. Like I said above, domestic and international family law is my legal specialty, what I've done every workday for the past couple decades. I've worked in dozens of US states, several Canadian provinces and then several law and legal translation offices overseas in Europe as well as (in 2016) in Cordoba, Argentina. My law partners and I have seen literally thousands of men in the US and Canada show up in our office, nervously asking about ways to protect their assets in the event of divorce, wondering about "the perfect prenup" or if marrying a religious girl in a religious ceremony, or a foreign girl protects them. (Short answer-- it doesn't, not if you're still living in North America or anywhere in the Anglosphere.) I'm sorry, but if you want to establish a meaningful relationship with a woman, have kids, start a family-- the things fundamental to any society for centuries-- there is now no alternative to becoming an expat outside the Anglo world. None.

The family law policies in the Anglosphere really have become THAT dangerous and perverse, and now with the #metoo hysterics and media push, it's only going to get even worse for men, families and reasonable women in the Anglosphere. I think other posts here have covered why, but if they haven't, here's the tl-dr: it's due to the particularities of Anglo common law (which is we learn from Day One in law school, is a whole different animal from civil statutory law), stare decisis and political/administrative inertia in Anglo legal tradition (feminists claiming female independence while clinging to "helpless wife" assumptions used to justify long term alimony), the oppositional essence of US law, media and culture (Appendix J2, pp.269-270).

Reading this, it seems to me as a legal layperson that Anglo-American law has become a misandrist weapon. Also, those men who marry foreign women and bring them back to the Anglosphere seem to be deluded in thinking that having a foreign wife will protect them from the vagaries of Anglo Divorce law. Legal Eagle seems to be presenting a more extreme variant of my original Thesis: for him, it is not so much the woman as the country one resides in. Common law and residual misandry are the defining factors, and these are defined by their geographical location in the Anglosphere. Inspired by Legal Eagle's commentary, a former American corrections officer called Lawrence described the legalistic misandry now rampant in the United States:

Here's some background. Before I myself went the expat route a few years ago, I had a job for about 10 years as a corrections officer, building up some savings and then later as a flexible shift job while taking correspondence courses in computer graphic and Web design and finishing a Master's in database management. I really wasn't a traditional fit personality wise for a corrections officer, I've always been bookish and nerdy and not really into rapping knuckles. But my family has been in law enforcement for a few generations and prison guarding can be a decently paid gig. So I used the job not only to make money but also observe the

US justice system up close, which I would later be able to generalize to much of the Anglosphere.

And here I have to warn you, if there is any job that will redpill you from your 1st month on the job into becoming an MGTOW, it's being a prison guard. Because you see the effects of the legal Weapon of Mass Destruction that is US divorce courts and family courts generally right up close. That's because the large, large majority of the prisoners we watch over in our jobs aren't violent, aren't dangerous, aren't even really criminal. They're either tossed in the slammer for the "crime" of minor drug possession (not dealing, just personal possession) or more and more, for contempt of court due to failure to make alimony or child support payments. And yes, this is a uniquely Anglosphere practice, mainly US, Canada and Britain. The rate of such imprisonments in France where I now live and work, and every other country in Europe? Or South America which follows French and Roman legal tradition? 0%. They simply don't do that to men here.

And yes it gets worse for anyone in the Anglosphere, like Legal Eagle said a terribly big fraction of the men in US or UK prisons for child or spousal support payments? They're wealthy and upper-class men, because their assets give the family kangaroo courts wide authority to impose outrageous and impossible payment demands on them. This is due to a family judge practice called "imputation", which essentially means the judge, completely ignorant of real economics of actual job and earning potential for a man hit with a divorce suit, can pull a random number out of her ass and tell the man, "this is what you should be earning". And this makes upper class and especially rich men particularly vulnerable to an enslavement by the family courts. While there are some idiot white knight male family court judges who do this, it's mainly naïve feminist female family court judges who see a man who's wealthy or has been at some point, and automatically assume the guy can grow money on trees. They're not only feminist idiots, they're ignorant about business, real hard work or what it actually takes to earn a lot of money, and how risky and uncertain, famine to feast a high-earning position or job is. So ironically it's the wealthier men who are hit the hardest by family court judgments since the judge can impute any ridiculous fantasy of what he "should" earn out of her ass, regardless of reality, and she'll always pick an outrageously high demand. Then with any dip in the man's fortunes or the broader economy, he of course can't make the impossible imputed payments, and then boom, it's off to jail for the "deadbeat" man even if he's been a model citizen. I saw this there in the prisons I worked at, day in, day out. And no, it's not a bug. It's a feature of the insane Anglosphere system (Appendix Q, pp.285-286).

Then, Lawrence exposes the Rosetta Stone that differentiates Anglosphere law from its non-Anglosphere counterpart: common law. For over a decade I have sought a well-defined, unambiguous factor that would explain the Anglosphere's unique misandry and institutionalised hostility towards men in general, and divorced fathers in particular. The Anglosphere's secular Puritanism is of course such a factor; but it is after all a generic cultural factor. By contrast, common law is not only unique to the Anglosphere, it has a direct bearing on the legal blandishments meted out to Anglo-American fathers in the divorce and family courts:

Practically speaking, "common law" means Anglosphere law, while "civil law" which comes from Roman law, is continental law, used in Europe, in South America which is continental-based, eastern Europe, and apparently in a lot of Asia, which for some reason has copied a lot of civil law practices. (I'm a lot less familiar with Asia so I'll trust Legal Eagle's word on that). In the USA, Canada, UK and Anglosphere generally, common law in practice means judges have much more latitude to impose harsh and arbitrary penalties, which they'll often feel free to do if they're riding political currents and punishing a group that isn't "politically correct". This also creates a toxic legal atmosphere in the Anglosphere which attracts the most militantly feminist female lawyers to become family court judges in a sort of selection process. Like I said I don't know the fine points of common law like Legal Eagle, but I did see how it played out in practice in US family courts when we were briefed on the court proceedings for inmates who had been confined for nonpayment of child support or alimony.

And it was very clear from the transcripts that the PC memes of feminist "you go girl" culture and the spewings of cultural Marxist academic journals had found their way into the American family court judges' rulings, where the man was automatically assumed to be a deadbeat and loser deserving punishment. Yes, even lifesaving surgeons with back injuries were thrown into this pile, and while misandrist feminist judges were the usual culprits, there were plenty of stupid male white knight family judges doing the same bullshit. I've heard some people claim that Jewish family court judges male and female were particularly inclined to go the misandrist route, but tbh I'm not sure I really saw this, I think they were maybe overrepresented in general among the lawyers and judges, but plenty among both the stupid white knights and the hate-filled feminist judges ready to incarcerate some poor ex-husband for child support or alimony arrears, were old fashioned Anglo Protestants. Especially up in New England where I worked early in my career as a corrections officer. It's clearly something in Anglo culture that combines with Anglo common law to fuel this insanity in the judges, possibly the strange combination of cuck-like chivalry by some men and zero-sum radical feminist hatred, unique to the Anglosphere, that maybe one of the other commenters made a note of.

The lesson to draw here is that it's the "playing with fire" basis of Anglo common law that makes this possible in the Anglosphere, as I'll explain, civil law countries reign in judges and don't let them do this. The essence of common law in practical sense, is that the law is based not just on prior court precedent but also— and this is the main point—on "broad political currents" in society that the court supposedly interprets. Despite the US Constitution, which is essentially statutory law, the common law, which predates the Constitution itself, means family court judges in the US and general Anglosphere can "go with the PC cultural flow" which family courts in France, Germany, Norway, Brazil, Chile and the non-Anglosphere in general cannot do. And when rampant misandry and "sock it to 'em"—even against a lifesaving surgeon whose gold-digging wife had 2 kids with other men—is the cultural current, US and Anglosphere judges have latitude to "go with it" and formalize the misandry in their decisions.

The common law, I suspect, is also why the Anglosphere, and I guess Israel from what Legal Eagle is saying (haven't been there so can't say personally), is unique in the way judges and the state have full purview to review and seize all of a man's assets. The civil law of the continent in Europe makes that a no-go because judges are handcuffed legally, while the common law gives Anglosphere judges a lot more power over men's finances. Combine that with the selection for feminazi lawyers to become family court judges, steeped in the latest misandrist bile from the media and women's studies journals from academia, and boom, you have a formula for turning "sock it to him" into formal rulings by judges to seize all a man's assets. Especially a wealthy man, who's a juicy and favorite target for the unholy alliance of radical feminist Anglosphere family courts with the profiteering lawyers and prison-industrial complex, particularly in the United States.

This is the "laymen's term" explanation for what Legal Eagle was saying: Anglo common law means that practically, a family court judge in the US and Anglosphere is a little dictator with uncontrolled and unappealable power to make state pronouncements that a man must 'pay up" unrealistic amounts that add up to more than 100% of his assets and salary. And make him a pauper. There is no restriction on the delusional imputation that a family court judge can do with spousal support and child maintenance expectations for a man.

The judge in the Anglosphere can cite, as precedent, both previous decisions but even "flavor of the moment" social movements like #metoo and whatever misandrist junk is being spilled out in US university academic feminist journals, since an Anglosphere judge has so much latitude.

Not so in the non-Anglo world, especially in Europe and South America which is continent-influenced and where civil law rather than common law prevails. This is really where continental civil law from Europe shows its virtues—it's in its essence more rational than Anglo common law, and by its very nature it imposes strict limits on what a judge can do, and how much of a man's assets a judge, and thus the state, can review and effectively take control of. Again guys like Legal Eagle will know about this more than I would, but after being in France for a while and trying to master my French, I read a French language book that talked about how the Romans came up with law. They were almost scientific about it, a lot of philosophy and long term thinking, and that's the heart of civil law that dominates almost every country outside the Anglosphere. Above all the Romans were realistic about how human passions of the moment could corrupt the law courts, and they were very frank about how women in particular, would too often get caught up in what we now know as misandrist hate campaigns like #metoo and the "sock it to him" hatemongering of divorce courts. That's why civil law in effect protects men from harm and makes marriage and family formation possible outside the Anglosphere, and that's true even in countries that, like in Scandinavia, have opened themselves up too much to many of the stupidities of Anglo-American culture. Despite this, the civil law tradition even in Scandinavia shields men in actual practice, something they don't have in common law-dominated Anglo countries.

In the practical terms of family courts themselves, family court judges in civil law countries are kept on a much tighter leash than common law Anglo countries, so the PC feminist "flavor of the moment" is irrelevant—the statutes are what matter, not vague prior "precedents" or media-driven memes like in the Anglosphere. That's why, like Legal Eagle said, child support in the non-Anglo world is strictly capped, why alimony is almost nonexistent. The non-Anglo world is much safer for men in general, especially for upper-class and wealthy men, because the caps are kept deliberately low by the civil law legislative process. This stupid Anglo standard, that after divorce "a woman should be entitled to maintain the same lifestyle as during marriage"? The non-Anglo countries call bullshit on that. By civil law codes, if a woman files for divorce, she then has to get off her ass and earn her money herself. And they HATE gold-diggers in Europe, which the civil law formalizes. It doesn't matter if the man has been a millionaire surgeon, like the poor unfortunate inmate I worked with, or a billionaire industrialist—a divorcing spouse is not entitled to his fortune, whether he made it before or during the marriage. She'll get only enough to provide basic support for herself and her kids given cost of living, and beyond that she has to work. A wealthy husband will customarily contribute more to help her get job prep at the start, and a husband who's having tough times or just lost his job will be given a break to get on his own feet.

Generally the civil law that Legal Eagle talks about, means that men in the non-Anglo world can marry, have kids, divorce if it comes to that, without putting their assets at risk. Because not only is there no alimony, but child support is kept low and works differently, as the woman filing for divorce is expected to work and do the supporting herself. Again this shows the rationality of the civil law which is developed by community leaders with long term thinking, as opposed to divorce law and family court judges with a feminist chip on their shoulder, swayed by the PC whims of the moment. The "playboy rule" that I and I think Legal Eagle are describing above, is done this way for a reason. It discourages divorce for one thing, so non-Anglo Europe and South America have much less of it than the Anglosphere. It also encourages shared custody, since a woman gets no advantage from profiteering through the child support bullshit which usually just supports a custodial parent's excessive lifestyle. It means men don't go to prison, since child support is low, it doesn't "rack up" and there's no alimony. It also means that lawyers, judges, states and the prisons don't get to be gluttonous greedy pigs like in the US, UK and Canada, since you can't profit from the divorce process, like I saw time and time again with all the poor ex-husbands sent to the prisons I was assigned to.

This in laymen's terms is what Legal Eagle was saying in his first point, the civil law of Europe, South America, east Europe, everywhere outside the Anglosphere is a far better protection of a man's assets, wealth and freedom than any prenup, because it totally changes the math and economics of divorce, takes away the incentive for it, prevents profiteering and makes custody shared. That's why, even if feminists and dumb Anglo culture get into non-Anglo countries, they're tightly shackled in what they can actually do. It really is true, I have seen this. Feminism and dumb Anglo-PCism are laughed at in France, Austria, Italy, Spain, Portugal, Holland, Belgium and east Europe, and whiny feminists especially here in France are vocally mocked and marginalized, but they do have some currency in Germany and Scandinavia, which makes them a little too vulnerable to stupid PC fads and feminist farts from the Anglosphere. (Although as I'll get to below, Nordic and German feminism really is a breed apart from misandrist Anglo feminism).

Yet despite this, the actual process of marrying and divorce in Germany and the Nordic countries has the same legal structure, with the same statutory protections as men enjoy in France and the Mediterranean, and it's because those countries also follow the civil law instead of the common law of the English-speaking countries. If the feminist harpies from the Anglosphere came to Germany or the Nordic countries, they could bleat all they want, but they have no power to ruin a man in a divorce as is routine in the Anglosphere. And so men in Germany and Scandinavia, especially upper class and wealthy men, have their assets walled off and protected from the state the same as we do in France. If a woman files for divorce in northern Europe as much as France or southern Europe, she doesn't get to do any gold-digging, and if she has a rich husband, she isn't entitled to his wealth. The statutory limit is deliberately kept low to discourage divorce and encourage custody sharing, and if she still goes ahead and files, she is responsible for getting off her ass and getting a job. No freebies on a husband's dime, whether he's rich or not so rich (Appendix Q, pp.295-301).

This remarkable exposition adds so much specific detail to my generic critique of the Anglosphere that it deserves a name of its own: The Common Law Thesis of Anglo Legal Misandry. Having lived in and experienced both America and the non-Anglosphere West, 'Lawrence' is uniquely qualified to comment on the legal differences between them. It would seem that the Anglo-American common law tradition negatively influences legal decisions against fathers (and men in general). By contrast, civil law codes persist in countries with a broader social base, where judges and other legal professionals come from more representative social backgrounds. Together with the pure and inviolate nature of civil law, this results in divorce settlements which are practical, fair and untouched by feminist ideology.

Clearly, common law is the soft spot in Anglo-American legalism – the unwatched gate through which feminism can pass without challenge to shape laws, judgments and sentences. A good analogy would be a small, unguarded gate in the wall of a great city; a gate through which an enemy can pass unseen to wreak havoc on the citizens within. Indeed, to pursue the analogy further, it may be said that there are traitors within the city, all too eager to open that gate. In fact, they ensured that the gate was present in the city's construction plans before it was ever built.

'Lawrence' then describes another problematic factor in the Anglosphere: the fraught and schismatic nature of much Anglo-American history. Because the colonial Anglosphere nations were built on slavery and dispossession, these countries harbour a good deal of unsettled resentment against the social order. Feminism was quick to exploit this resentment, which facilitated its rapid growth throughout the Anglo cultural establishment:

So North America, in particular, has had this nasty history of rival ethnic and racial groups, displacing the natives and fighting bloody wars against each other, and never came to an understanding about it. And then cultural Marxism came, whipping up and playing on these conflicts as a wedge against the West, and it found its most fertile ground in the Anglosphere. The malicious Anglo feminists of US divorce courts and #metoo seem to borrow a lot of that group warfare language, and maybe that combined with the Puritanism has made the Anglo strain very ugly and hostile (Appendix Q, p.304).

While this is true, it has to be pointed out that many early Anglo feminists were explicitly racist and fascist. Indeed, white women in America seem to remain as racist as their antebellum forbears, judging by the low rates of cross-racial marriage in the modern United States.

An ex-military expatriate calling himself 'Ranger' confirmed Lawrence's claims from a practical standpoint. He makes it absolutely clear that divorce in the non-Anglosphere West is a completely different animal than its Anglosphere counterpart:

On divorce here? Yeah it happens, but in Germany and Europe, it is true, divorce is just a bump in the road, nothing like the total wreckage you suffer in the US. They don't even really have family courts here, it's all a "mediate it and be done with it" thing. You don't lose your kids, you keep your house and car, you keep what you've earned and saved in your profession and your hard work. No alimony. CS is a max amount and you don't get gouged. So a girl can't gold-dig here, a lot more incentive to work things out if things get rough. I've known hundreds of American guys who came to Europe, got hitched, some got divorced. Not one single one got ruined. They don't want people to divorce here, so the laws make sure you can go without hassle (Appendix O, p.278).

When I began my research a decade ago, I never expected scholars from other disciplines to be inspired by it – much less make the extensive contributions they have. My intentions were humble and pragmatic: to show men that Anglo feminism was merely part of repressive Anglo-Saxon culture, and thus uniquely sex-negative, strident and misandrist. Additionally, I wanted to show that Anglo-American women were also marked by this repressive culture, which made them unsuitable mates for honest and reasonable men.

I considered these facts self-evident; but when I began, few did so. That has changed. Now it may be seen just how influential my ideas have become. The misandrist nature of Anglo-American common law is a complete revelation to me, and my learned correspondents have forged an entirely new branch of my original thesis. Today, my work is cited around the Anglo-American world in a wide variety of contexts: elite Anglo American universities and Law Schools as well as the top manosphere blogs and websites. Like Darwin or Feynman, I was happily granted insights denied to far cleverer men. For great original contributions depend on luck and circumstance as much as on 'mechanical' intelligence or acquired knowledge. A true originator is as much the product of unique cultural circumstance as his personal qualities.

Part Four

Sexual False Consciousness

How Sexual False Consciousness Maintains Gynocratic Agendas across the Anglosphere

4.0 Introduction

In Greek mythology, King Tantalus was tortured for his cruel deeds by a terrible punishment in Hades. A lake of wine surrounded him, while a vine of grapes hung just above his head. Every time he stooped to drink the wine, it ran from him. Every time he reached up to eat the grapes, they swung tantalizingly out of his reach. And so he was doomed to suffer terrible hunger and thirst, for all eternity. As we shall see, this tale reflects the lives of most Anglo-American males. Unlike Tantalus, however, their punishment is no fault of their own.

From birth to puberty, most Anglo-American men tend to 'swallow' the myths of childhood. That is, they grow up believing that the world is a 'fair' place; that adults 'knows best'; and that organized religion – in its various forms – approximates truth.

At puberty, various physical/hormonal/psychological changes kick in. For most males, these shatter the old pre-pubescent world-view. As Professor Richard Lynn observes, the sudden spurt in IQ at this time leaves most self-aware young people either atheist or agnostic (Paton, 2008). The 'class-blindness' of childhood gives way to an awareness of socio-economic distinctions – and the piercing revelation that life is unfair. It is no surprise that the disenfranchised typically 'switch-off' education at this time, clearly perceiving the vast socio-cultural obstacles they face in pursuit of upward mobility. For adolescent males, the emergence of a sex-drive replaces childhood pursuits with deep, carnal yearnings.

In sum, the self-aware youth has his world-view completely restructured in the space of a few years. This transformation typically occurs without any meaningful guidance from any quarter save the mass media. Indeed, 'mainstream' Western society continues to peddle pre-pubescent themes to young people long after adolescence – with ever-diminishing returns. Perhaps this is yet another expression of the Anglosphere's latent Puritanism and fear of adult sexuality? But I digress...

The media, of course, has always been quick to exploit the changes associated with adolescence. The West's 'youth culture' is really a 'post-pubescent youth culture', after all. Video games, popular music and films all bombard the young with images of a sexualized, liberated 'adult' world that waits beyond the pre-pubescent confines of school and the parental home. Rap and rock music videos, for instance, invariably parade hordes of nubile, scantily-clad women as 'available' appendages to 'adult life'. These images raise the adolescent male's expectations of adult sexuality to priapic dimensions. In good faith, he truly thinks that armies of sexualized women await him in the adult world, eager to be plucked like fruit from a tree…

Well, they do if he is a swaggering plutocrat or sadistic thug, or blessed with outstanding good looks. For the vast majority of males, of course, they *don't*. And so many young men suddenly find themselves as confused and challenged by adult life as they were by adolescence. In childhood, they were told a pack of convenient lies that they discarded at puberty. They then find that the 'adult' world-view they adopted in adolescence was a pack of lies, too. Like Tantalus, their wine and grapes have been snatched away - *again*.

And this is the root of the 'male crisis' that stalks the modern western world: a breakdown of certainty, a failure of trust. Having been deceived twice in rapid succession by the social order, Anglo-American men are increasingly distrustful of all received wisdom and advice. Hence, the explosion of the online manosphere...

Indeed, it must be admitted that much 'manosphere' activity represents an attempt to manage the disappointment and alienation of Anglo-American men. On the one hand, the PUA gurus offer Incel men 'restorative justice' – a way to realize the 'adult' dream of effortless sex that haunted their adolescence. On the other, the MGTOW crowd present a more radical alternative: complete rejection of a deceitful social system. Last but not least, the conservative MRAs promise retribution against women and a social order that allows them to indulge in selective hypergamy. However, at base, all these responses are designed to redress the justified sense of betrayal that currently besets all but a small minority of Anglo-American males.

4.1 What is Sexual False Consciousness?

According to Karl Marx, the broad masses in capitalist societies are coerced by what he termed 'false consciousness'. In this view, the exploited and disenfranchised internalize the world-view of the dominant class, even where this works to their detriment. Hence, the blue collar masses in North America often vote Republican, even though this results in reduced life-chances for people in their socio-economic bracket. Similarly, the British underclasses are often fanatical defenders of the social order, despite being firmly fixed at the bottom of it. Neo-Marxists such as Antonio Gramsci claimed that the complex mass media in Western societies are largely responsible for maintaining 'false consciousness' among the masses.

While some researchers have questioned whether false consciousness really exists, I believe it is alive and well. It has just transformed into something else in the post-Marriage era: namely, sexual false consciousness. While disenfranchised men have a relatively clear grasp of their economic situation, they now suffer from sexual self-delusion. And this is a logical progression, in that status in western countries is now expressed sexually rather than economically. This change has shifted the locus of false consciousness from the economic to the sexual sphere, since the sexual sphere is now more important. Indeed, as the British writer Colin Wilson avers, the sexually disenfranchised are the new underclass, whatever their economic situation. Hence, an incel doctor has lower status than a tattooed thug in a housing project, if the thug is enjoying a surfeit of sex.

As we all know, the Anglo-American world is a dating nightmare for men. More than half of all American women are obese; most women over 35 are 'past it' from a sexual stand-point; and the few attractive women are entitled, unpleasant and only interested in thugs on Death Row. Men who want sex with the few eligible females have to work hard at it: study Game, hit the gym, eat right – and as the guys at PUA Hate argue, even all that effort guarantees nothing. So, aside from fucking whores and pursuing foreign women, the sexual options for the average Anglo-American male are, basically, dire. For a start, there are too few eligible women. And the eligible women that do exist generally hate men who aren't 'exciting' (i.e. tattooed, psychopathic thugs or wealthy celebrities).

Despite this gritty reality, most Anglo-American men seem to live in a world of endless sexual bounty, having sex with teenage models every few days (at least according to themselves). Even old, ugly men with menial jobs claim to be doing this, in the face of all rational evidence.

That is sexual false consciousness, in a nutshell: rampant self-deceit about one's sexual chances, options and achievements. Men suffering from this malady are fairly ubiquitous in the Anglosphere. They are particularly common among the lower social strata, especially the type hitched to obnoxious land whales. If we examine their claims objectively, they have to be bullshit: otherwise, the Anglosphere's tiny minority of beautiful women would be having sex with thousands of men every day.

False consciousness has a purpose. It deludes the masses into thinking they are living in mansions, not hovels; that they are driving Maseratis, not Volkswagens. Similarly, sexual false consciousness deludes men married to past-prime blimps that they are having sex with 18 year old models; or it deludes hardcore incels that such escapades are a serious possibility. And so such men stumble on through lives devoid of all sexual prospect, keeping corporate capitalism ticking over as workers and consumers.

The case of Elliot Rodger shows what happens when sexual false consciousness breaks down, or fails to form in the first place. Instead of padding his mind with ludicrous pipe-dreams, Rodger confronted his incel status every hour of every day. Rather than being 'crazy' or 'insane', he was, in fact, entirely grounded and objective: far more sane, in fact, than men trapped in sexual false consciousness.

Rodgers' only insanity involved his acceptance of Anglo-American Puritanism as the limits of his psycho-sexual world. With his money, he could easily have hired a bevy of silicon-enhanced hookers for sexual relief. Better still, he might have just journeyed to a foreign country where women are thinner, prettier, less entitled and frankly, less misandrist. To illustrate the point, let my learned correspondent

Lawrence describe the appalling state of gender relations in the contemporary Anglosphere:

And now, in the ugly aftermath of #metto, #timesup and #nameandshamehim, you don't even have to get married or have a kid in the Anglosphere to become a slave. Any interaction with a women, even something as casual as a glance or an innocent conversation, opens you up to charges of harassment and sexual misconduct. And given that as much as half of young white women in America find even innocent male female interactions to be harassment, you're in great danger at any moment. Many harassment and misconduct changes now are being assembled by our corrupt legal-prison-industrial complex system to become prosecutable offenses. But even short of that, the witch-burning in social media means that any vague accusation, whether recent or months or years ago, will make you unemployable and a social pariah. You'll lose your health insurance and ability to earn a living, and then the state will have all kinds of additional ways to brand you a criminal and toss you in jail (Appendix Q, p.294).

Had Rodger left this cloying cesspool of repression, paranoia and institutionalized misandry, his lapse into murder-suicide would surely have been permanently arrested.

4.2 How does Sexual False Consciousness Work?

A revolution is sweeping the English-speaking nations, especially the United States. Reality, so long suppressed and devalued by the lame-stream media, is reasserting itself. Nowhere is this truer than in the field of sexual relationships. The Internet now allows men to discuss such matters without upper-middle class censorship and the results are a revelation. Most American males are NOT living Don Draper lives, with bosomy models tapping them on the shoulder for sex whenever they walk into a bar. Indeed, most American women are not bosomy models at all; they are mostly obese, ugly and frigid. And the few sexualized, thin and attractive American women are (at least in their prime years) attracted only to violent, mumbling thugs.

Despite these harsh realities, most Anglo-American men are insistent that they are having sex with 17 year old models on a regular basis. This is especially true of blue-collar, middle-aged males who are clearly of no interest whatsoever to the small minority of attractive American women. Indeed, many a hard-core incel shelf-stacker seems to think he 'has a chance' with girls who would, in reality, not deign to spit on him.

Surely the broad masses embrace such fantasies in order to make their pointless lives endurable. In this section, I offer a theory as to how Sexual False Consciousness is maintained on a daily basis.

In Britain, one of the most interesting entertainers is a fellow called Derren Brown. A mentalist stage magician, he is known for feats of memory, sleight of hand and mental manipulation. I recently read his thoughts on stage hypnotism and they went some way to explaining how Sexual False Consciousness operates in practice (Brown, 2007). According to Brown, nothing 'happens' to the subjects in a hypnotist's show. For the most part, the participants eating onions, singing arias and dancing the polka are their normal selves. Their enthusiastic participation relates more to a deep human need for social conformity than any real change in their mental condition. That is, they do not want to upset the audience/hypnotist/other participants by failing to 'act up to' expectations. Brown uses the famous Milgram Experiment to illustrate this deep human need to conform. When test subjects were told to administer imaginary electric shocks to an actor, most of them did so without demur. Even when the actor was howling in mock agony, the subjects did not desist.

It occurs to me that this deep human need not to 'rock the boat' explains Sexual False Consciousness. Blue collar males who never have sex (certainly with 17-year old models) maintain that they do for the same reason 'hypnotized' people dance the polka. Since the late 60s, a pan-Anglosphere myth has arisen that women are having sex with everybody; that post-feminist society is overflowing with sexual opportunity. This myth is maintained by the media at every turn - by rock music, rap music and TV shows like Mad Men. In short, there is considerable societal pressure placed on men (in particular) to pretend they are having sex with models every day of the week. To admit this is not happening is 'spoiling the show'; an unforgivable crime.

By extension, it occurs to me that males who are drawn to this site and the Men's Movement in general possess, for one reason or another, stronger personalities than most. Perhaps some are immigrants to Anglo-Saxon countries and thus less troubled by non-conformity. Perhaps the anonymity of the Internet facilitates an honesty and self-awareness that men hesitate to show in their normal lives. Whatever the cause, reality is flourishing and there isn't a damned thing the Anglo Power Elites and their lackeys in the lame-stream media can do about it.

And long may it continue.

4.3 How is Sexual False Consciousness Maintained?

Sexual false consciousness is the widespread male delusion that young, attractive women hand out sex for free. Moreover, not only do they spend every hour of every day handing out free sex, they give it to aging, blue-collar schlubs in pick-up trucks. All utter nonsense, of course: and yet such delusions are ubiquitous among blue collar males, who truly believe that 18 year old models are gasping for sex with mechanics and road-sweepers.

If we accept that the legacy media is largely responsible for sexual false consciousness, a question presents itself: how is it infiltrated by such an agenda? Why do celebrated TV shows like Mad Men describe sexual experiences completely detached from practical male experience?

The answer is relatively simple. The mass media – and especially the Anglo-American mass media – tend to extol the views and experiences of unrepresentative minorities. This is partly because the people who create and finance TV shows like Mad Men are simply not representative of most people. The same is true of those who create Hollywood films, or BBC costume dramas. Like Anglo politicians, they are overwhelmingly upper-middle or upper class in origin. They will generally have had very limited contact with anyone outside a small, relatively privileged social circle. In his superb book Hollywood Versus America, Michael Medved cites examples of American TV executives thinking routine office workers earn millions of dollars a year. If someone can believe that, they can also believe road sweepers are having regular sex with supermodels.

The British sociologist Anthony Giddens explains the effects of this hermetic self-isolation via the concept of 'structuration'. In this view, English-speaking countries are characterized by extreme self-segregation between different economic strata, age-groups and ethnicities. This leads to widespread delusions about the nature of society. For example, half the British underclass think that everyone in Britain is like them - that is, unemployed and living in social housing. Similarly, American liberals assume that 'everyone' is left-liberal, because they only mix with other left-liberals. In sum, then, Anglo-Saxon countries are characterized by extreme 'structuration'. Because different social groups have little in common and no shared experiences, social subcultures tend to massively exaggerate the status of their own worldview. Given such a bizarre situation, it is little wonder that wealthy media executives tend to over-promote their experiences on the casting-couch.

So when we see Don Draper being approached by models for sex on an hourly basis, we must remember that those who created this scenario are overwhelmingly rich, privileged and socially unrepresentative. It may well be that they are having lots of 'casting couch' sex themselves – but that is hardly true of most men. Moreover, their social insularity deludes media executives into thinking that mechanics and road-sweepers are indeed having regular sex with supermodels. Much like 'everyone' took drugs in the 60s, or made millions on Wall Street in the 80s, so 'everyone' is having sex with elite women in the mad, weird world of the Anglo-American mass media.

Having explained the idiomatic, fantastical content of the 'mainstream' media, we must ask: why do the masses accept such blatant lies so readily? Why do frigid, hypergamous women watch Sex and the City (a hyperreal fantasy if ever there was one)? Why do incel computer programmers enjoy watching Don Draper bang his latest playmate? If the media does not reflect reality, why are the masses so readily seduced by it? Perhaps because it is *not* reality. Like porn, maybe its appeal relates more to vicarious wish-fulfillment than personal identification. As boxing fans emulate the punches of their heroes in the bathroom mirror, TV and film audiences derive voyeuristic pleasure from the priapic escapades of their media idols.

Knowing this, the media has developed conventions to maintain its hold on the mass mind. American TV executives clearly have an informal agenda to elide the old, the ugly and the poor (Medved, 1993). For seldom if ever do we see Anglo-American TV shows starring anyone over 50, crippled or possessing a socially critical outlook. Everything conspires to banish reality in favour of an upper-middle class, hyper-sexualized fantasy world full of grinning, youthful automatons. No producer will break ranks to create a show bucking those conventions, since money is king.

However, the broad masses go beyond simple voyeurism in their appreciation and consumption of 'mainstream' media. Many of them come to internalize such delusions as 'reality'. Indeed, people like ourselves who dare to question this 'reality' are viewed as embittered eccentrics and dangerous malcontents by guys who, frankly, will never have sex with a model in their whole lives.

Perhaps we need to remember that the 'mainstream' media has been pumping out these 'libertine' messages since the mid-60s. Three generations of men have grown up knowing little else. Since infancy, the notion that 'everyone' is living in a mansion and having daily sex with models has been drilled into them, without pause. Such ceaseless indoctrination has surely clotted all capacity for critical thought on these issues. Hence the innumerable blue-collar incels who serious think they can bed models and actresses, or white-collar men who seriously think women view them as something more than walking ATM machines.

Only with the rise of the Internet has sexual false consciousness been offered any challenge since the mid-60s. Little wonder that educated males from generations Y and Z are the first to begin throwing off its brain-rotting yoke.

4.4 Is the Blue Pill Really Sexual False Consciousness?

What the radicalized manosphere calls 'Blue Pill Nonsense' is really better described as Sexual False Consciousness. The latter concept has much greater depth and explanatory power because it is rooted in a long-standing body of discourse originating in the nineteenth century, not something recently devised to cope with the vagaries of female mate-choice.

What is false consciousness? For Karl Marx, false consciousness denoted the widespread tendency for low-status, exploited people to 'buy into' the values/ideology of the ruling elite. Of course, the elite use all their power to maintain false consciousness – compulsory state education and the mainstream media represent the two potent mechanisms of mass indoctrination. Not, of course, that Marxism is a viable philosophy; only in this narrow area has it value or significance.

Noam Chomsky has applied the concept to modern America, showing how the Anglo-American media 'manufacture' consent for foreign wars, coercive policing and other abuses (Chomsky and Herman, 1995). The Italian neo-Marxist Antonio Gramsci pushed the concept of false consciousness in another, more abstract direction: he argued that advanced societies were forged from ideological 'cement' called 'hegemony'. Consisting of language, laws, conventions and customs, hegemony represents 'common sense' at any given moment. Of course, national hegemony is subject to continual revision: in 50s America, marriage and heterosexuality was immutable norms, not mere lifestyle choices. And while provisional acceptance of a given hegemony represents a certain degree of false consciousness, coercion of the masses can never be total.

Why am I explaining this? Because Blue Pill/Red Pill terminology is much better understood when redefined as false consciousness; or its opposite, revolutionary consciousness. Swallowing the Blue Pill means accepting the mainstream narratives associated with the prevailing hegemony; swallowing the Red Pill means rejecting such narratives and accepting one's true, disenfranchised situation (and of course, acting to remedy it).

The manosphere has a specific interest in defining gender relations in Red Pill/Blue Pill terms, of course. However, even this development is not entirely new. The British crime writer Colin Wilson developed the concept of 'sexual disenfranchisement' several decades before the Manosphere even existed (Wilson and Seaman, 1990). He argued that men have traditionally displayed status via wealth, power or even spiritual standing. However, in the modern era they principally display their status via sexual conquests of the young and beautiful. In short, the American Dream has become the American Sexual Dream. Consequently, the nature of revolt has changed. When wealth was the principal source of social status, revolutionaries like Che Guevara clamored for economic equality. However, now sex is the chief marker of social status, revolutionaries see the equalization of sexual resources (typically young women) as their main goal (PUAs are a good example of this trend).

Hence, in the modern era 'sexually disenfranchised' men are the principal revolutionary force in advanced industrial nations. According to Wilson, sex criminals are males who have seen through the hegemonic smoke screens erected by the mainstream media; and, having realized their sexual exclusion, set about remedying it via sex crime (or, more recently, game). In other words, they have rejected the Blue Pill of sexual false consciousness for the Red Pill of strenuous resistance. Wilson calls this process of realization 'switching on the dark'.

Redefining the MRA Blue Pill as sexual false consciousness greatly expands its explanatory power. The Manosphere is no mere collection of incel misfits – it is a counter-hegemonic movement. Males such as Elliott Rodger or Cho Hui Seung were not mere psychotics – before death, they achieved a certain insight into their sexually disenfranchised condition. And the Anglosphere's myth of universal sexual liberation/bounty is no mere chimera – it is a contrived hegemonic narrative maintained by the elite to nullify the male masses.

And so on.

Sexual false consciousness is the erotic expression of the American Dream and it serves the same purpose in neutralizing the masses as its economic counterpart. Low income Americans vote Republican because they spuriously believe they are only 'temporarily' poor; that someday, despite all evidence to the contrary, they can be rich. Like the American Dream, SFC encounters little resistance because most American males have bought into the delusion they can achieve it. And because the sexual rewards for success are so alluring (and the price of failure so catastrophic), they cannot accept that most of them will never have sex with actresses, models and other attractive women. Like the blue-collar schlubs who seriously think they have a chance with models and actresses, the average American male would sooner wallow in delusions of sexual success than accept his incel/landwhale-fucking reality.

The dream of sexual success hangs before every American man like a shimmering mirage, binding his consent to elite narratives even as he studies and toils. In fact, SFC is now the true opiate of the male masses; their primary existential motivation.

Interestingly, Philip K Dick saw his sci fi novels as metaphors for false consciousness and counter-hegemonic resistance. The Pill trope had its first cinematic outing in Total Recall, a film inspired by one of Dick's short stories. In short, the Blue Pill and sexual false consciousness have always been one and the same.

4.5 Female Sexual False Consciousness

Male Sexual False Consciousness is a well-described phenomenon in my writings. Blue collar males in the midst of decade-long sexless 'dry-spells' talk and act as if they were bedding models every night. Nor is this mere bluster and persiflage; many celibate males really believe they *are* having sex with teenage pop singers and actresses, women who would not spit on them if they were burning. Male SFC is a product of Anglo-American reality avoidance, 'lamestream' media manipulation, simple self-delusion and (concealed) shame. In any case, most males in the Anglosphere are so psychologically damaged by institutionalised misandry that they cannot think rationally about their sexual situation.

What about female SFC?

Women's magazines, TV shows and books are full of sexual tips and spine-tingling accounts of multiple orgasms with alpha paragons. However, this priapic narrative contrasts hugely with serious research into female sexuality, most of which finds that a huge minority (around 40%) of Anglo-American women have little or no libido. At a practical level, the average Anglo-American woman presents as a classic 'Anglobitch' – frigid, arrogant, misandrist, entitled, vindictive and snotty. This holds as true for the ugly, obese and post-Wall variety as it does for young and attractive ones.

So much for the boundless 'liberation' endlessly extolled by the 'lamestream' Anglo-American media.

Most Anglo women dress like ten-dollar whores, read and talk about sex all day, even consider themselves intensely sexualized – yet are, in truth, as frigid and repressed as their grandmothers. Young males are rightly baffled when young girls dress provocatively yet resent all expressions of sexual interest: they seem to inhabit a state of 'sexualized frigidity', flaunting sex yet hating it too. What are the best explanations for this glaring contradiction? Why do so many Anglo women strive to talk, dress and look 'sexy' while being volcel or even actively hostile to sex?

The answer is complex. Unlike male SFC, the female form of this condition derives from the specific vagaries of female psychology –

namely solipsism, the herd instinct and greater psycho-sexual plasticity. However, the fact that priapic gay men design female 'culture' in their own image is also highly significant.

Many gay men adopt homosexual lifestyles in the repressive Anglosphere to gain easy access to sex – as a group, they are disproportionately self-selected for hyper-sexuality. In short, gays are the kind of males who will project sex onto everything they see. Since such men are largely responsible for female fashion, television, music and 'culture' in general, they inject these things with their own sexual obsessions. Lacking the merest shred of creative originality, women have yielded control of all these activities to infinitely more creative and intelligent gay men. And gay culture is suffused with – indeed, defined by – sex. Assuming women to be female versions of themselves, these men have plastered the bare wall of female sexuality with their own erotic obsessions – obsessions Anglo women almost completely lack. In this view, frigid women do not dress provocatively to attract elusive 'alphas' – they dress that way because hyper-sexualized gay men told them to. After all, the average Anglo woman derives no more pleasure from the concept of 'man' than she does from a dose of hives.

In many ways, this gay domination of female culture is at the root of female SFC. It surely explains the massive gulf between sexualized female rhetoric and the frigid, uptight and misandrist reality. Female sexuality seems to be a provocative simulation of gay male sexuality, a frigid caricature. However, there are deeper issues in play. The female herd instinct is also implicated, as is female solipsism. If some trendy magazine or television show tells its female audience that the moon is made of cream cheese, their default compliance to authority makes them automatically believe it. Moreover, their infantile solipsism impedes women's ability to check such claims against reality; to a solipsist, reality is what one feels on any given day.

Solipsism distorts women's views in another way. Because most women can get sex relatively easily, they assume the same must be true of most men. This is utterly bizarre when one considers the contempt Anglo-American women typically harbour towards most males; but being entirely self-absorbed, they never link their own sexual elitism to the reality of male experience. Hence, women quite readily assume both genders have equal access to sex, even as they mentally excise the vast majority of males as potential sexual partners.

So, while male SFC is largely a product of shame and insecurity, low self-awareness plays a much greater role in female SFC. As for the minority of sexualized Anglo-American women (yes, they do exist) – typically damaged, addicted, working class and Dark Triad (narcissistic, borderline and histrionic) – they are just as confused as their frigid sisters. Their SFC typically involves confusing abuse for love – something pimps, thugs and other male sociopaths are adept at exploiting. Essentially, sexualized Anglo women are so fucked in the head that true sexual false consciousness eludes them; they have no 'real' sexual identity to compromise. Their SFC concerns not sex itself, but a deluded interpretation of human relationships.

Female sexuality is a juggernaut that carries all before it, and even disabled women can still attract male attention. This is especially true in the repressive Anglosphere, where sex is a culturally restricted commodity. Consequently, while male SFC conceals sexual 'inadequacy' or inceldom, female SFC takes a more complex form. Unlike male SFC, it originates in female solipsism coupled with mental malleability, hyper-hypergamy and sheer hypocritical stupidity. Yet it has immense impact on men, since women regulate all sexual access in the post-feminist Anglosphere.

The only effective and rational responsive is planned departure to liberated, man-friendly shores.

Part Five

Exporting Anglo Feminism

How the Anglosphere Exports the Five Pillars of Feminist Dysfunction

5.0 Introduction

Because of its unique alignment with the dominant culture and its values, Anglo-American feminism has been uniquely successful. Men in the Anglosphere are failing in record numbers while women monopolize education, law, media and the socio-cultural cathedral. Having achieved such success, and given the distinctive colonial history of the Anglosphere, it is inevitable that Anglo feminists will seek new fields to conquer. As we shall see, this expansionist programme is already well-advanced and will likely achieve even more success in the decades to come.

5.1 The Hillary Doctrine

In 2016, the future of the whole planet hung in the balance. After months of campaigning, Clinton and Trump at last faced up to one another in the Presidential election. While Trump had his faults, they paled into insignificance when compared to Clinton's criminality, deceit and chilling sense of entitlement. Worse still, Clinton is a rabid feminist who, if elected President, fully intended to use America's power and influence to advance her warped agenda. For the whole thrust of her foreign policy was no less than the brutal imposition of misandrist Anglo-American feminism across the globe. This heinous agenda, known as the Hillary Doctrine, simply represents an international war against male rights and freedoms. Here is Clinton speaking at a TEDWoman conference in Washington DC:

So the United States has made empowering women and girls a cornerstone of our foreign policy, because women's equality is not just a moral issue, it's not just a humanitarian issue, it is not just a fairness issue; it is a security issue. It is a prosperity issue and it is a peace issue. … Give women equal rights, and entire nations are more stable and secure. Deny women equal rights, and the instability of nations is almost certain. The subjugation of women is, therefore, a threat to the common security of our world and to the national security of our country (Hudson and Leidl, 2017: p.3).

On paper, it all sounds fair enough. However, as we all know, the reality of male life in the Anglosphere is systemized persecution and discrimination across a huge range of factors, from criminal sentencing to schooling and health care. Because of their Puritanical history, the Anglosphere nations exalt women on blameless pedestals while castigating men for possessing an active sexuality (interestingly, Clinton and her chorus lines in the 'mainstream' media criticized Trump for no more than being a 'sexual' man – hardly a federal offence). What Anglo feminists really mean by 'gender equality', of course, is a feminist dictatorship wherein men are third class citizens deprived of the most basic human rights; where all forms of sexual expression – pornography, prostitution, even game – are ruthlessly quashed; where women are parachuted into positions of power and influence by mere virtue of their gender; and where men are drafted to advance women's 'rights' while being systematically robbed of their own. This is not a world I (or any sane man) wants to live in, when viable alternatives exist. Here is one of my correspondents, Lawrence, on the key difference between Anglo countries and those in the non-Anglo West:

For most potential hazards, your wealth and assets protect you, but it's the opposite in the upside down world of Anglosphere family law. For wealthy and well-paid American men and their peers in the Anglosphere, marriage, having a kid and yes, now in #metoo world even striking up a conversation or hooking up with women paint a huge, ugly red bullseye on your back for the lunatic family court system in North America to come after you and profit at your expense. Not just to take your assets and impoverish you, which they absolutely do and which family law gives them full power to do, but also to toss you into prison. Yes, rich, upper-class and professional men not only robbed of their assets under full cover of law, but also thrown in jail, a tyrannical practice unique to the Anglosphere (Appendix O, p.284).

However, had Clinton won the election the misandrist US common law legal system would doubtless have become the preferred model for judges, jurists and juries across the globe. For Clinton, reducing all men to serfdom is central to her design. What she wants – what all Anglo feminists want – is a planet where sexual scarcity has reduced all men to denatured, pussy-begging maggots or deluded femiservatives; a world where men are expendable slaves or beasts of burden, as they are in the United States. A world where every female is a princess walking on air and all men disposable fodder. In Hard Choices (2014), Clinton's demented political memoir, she explains her agenda in greater detail:

... It was no coincidence that the places where women's lives were most undervalued largely lined up with the parts of the world most plagued by instability, conflict, extremism, and poverty. This was a point lost on many of the men working across Washington's foreign policy establishment, but over the years I came to view it as one of the most compelling arguments for why standing up for women and girls was not just the right thing to do but also smart and strategic ... the correlation was undeniable, and a growing body of research showed that improving conditions for women helped resolve conflicts and stabilize societies.

"Women's issues" had long been relegated to the margins of U.S. foreign policy and international diplomacy, considered at best a nice thing to work on but hardly a necessity. I became convinced that, in fact, this was a cause that cut to the heart of our national security (Clinton, 2014: p.469).

One only has to look at the chaotic state of the Anglosphere nations to see the real fruits of feminism: a criminal, welfare dependent underclass; an ailing, non-productive economy; institutionalised anti-male discrimination; record male suicide rates; and near-ubiquitous male alienation. How any of this can be equated with prosperity or stability, I leave for the reader to judge. Here is one of my expatriate correspondents, Phil, describing the #metoo nightmare that is modern America:

So, I guess here's the summary-line for you poor souls cursed with a Y chromosome living in the US or Canada, and it sounds like Israel or Britain too. In the #metoo era, your next date, work place interaction, water cooler conversation, any interaction private or public with a women even if it went well- it's now fair game to be "outed" with your name and pic attached, on social media, by these lynch mob witch hunts. That's seriously where the media and movement are going. I kid you not. And it's dangerous. In polls done of Millennials, almost 40 percent believe even a guy just winking or giving a compliment on appearance to a woman is now sexual harassment. Note the poll's of both sexes, and since men overwhelmingly disagree, that means a scary huge majority of young women think this. Plus, black and Latina women are actually more sensible when you break down the poll's tabs, they don't subscribe to the "everything a man does is harassment" line and a much smaller minority of them say this. So, when you break the poll numbers down, 80 percent of Millennial white girls in the United States and Canada are ready to spring sexual harassment charges on you if you just wink or them, hold a door for them or say they look nice. And even worse, to publicly humiliate you by name in social media and make you a pariah and unemployable. Stay away from Anglo girls if you're in the US, Canada or UK, you're inviting disaster! (Appendix E, p.236)

The overwhelming support Clinton enjoyed during her losing election bid from the mainstream media, Wall Street, academic commentators and everyone apart from the electorate did serve one useful purpose: to illustrate that the United States is an unabashed matriarchal oligarchy. Feminism in American is not marginalised at all; the Anglo-American establishment is thoroughly committed to the Anglo-Feminist agenda and views it as the primary ideological weapon in its international culture-war against the world's patriarchal nations and regions.

However, Clinton's resounding defeat also demonstrated that these agendas are increasingly opposed by enlightened men within the United States itself. The establishment consensus was that Clinton merely had to 'show up' in order to win the Presidency with a landslide majority; indeed, the result was presented as a foregone conclusion. Perhaps the dissident manosphere has more influence than we dare to believe.

5.2 Foreign Interference

Anglosphere countries have a persistent habit of interfering in the affairs of foreign nations. This is not just in the military sphere, but also in the fields of culture, economics and even law. Not a day goes by without the Anglosphere threatening sanctions or military action against some sovereign state and its people. Where does this cultural arrogance originate?

Because the Anglo-American mentality lacks existential self-awareness, the assumption that corrupt, repressive, divided, racist countries like the US, UK and Australia occupy some lofty plane of moral perfection goes largely unchallenged in the world. The elitist Anglosphere media are primarily responsible for maintaining these delusions; by focusing on the rosy lives of unrepresentative economic elites, they hide inequality, injustice and repression behind a cloak of dreams. This is why visitors to Anglo-American nations are invariably astonished by the vast gulf between real life in those countries and the media's carefully-crafted illusions: they seem to be different nations, with the Blue Pill simulation completely at odds with the Red Pill reality.

While the Anglosphere nations continually excoriate foreign cultures; it never occurs to them that Anglo culture is in itself riddled with dysfunction. Aside from a few private schools and elite universities, most Anglo-Americans remain resolutely anti-intellectual, even anti-intelligence, focused on absurd fantasies of self-aggrandisement and largely unfit to make any socio-economic contribution. As is well known, the Anglosphere contains a large, uneducable underclass prone to crime, Welfare dependency and drug addiction; a costly burden in social, legal and economic terms.

However, it is in the area of gender-relations where Anglo-American self-delusion reigns almost totally supreme. We could immediately turn point out the massive rates of singleness, childlessness and divorce that define the Anglo world (certainly the white majority within that world). Instead of blonde, lissom cheerleaders giving free sex to everybody, foreigners find the frosty Anglobitch in all her borderline, entitled glory; a misandrist legal system; high levels of male school failure, homelessness and suicide; and an endless torrent of false abuse allegations directed at men for the 'crime' of having a sex drive. In some ways, seeing the real Anglosphere is like Neo awakening from the Matrix to find his real body immersed in a vat of chemicals. Here are the searing words of an anonymous American correspondent comparing his homeland to his adopted country, France:

I'm one of the "exiles" from the failing and falling down Anglosphere, moved from the US to southwestern France over a decade ago and it's been a blessing in every dimension: career, love life, family, life quality, health, education, food. Everything. I was part of a big movement of Americans and Canadians who made our exit right around the start of the great Recession. The Silicon Valley press never had a precise name for us, but most of us made our fortunes in the software industry, saw writing on the wall and cashed in our stock options before the big crash of the S&P and Nasdaq in 2008.

But after dodging one bullet, we were left pondering why we should risk everything again in the even more dangerous and unpredictable world of US divorce courts. Many of us had seen multimillionaire colleagues reduced to poverty and misery in US family courts after their wives sued for divorce. And slowly but surely we realized the problem was more than a few isolated cases or soothing marriage counselor platitudes. It was in the broader American, and more generally Anglophone culture itself. And in the brainlessness of the courts that give carte blanche to the most parasitic women to leech off their spouses who contribute to society (Appendix B, p.224).

Despite this grim reality, the Anglosphere countries unthinkingly assume they have a right to 'correct' other nations and show them the way on every issue. Quite how the Anglo-American elite feel they have a right to impose their toxic values around the world only becomes clear when we examine the underlying pillars of Anglo-Saxon civilization. The most important of these is the extreme class distinction that characterizes the Anglo-American world, which has comparatively limited social mobility despite endlessly bleating about 'equality', 'rights' and 'justice'. Simply put, Anglo social elites never encounter the uneducable underclass, falsely-imprisoned men and fatherless children their repressive culture creates, and consequently believe that culture must be perfect. The British sociologist Anthony Giddens calls this Anglo tendency 'structuration', a kind of social apartheid that cuts across every area of social life. Briefly put, if the Anglosphere elite had even the most rudimentary knowledge of their own societies, they would never assume an attitude of cultural superiority.

Another factor in play is the dominance of the empirical tradition in Anglo-Saxon intellectual life. While the concise rationality of philosophical movements such as American pragmatism or British logical positivism is intellectually admirable, the dominance of such empirical movements indicates a certain lack of self-awareness among the Anglo-American intelligentsia – and by extension, Anglo-American civilization in general. When analysis is one's sole intellectual and cultural recourse, it inevitably leads a culture away from introspection or healthy self-awareness. For example, contrast the deep German shame over the Holocaust with the glib glossing of Britain's pivotal role in the slave trade – whole cities like Liverpool and Bristol grew fat on this vile trade, yet Britain's guilt about its complicity remains disturbingly negligible. In modern times, the same lack of Anglo self-awareness characterizes not only politicians and thought-leaders but Angloskanks themselves – how can men not be attracted to their borderline personalities, overbearing sense of entitlement and landwhale dimensions? No, guys that flee (or want to flee) the Anglo-Feminist Plantation must be mad, blind or gay.

Rightist writers in the dissident manosphere talk a lot about the mainstream media's abuse of Hegelian dialectic in the cultural war that engulfs us. Create a false flag threat of some kind - then concoct repressive measures to 'counter' and 'protect' the masses from it. By this means, the masses gleefully accept the terms of their own coercion; a good example being the recent 'sex abuse' hysteria. However, the same method can be deployed strategically: for example, the Anglosphere has used the Holocaust to deflect criticism of its own historical misdeeds for many decades now. Yes, the Holocaust happened and it was wrong; but the Anglosphere nations have gleefully seized on it as the 'greatest evil' in history to hide their own crimes against blacks, Indians, Scots, Jews, Native Americans and other indigenous peoples. A whole conceptual climate has been cleverly built on Anglo-Saxon opposition to Nazi Germany, which gives underhand legitimacy to modern Anglo-American imperialism and its warped mission to impose repressive Anglo-feminism across the globe.

5.3 Handmaid's Tales

Women are now so exalted across the Anglosphere, so obviously advantaged in every sphere of life, they can only feed their need for victimhood by retreating to a fictional world of imaginary persecution. The triumph of Anglo-American feminism has been so total that its devotees can only maintain their cherished victim status by confusing fantasy for reality.

The television series The Handmaid's Tale is all the rage among Anglo-American women in 2018. Everywhere I go they seem to be babbling about it - as if, at literally any moment, they were going to be stuffed into Victorian dresses and forced to bear rich men's children. In truth, The Handmaid's Tale is failed science fiction: despite falling birth rates around the industrialised world, no advanced democratic country has done anything to limit female reproductive freedom. In fact, most countries have actually extended it (Ireland being a notable recent example). Moreover, the West is becoming more secular on every measure, with the average Christian now an affluent white female (the same demographic who watch The Handmaid's Tale, oddly enough).

So why, then does this lame 80s novel and its various televisual spin-offs retain such a strong hold on the female imagination? It bears no relation whatsoever to existing affairs and social currents are moving ever further from the scenario it describes.

In reality, the Anglosphere is now an open matriarchy where women can get away with literally anything, including the sexual abuse of minors, fake accusations, racism and even murder. Given the well-attested privilege women are shown in the education system, in job selection, in the media, in reproductive matters, in healthcare and before the law, one is left completely baffled by the popularity of The Handmaid's Tale. In reality, female power and privilege expand with each passing year. The Anglosphere is an openly misandrist, gynocentric matriarchy, yet Anglo feminism still insists – or needs to insist – that women are somehow sexually oppressed and downtrodden.

The Handmaid's Tale is merely the next step in this project of obfuscation and self-delusion, with a hypothetical fantasy world replacing the 'global misandry' so loved by Anglo feminists. However, the Anglo-American fixation on meddling in the affairs of other countries is similarly designed to mask the various dysfunctions of the Anglo-American bloc itself. This fixation allows white Anglo feminists to claim female oppression in Mozambique or Iran somehow applies to themselves (as 'women'), thereby occluding the gynocentric misandry that prevails in countries like Australia and the United States.

By focusing on misogynist crimes supposedly committed in non-Anglosphere countries, the Anglo-American matrix seeks to paint itself in heroic colours while engaging in military piracy for oil and other natural resources. One recent tool of these matriarchal agendas was a Pakistani girl called Malala Yousafzai, supposedly shot by the Taliban for attending school in 2012. Never mind that the Taliban offer at least as much violence against subaltern males in Afghanistan – *all* males are the enemy to the misandrist Anglo-American media, and thus unworthy of consideration or sympathy. A vast outpouring of sympathy, advice and financial assistance poured out of the Anglosphere to give her the best medical treatment and support.

With popular support for the unwinnable wars in the Near East waning, the Anglo-American media is redefining those wars in terms of a matriarchal crusade against 'patriarchal barbarism' in a vain attempt to hide its own internal problems. Yet mass alienation among educated Anglo-American males and an increasing exodus of the most able and intelligent men from the misandrist Anglosphere can no longer be disguised, nor their effects denied:

Some of these self-claimed conservatives will whine about how ditching the Anglosphere means the Muslims, Africans and Latinos will take over, but at this point it doesn't matter, and it's too late to stop it anyway. Anglo civilization has slit it's own throat with this insane Puritanism and misandry. Winston Churchill was sadly deluded with all his triumphalism in the history of English speaking peoples, the civilization may have been sustainable back then before feminism and cultural Marxism infected the media and universities of the Anglosphere. But in combo with the cuck chivalry and Puritanism of the Anglo world, made worse by the profiteering of the common-law system, it means the ugliest decline and fall, and for the Anglo world it'll be a lot worse than what the Romans saw. The birth rate and marriage rates of the Anglo populations in the Anglosphere keeps plunging farther and farther as the misandry of family courts and the overall culture continues to take it's toll, so much so that Anglo families can survive only in the non-Anglo world now (Appendix A, p.222).

The ultimate problem with their crooked agenda is this: very few Anglo-American men want to die for the matriarchy. Apart from deluded White Knights and lumpen working-class idiots, most educated men rightly view feminism as a threat to their lives and liberty. Having seen so many fathers, uncles and brothers crash and burn in 'no fault' divorces, not to mention having experienced discrimination in every sphere of adult life, very few Anglo-American American males will be signing up to defend women's 'rights' any time soon. If feminists want to expand the matriarchy, perhaps they should do it themselves?

In any case, giving non-western women access to education will not neutralise terrorism in those countries. To the contrary, female hypergamy will only result in more men becoming sexually disenfranchised and alienated from the social mainstream, resulting in heightened alienation and even higher rates of terrorism by men with nothing to lose.

5.4 Advancing Gynocracy

Of course, part of the Anglo feminist agenda involves exporting the values and institutions that have made Anglo-Saxon civilization unliveable for most normal men. Anglo-American culture comprises five distinct interlocking memes or pillars, which will be discussed at length in a section of their own. These pillars cohere like links in a chain to promote feminist agendas at male expense. A further factor in play is that the five pillars are so deeply embedded in the culture it is almost impossible to resist them.

The Pillars are:

Class distinction
Social Isolation
Materialism
Puritanism
Common Law

An obvious agenda of the matriarchal Anglosphere is to impose its values on the rest of the world. Lacking any self-awareness and blinkered by naïve elitism, its leaders cannot see that other countries do not want or need the chronic dysfunction associated with its civilization. However, the Anglosphere not only exports the Pillars via direct military conquest, it also uses 'soft force' to impose its values.

Perhaps the major gynocratic meme exported from the Anglosphere is its repressive puritanism. The Anglo-Feminist obsession with suppressing sex work via false flag trafficking hysteria represents a potent stand of this agenda.This makes much sense, since puritanical repression is the cornerstone of Anglo dysfunction; the key to the five pillars, the true nexus of misandrist Anglo feminism. From religious Puritanism sprang its modern, secular form; and third/fourth wave feminism is its ultimate expression.

Not even Anglo feminists can still pretend that women face serious structural discrimination in the Anglosphere. It is entirely obvious that men are getting shafted in the divorce courts, in education, in employment, in healthcare, in the media and pretty much everywhere else. So obvious is this structural injustice, in fact, that its continued denial would result in mass cognitive dissonance and overt ridicule of feminist agendas. Hence feminists have shifted focus to regions where women do face real oppression (although they are still quick to deny male oppression in the same places).

This serves two purposes. First and most important, it diverts attention away from male suffering and female privilege within the Anglosphere itself. Consider it a feint or demonstration, a gesture designed to mislead. By focusing on places where women have no reproductive rights, women can continue to promote the illusion that women are still oppressed as a class even when this is longer true in the Anglosphere. Second, Anglo feminists have a genuine desire to 'reform' regions still governed by traditional gender relations. Having turned Anglo males into third class citizens, Anglo feminism is turning its eyes to new fields it can conquer. It is like a tumour senselessly devouring global civilization until only matriarchal, gynocentric barbarism remains.

The first target is the non-Anglosphere West. The second target is the rest of the world. Both places lack the Anglosphere's characteristic Puritanism and also have a civil law code impervious to feminist manipulation (on which much more later). While much ink has been expended on the subject, Lawrence (an expat former corrections officer) explains the difference:

I know Rookh was bringing this up as a main topic, and when it comes to things like sociology and cultural history I'm really not too familiar, so I can't really comment with the depth a lot of you guys have here. But I can say this from direct observation, the feminism of Scandinavia and Germany really is a world apart from the hate-filled, virulent misandrist madness of the Anglosphere, and ironically it further serves to help northern European men and protect them from divorce or #metoo-like harassment witch hunts. This isn't so easy to explain to people in the Anglosphere because the cultural framing of reference in Europe is so different, but I guess here's the essence of it.

Consider for a moment a European country infamous for its loud, obnoxious feminists, say Norway, Sweden or Finland. For the poor guys stuck in the Anglosphere, as I was until I expatriated, when we hear "feminists" even overseas, we instantly think of the vitriol-filled, openly misandirst American, Canadian or British harpies like Emily Lindin at Teen Vogue. For those who don't know, she was the disgusting bitch in the middle of the #metoo witch-hunting who wrote on Twitter a few months ago, "if some innocent men's reputations have to take a hit in the process of undoing the patriarchy, that is a price I am absolutely willing to pay." This is the character of Anglosphere feminism: it's shrill, resentful, spiteful, malicious and clearly full of hatred, less concerned with helping women than with doing damage to Anglo men in any way possible. (If these crazy feminists really wanted to help women, they'd campaign against the oppression in Muslim countries like Saudi Arabia).

So what about the feminists in Norway, Sweden, Germany, Denmark and Finland which had feminist traditions even before North America? It really is a totally different form of feminism. The feminists up there in Nordic-land and Germany can be shrill and loopy in their own way, yes. But up there, the feminism isn't misandrist, and they aren't obsessed with this "evil oppressive patriarchy" the way Anglosphere feminists are. For the Nordic feminists, it's more about true independence, sexual freedom and yes, actual egalitarianism. They hate the #metoo thing up there because they think it makes women look weak. They hate alimony for the same reason, in fact of all ironies, it was Nordic and German feminists who led the push decades ago to abolish alimony and restrict child support. And even to help institute paternity leave as well as maternity leave to encourage fathers to be with their young kids. It sounds crazy to us in the Anglosphere because "feminism" here is something so much nastier and misandrist by definition, but the feminists up in Nordic-land in Germany in general aren't misandrist and in fact do a lot of things that are very husband and father-friendly. Yes, they can irritate sometimes with their own "you go girl" talk and be a little standoff-ish at times, but to a surprising extent, most of them are actually reasonable, and mainly focused on making sure that girls and women have opportunities to explore and be creative—without doing this at the expense of boys and men (Appendix O, p.284).

Yes, it really is different. The correspondent is an American expat with extensive personal experience of both North America and Northern Europe. Why would he lie? The simple fact is that Anglo feminism is a completely different animal to its Continental European or Scandinavian counterparts. I have always said that the misandrist nature of Anglo feminism derives from the Anglosphere's repressive values. Ultimately, Anglosphere puritanism leads to an all-pervasive misandry which punishes men however they conduct themselves. It also places impossibly unrealistic expectations on marriage and relationships, which make divorce all the more likely when reality intervenes. Here is the Law Professor on how such puritanical delusions impact on Anglo-American divorce and its destructive outcomes:

A straying or dissatisfied wife outside the Anglo world will possibly sleep with the muscleman washing her car at times, take on a secret identity or even try an open relationship or swinging. (This is reasonably common in Europe and some portions of South America to ease relationship tension, as they are less puritanic in culture and seem able to grasp and hold to a bigger picture.) But the part that matters, is that the marriage will stay intact despite the straying, because the woman, the lawyers and the courts have no profit incentive to encourage it. And if it does happen, she will still need to take responsibility and become an earner, which fortunately, those societies also provide an assist for, in the interest of making sure everyone comes out OK (Appendix O, p.303).

If Anglo feminists like Catherine McKinnon had her way, humans would be conceived in test tubes and raised in artificial wombs. Anglo-American feminism is not against abuse, it is against sex itself. It may target its rhetoric against 'abuse' but its real target is heterosexual sex - exactly like the Victorian patriarchs they claim to despise. And this is what makes gender relations in the non-Anglosphere West so attractive to men, in countless ways:

And the different, more freewheeling attitudes of Europe towards sex and sexuality are truly a lot different, which probably steers the culture sharply away from Anglo-style feminism, even among the feminists there. Before my fiancée joined me in France—and I'll admit it here, even after we got married—one of the places I loved to go was up In NE Germany. Tbh German, Polish, Czech, Swedish and Finnish girls are sexy as hell in general, something about that Baltic area, and these gorgeous ladies never have hang-ups about being sexy, attracting men, even being nude or out in thongs in public. When you talk to them, many will say they're feminists, but their coziness and lack of frigidness around being sexual totally changes what feminism means to them. FWIW I see the same kind of thing down in South America when I've been there, particularly down in Brazil, which is the one country I would have chosen if I didn't wind up in Europe. Crazily hot women, independent, often say they're feminists but it all means something a world away from Anglo feminism. (In Brazil, when a girl says she's feminist what she really means is she likes to be the one in control in bed). So from that observation I think you guys are right, the way that Anglo feminists have been conditioned to view sex itself as dirty and nasty, a hang-up from our Puritan tradition, may contribute a lot to the nastiness and misandry of US and Anglo feminism (Appendix O, pp.303-304).

Precisely – feminism does not have to be the strident, sex-negative, zero-sum game it has become in Anglo-Saxon countries. In fact, the greater liberation of the non-Anglo West makes foreign women in general more personable, rounded, intelligent and reasonable. Because sex is not the elusive commodity it is in the Anglosphere, it is not the sole determinant of female worth outside Anglo countries. This is why non-Anglo Western women are not trapped in the Borderline, homosocial twilight their Anglo sisters reside in – they are of far higher quality in every respect: intellectually, culturally and socially. Another side-effect of Anglo repression is chronic obesity; lower class Anglo-American women happily eat themselves into elephantine obesity because they still retain female 'worth' (i.e. a vagina) whatever they look like. Where simple 'ownership' of sex is less significant, as in Scandinavia, women are compelled to maintain a human size. In England, probably the most repressed of the Anglosphere countries, women with a normal body weight are now a rarity: surely no coincidence.

Sexual repression coheres with another of the pillars, class distinction, to produce another unique Anglo-Saxon phenomenon: hyper-hypergamy. This is a term I coined to denote a hypergamy which focuses on unreal beings from fiction, such as vampire princes, swashbuckling pirates and flawless knights. Huge numbers of Anglo women waste their prime years lost in such febrile fantasies, which no real-world male can ever match. This dysfunctional female desire for unattainable ideals is a direct expression of the sacralised status all fertile women enjoy in Anglo culture. This sacralised status amplifies innate female tendencies such as conformity and materialism into unnatural caricatures which inhibit normal relationship formation during a female's prime reproductive years.

Of course, Anglosphere feminism hates Europe's sexual freedom and is doing all it can to taint and subvert it. Already we can see liberated countries like France moving to ban prostitution, typically at the instigation of Anglo-American feminists. European men need to fight this attack on their sexual freedoms tooth and nail – and the same goes for expat Anglo-Americans enjoying new lives in European lands. That said, the well-developed legal, economic and political systems of the non-Anglosphere West make the Anglo feminists' task much harder than it is in developing countries, where the native culture is a more of a *tabula rasa*. Anglo feminists can hope to advance only the Puritan pillar of dysfunction, using only soft power (principally, the media). One aspect of this involves the mainstream Anglo media misrepresenting Europe's sexual freedoms with hysterical lies and distortions. George, one of my correspondents, writes:

Picking up at least some of the language is also a plus to help dispel all the bad information and fake news about Europe that's all over the US and UK, including in MSM outlets. Like the OP was saying Breitbart does tell a lot of un PC truth but they've got a serious blindspot on Europe. Both Breitbart and liberal mainstream media like CNN, Time Magazine, Guardian and NBC ran some completely made up story about how Sweden had passed a law requiring a formal signed written contract to have consent for sex. Because I'd learned Swedish I instantly knew this whole claim was absolute bullshyte, turned out there were a couple Swedish tabloids that put up salacious stories about a proposed law in December that was focussed on protections in the adult film and other industries. And it didn't even take the form of a law, just proposals and increased protections (Appendix C, pp.229-230).

However, soft power is a dangerous channel to rely on, since it runs both ways and is therefore open to infiltration and critique. This is why the Anglo-Feminist matrix is focusing its efforts on the developing world, as we shall now observe.

If elected President in 2016, Hillary Clinton intended to use America's power and influence to advance her warped agenda. But even though Clinton lost, her feminist cohorts are still striving to impose her feminist imperialism around the world.

As First Lady, Clinton characterized the 2001 war in Afghanistan as a war for women's rights. However, this tendency to characterize Anglo-American imperialism goes back rather further: the Bush administration (specifically Barbara Bush) characterized the War on Terror as a struggle for the rights of women. Cherie Blair, wife of British Prime Minister Tony Blair also described the War on Terror in these terms. Indeed, the Anglo nations are especially prominent in these campaigns, even fabricating forensic evidence to initiate them. This rhetoric helps to legitimize these imperialist ventures among the Anglo-American masses, for which women are sacred deities. Western media typically gloat over the vast numbers of foreign men killed by 'Our Boys' (the unemployable Anglo-American underclass) while emphasizing attempts to minimize female casualties. Though illegal acquisition of oil and natural resources plays a major role in these campaigns, they are also motivated by the Anglosphere's presiding motif: the sacralised human female. It is notable how American bomber crews in World War Two frequently decorated their planes with paintings of nubile women displaying their breasts and legs. It is also interesting how many Nevada brothels offered helicopter crews free sex during the first Gulf War, as if rewarding sex-starved devotees in some gynocentric cult. One is reminded of the ancient Assyrians and their blood-eyed war goddess, Ishtar, in whose name they sacked countless cities and conquered dozens of peoples.

The Anglosphere also attacks the developing world using the media's 'soft power', just as it attacks the countries of the non-Anglo West. Digital communication permits the global proliferation of films, TV shows and news channels as never before, and the Anglosphere countries remain the preeminent manufacturers of these media. One aspect of the Islamic world is strikingly reminiscent of the Anglosphere: Puritanism. While woman-worship does not dominate Islam for a host of peripheral reasons, its puritanical repression is an obvious schwerpunkt (weak point) in its ideological armour. Once Islamic women gain a certain degree of economic and social autonomy, they might quickly gain the sacralised status of Anglo-American women. Already, Hollywood is lining up an 'empowered' female Muslim superhero to advance this agenda. If this subtle subversion programme is successful, one might soon find Anglo women relocating to the Islamic world in droves to enjoy even loftier pedestals than those they already occupy.

5.5 The Military Export of Male Sexual Disenfranchisement

Anglo-American sexual repression is clearly linked to Anglo culture's fatal obsession with consumerism and debt slavery. And yes, it is obvious that blue-pilled males slave their pointless lives away for branded commodities assembled in Third World sweat shops to 'win' (or try to win) some frosty Anglobitch tail. Of course, both women and the Matrix have vested interests in maintaining this situation. Women get raised onto marble pedestals by their beta lackeys and the system at large; and by selling debt and dross to pussy-starved betas, the Matrix secures its existence for the foreseeable future. A win-win situation for both parties.

However, sexual repression in the Anglosphere serves an additional purpose: it creates a ready supply of frustrated cannon fodder useful for imposing Anglo matriarchy of other parts of the world. As well as making these deluded Gammas more reckless, prolonged sexual deprivation makes them exalt women as goddesses worth fighting and dying for. In sum, withholding sex from Anglo-American males not only serves the Matrix within the nation state; it helps the Matrix expand its gynocentric agenda beyond the Anglosphere.

As we have seen, class distinction is one of the five pillars of Anglosphere dysfunction. The socio-economic power-distance deliberately fostered by every Anglo-Saxon nation produces a large, alienated underclass defined by low intelligence, limited horizons and cynical conformity. In the UK for example, one third of the population cannot divided 65 by 5 with pencil and paper and almost 20% are functionally illiterate. Research continually shows how clueless most Americans are about the wider world; only 1 in 3 Americans can find Great Britain on a map, for instance. With illiterate mobs coexisting alongside privileged elites, the major Anglosphere nations are more like Third World countries than progressive states such as Norway, Germany or Japan. However, this retarded Anglo underclass does serve one useful purpose: as willing fodder for the military-industrial complex.

For these bone-headed clowns join the military in droves – what other career, apart from criminality, is available to them? And this is where good ol' Anglo sexual repression kicks in. Sexually disenfranchised males are far more likely to risk life or limb than males with a reproductive stake in the future. Widespread sexual repression not only makes the rabble take risks; it transforms women into semi-divine beings worthy of worship and self-sacrifice. Together, these factors create the perfect background noise to Anglo-American campaigns in 'patriarchal' regions.

And these ugly clowns are perfect cannon fodder, if nothing else. Blue collar males in the Anglosphere are deeply damaged by institutional misandry and gynocentric discrimination; they commit suicide in droves; almost 40% die single and childless; their lives are holes of self-loathing concealed by sexual false consciousness and infantile bluster. Largely deprived of the basic human need for sex, they constitute a reserve army of lemmings desperate to escape their tortuous celibacy; even a sniper's bullet is preferable to that walking death. Keeping these gammas in a constant state of sexual thirst thus serves the Matrix not only in economic terms but in military terms, too. Being rabbit-brained shills and incapable of rational thought, Anglo women effortlessly conflate their own role in the military-industrial complex with the trendy liberal pacifism they picked up in college (perhaps it should be renamed the military-industrial-sexual complex – an interesting concept indeed).

Meanwhile, the 'lamestream' media skews all international news with explicit feminist and misandrist narratives, further exciting our incel White Knights with chivalrous indignation. A good example would be Boko Haram, the African Islamist outfit whose massacres of boys are conveniently omitted in most western reportage. Instead we are treated to endless 'Find Our Girls' headlines calculated to stir the average Anglochump's 'protective' instincts towards stainless damsels. And so we are left with an ignorant, sexually frustrated horde of unemployable dolts fired up by feminist propaganda to support whatever illegal invasion the Matrix dreams up next...

Truly, the Anglosphere sets all standards of economic, educational and social progress.

I am well-known for my cynicism about Men's Right's Activism. Not that their views are wrong – they are not – I just don't think they can change anything. The reason is not wholly biological, although gender biology plays a role; it is rather that the Anglo-American Matrix is too well-organized and powerful, too integrated and efficient a system to be easily overthrown by AVfM and 'gender justice' groups of that ilk. The Matrix can be compared to an organism that has successfully weathered centuries of evolutionary and environmental pressure and has developed countless defensive mechanisms to secure its own existence. It utilizes gender biology, mass psychology, media, technology, education, money and language to defend itself in ways that are beyond any individual human consciousness (including mine) to completely unravel.

So we in the manosphere need to transcend outmoded narratives of 'justice' and 'fairness', or the notion that being intellectually 'right' makes victory inevitable. We can be proven 'right' a thousand times but if nothing ever changes – and it never does – none of it matters. A more effective course for the awakened man surely lies in self-development (separatism, minimalism, personal growth) and building a new life outside the Anglo-American Matrix.

Part Six

Pan Anglosphere Dissidence

The New Challenge to the Anglosphere's Toxic Women, Sexual False Consciousness and Institutional Misandry

6.0 Introduction

The 'old school' or 'first wave' MRAs who believed the Anglosphere could be reformed and remoulded along less misandrist lines are looking so dated. Yes, a lot of what of A Voice for Men, Warren Farrell and Angry Harry talked about is essentially right (and they deserve respect for that): but so what? For all their efforts, these guys did not change a single thing in the lives of real-world men. Men still get ass-raped in the divorce courts, the 'lamestream' media still set women atop pedestals and men are still ten times more likely to get a custodial sentence for a criminal offence.

The great problem with those 'first wave' Manosphere writers is that they failed to see what we Pan-Anglosphere Dissidents see all too clearly: that Anglo-Saxon culture is inherently misandrist and, as such, is inherently impervious to pro-male reform. In a nutshell, that is the big difference between us second-wave Manosphere writers and the 'old school' MRAs already alluded to. They believed reforming the system was possible, while we (in our various ways) have concluded that it is not. Essentially, the Anglosphere is built on gynocentric, misandrist foundations and, barring a complete cultural overthrow, that is how it is going to stay. An awakened male can either remain as a malcontent within the Anglo-Feminist Matrix; he can exploit the Matrix to fund an alternative lifestyle; or he can leave it altogether. Those are the real choices available to red-pilled males; reform is an 'old school' pipe dream.

The 'old school' men's rights activists always assumed that if only they highlighted the iniquities of an anti-male judiciary, education system and mass media then – as if by magic – reform would inevitably follow. In reality, Anglo-American civilization has just carried on in the same old misandrist way because misandry and gynocentrism are embedded in its socio-cultural DNA. And that is why the 'old school' MRAs could no more reform the Anglosphere than they could hold back the tides of the sea; and why their efforts to do so were doomed from the very beginning.

MGTOWS are deluded in a different way - they claim to shun Anglo women who already view them with utter contempt: not much of a protest. In truth, with their rampant misandry, fridigity and hypergamy, entitled Anglo-American females positively welcome the self-removal of such low-status 'losers' from their lives (if they even notice their absence at all).

When I began this project – if it may be considered such – I was a fairly marginalized figure in the Manosphere. The old school reformists held sway. At first, I even had to call myself an MRA; a decade ago, no terminology existed to properly describe my unique vision. Gradually, though, a coherent terminology began to emerge through ceaseless argument and discussion, through mimesis and mutation. And so the Pan-Anglosphere Male Resistance Movement, with its distinctive terminologies and modes of thought, came to be. And here we are, our understanding of the true situation perfectly developed. Lawrence, one of my voluminous correspondents, presents the essential argument:

But it's really the legal structure that matters most in making things so lethal for Anglosphere men compared to the protections of the non-Anglo world ruled by civil law. Even if I don't know the fine legal points of common law against civil law like Legal Eagle, I can tell you pretty specifically how they're so different in practice, and why the civil law countries are a far better choice for Anglo men and sensible women, above all for professional and wealthy men, to expatriate to, settle down and have families (Appendix Q, p.295).

In sum, the Anglosphere is just one cultural bloc among many cultural blocs and should be seen and criticized as such; there is nothing 'special' about it. The Anglosphere's era of dominance in the late twentieth century was more the result of historical accident than anything else; and its future decline looks assured. The motor of this decline is misandrist Anglo-American feminism and the social dysfunction – not to mention male alienation – it leaves in its wake. But this decline cannot be arrested, nor should it be; it is the inevitable fulfilment of the Anglosphere's misandrist destiny. Low trust relationships, political alienation, a costly underclass and educational failure already blight the Anglo-American bloc, and will only worsen; but this is to be celebrated. Men cannot arrest the slide into barbarism, even if they wanted to; no, they must look to foreign shores for fulfilment, peace and pleasure. A single mercenary male without social ties has the Anglo-Feminist Matrix at his mercy; he is untouchable, boundless, almost a god.

That is our movement's unique insight.

6.1. Why is America so Receptive to Male Dissidence?

If we consider the contemporary manosphere, it must be said that the United States is the Anglo-American nation most receptive to the 'male dissidence' message. This is not merely due to its size or ethnic diversity, but rather because America's distinctive puritanical history coupled with sex-negative feminism have created a society uniquely hostile to men.

America was founded by religious fanatics – people who fled England in the seventeenth century because it wasn't repressed enough. It was said that English puritans wanted to ban bear baiting not because it gave pain to the bear, but because it gave too much pleasure to the spectators. Even today, the United States is the only Anglosphere nation with mass religious belief, high levels of church attendance, and so on. Although new cultural currents have arisen, these are still defined by sexual repression and institutionalized misandry (liberalism and feminism being good examples).

Because of its secular puritanism and a 'mythical' media which sets women on pedestals, the gap between male expectations and reality is greater in the United States than any equivalent nation. American men are conditioned by movies, rock music and TV shows to believe all women are slim, beautiful, articulate goddesses offering free sex to everybody. As children, they are led to think they will be sleeping with models and actresses the minute they hit sixteen. This makes the reality – obese, ugly, selfish, man-hating harridans exclusively obsessed by billionaires and mass murderers – all the harder to take. Instead of enjoying free sex with models every night, American men find themselves paying their hard-earned bucks to watch the few slim, attractive American women cavort in sordid strip clubs: so much for the 'sexual revolution'.

Society works because its members are prepared to 'take hits for the team'. For the past 50 years, men have been expected to take all the hits while women take none. Men do all the most dangerous jobs, get shafted in no-fault divorce settlements, are arbitrarily imprisoned in pseudo-correctional rape factories, have little control over their reproductive labour, live shorter and less healthy lives, are far more prone to suicide and homelessness – yet Anglo-American society still expects them to 'man up' and take all the hits while giving nothing back in return.

The minimalist blogger Relampago Furioso deftly describes the situation in words fit for the ages:

Traditionally, for our peaceful participation in society and going along with its schemes, men have been awarded control and decision-making status over women, family and society. This has been loosely defined as a social contract in civilized societies from Greece and Rome to present day Western society. The crucial part of this "social contract" that statists are so fond of referring to, was that for participating in society, being subjected to its legal demands, and supporting it, men received certain incentives. These incentives include:

- *Culturally and legally enforced female monogamy*
- *Guaranteed paternity*
- *Decision making authority as the head of the household*
- *Exclusive sexual access to a wife, i.e. a virgin bride*
- *As house-band (husband) culturally and legally enforced obligation for wives to remain in the relationship (i.e. no flightiness or "finding herself")*
- *Culturally and legally enforced responsibility for women to be good mothers*
- *As defined in the Christian bible, the responsibility of a woman to respect and obey her husband*

In exchange for these accommodations, men were expected to give their lives and their labor for the protection and benefit of their wives, families, and communities. However, since feminism the incentives for men to go along with the deal have been removed, while the demands for men to sacrifice their lives and their labor for the benefit of society have increased (Furioso, 2016).

There it is, in a nutshell. And the key difference between the old social contract and the new is the presence/absence of religious belief. While the old religious Puritanism granted men a certain intrinsic status for being fashioned in God's image, they have no standing at all in the new secular Puritanism. Anglo feminists expect men to accept their traditional obligations, even while they practice witchcraft, lust over criminal thugs and murder their own babies. Disney is the darkest embodiment of this new ideology – an endless celebration of asexual, pedestalized princesses in a homosocial, lesbian world of boundless 'empowerment'. Similarly, the Roe-Wade case granted women omnipotent reproductive power while reducing men to ephemeral sperm doners and disposable ATM machines. Then there is America's ongoing war against prostitution – transsexuals can 'transition' on the public purse but consenting adults exchanging sex for money are hunted like sick pariahs. But aside from secular Puritanism and its manifold evils, can any other factors explain America's emerging 'gender crisis'?

Over the past forty years, it seems that America has fallen into line with other industrial countries in terms of social inequality, intergenerational mobility and so on. Somehow, the American Dream has come undone and America now resembles 'old' countries like France or Britain, not the energetic America of the twenties, fifties or eighties. A socialist like Bernie Sanders would have been arrested for Un-American Activities a few generations ago; now he is hailed as a serious presidential candidate. Similarly, the plight of 'the White Working Class' is now a topic of mainstream political discussion – unthinkable in the Reagan era. Films like 'Manchester by the Sea' could have been shot in class-bound Britain – indeed, the film's very title invokes the British working class and their lives of cheerless toil. In sum, American Exceptionalism has ground to a halt and Americans are behaving more like other peoples as a result.

This 'Brazilification' of American society during the 1980s granted a cartel of narcissistic oligarchs ever more wealth, status and power, while systematically shrinking the middle class. The halcyon post-War days when a factory worker could buy a house, run a car and send two kids to college are long gone. It is no surprise that feminism has waxed since Brazilification began, while male fortunes have waned. In simple terms, any elite has to keep women 'onside' in order for society to reproduce itself; but no such tender mercies are afforded low-status men, whom the elite see as dangerous fodder. And since Anglo-American Brazilification began in earnest, ordinary American males predictably find themselves enslaved by the divorce courts and the prison-industrial complex in unprecedented numbers. Of course, MGTOW and other forms of male dissidence represent the inevitable 'fight-back' against this gendercidal programme.

Another anti-male factor specific to the Anglosphere nations in general (and America in particular) is a dysfunctional, non-selective state education system. Most European countries have selective secondary education, which reduces the psychological and emotional damage done to clever children by jail-bound morons. In America, intelligent males typically emerge deeply alienated from the social order because of their school experiences – just consider Klebold and Harris, not to mention a host of other school shooters.

The foregoing discussion explains why the United States is ready for male revolt above all equivalent nations. Puritanical repression and male alienation are like nitric acid and glycerol – a lethal mix of discordant elements ready to explode.

Amidst all this woe, can we extract anything positive from America's burgeoning male dissidence? Of course: America's unique tradition of liberty gives American men greater psychological autonomy than men in other nations. Together with its rich entrepreneurial heritage, this thirst for freedom has already created an online resistance movement which the authorities hate and fear. In sum, the American male will never be wholly subdued by the Anglo-Feminist Matrix – many of the Founding Fathers were genuine radicals, and the 'freedom memes' they planted in their young nation will never perish.

Similarly, American cultural pluralism presents an insurmountable problem for the Matrix: although the original Anglo-Puritan elite tried to define America in its own joyless, workaholic image, later migrants brought alternative cultural traditions which continue to inspire them.

6.2. The Anglosphere: Inherently Anti Male

The Anglosphere harbours a unique hatred of heterosexual men that is best explained by the unique dynamics of the Anglo-American world. Of course, puritanism is the first and foremost of these factors, but the other five pillars of Anglosphere dysfunction also play a role. These factors interact with its oppressive colonial heritage to create an environment uniquely hostile to heterosexual men. For example, the Anglosphere's colonial heritage coheres closely with its puritan traditions to exalt women as faultless deities while stigmatising men as sex criminals subject to eugenic regulation.

In a post on his Men-Factor Blog, Richard Scarecrow drove right to the core of the ineradicable Anglo-American problem - hatred of men:

The core issue that is not addressed often - is HATRED OF MEN. Get ready for a long-ass rant. One that you've heard before if you read my blog.

When I was in college, my friends and I had the typical attitude, "Don't hit a women, Scold any scum man that hits his wife/girlfriend" etc...(sound philosophy to be sure - one I still uphold today - I will not hit a woman unless my life depended on it). Then, Lorena Bobbitt happened. We all noticed how radically different women thought than men - they all had a "You Go Girl!" attitude towards the incident. This stumped all of us. We despised any man who engaged in physical violence against a woman. Women were applauding a woman who sexually mutilated her husband - and knew NOTHING about the situation... That is when we started realizing how deep this hatred ran.

We were all beaten (metaphorically) over the head with "be nice to girls" talk growing up. When we were in our twenties we were all scratching our heads wondering why women were so malicious, callous, and sadistic towards men, while men were the opposite towards women. Quite a wake up call. Once divorces started happening, the hatred of men (insane rage, relentless baseless vindictiveness, and sadism) became more apparent. More of my friends got divorced, and more of my friends got into drugs and liquor to sedate themselves from the insanely hate-filled women in their lives (and to think - for a while - I felt left out!!!). Of course, this happened all over again with the Katherine Kieu Becker incident - a "superior" Asian woman who doesn't hate sexually mutilated her husband.

You can change divorce laws all you want. You can bias them in favor of women - it takes evil sadistic women to exercise those laws. The problem is not any laws on the books. The problem is the sadistic women who enjoy the privilege of those laws (99.999999%). Women who have the doors held open for them - Women who have 30-40 guys pining for them - Women who can get sex anytime they want for free - Women who can treat a lot of men like crap and get away with it - Women who get gifts and money showered on them in some misguided attempt to get laid - Women who are in fact privileged and pedestalized. NOT NOT NOT women who are abused (verbally or physically), raped, tortured, insulted every 5 minutes, cussed at etc... No - those things are reserved for men (Scarecrow, 2017).

While there is a biological foundation to social gynocentrism, the residual difference between the Anglosphere and other cultures is unduly extreme. This residual difference in the Anglosphere is so great that it surpasses the biological differences: men are ostracised and hated while women are exalted as deities on pedestals. Indeed, gynocentric misandry is now the Anglosphere's default ideology. As we shall see, Anglo-feminist assumptions about the current state of society are bizarre inversions of a grim misandrist reality.

While feminists always rail against 'the patriarchy' and successful, wealthy men, such men are in fact the primary *targets* of the Anglo-American prison-divorce complex. Male celebrities are not safe – indeed, they are the primary targets of this complex. Such victims of gynocentrism serve to terrorize other men into gynocentric conformity. Robin Williams is the most prominent of these 'sacrificial victims' in recent years. His suicide was entirely the result of unreasonable demands by the Anglo-American court-industrial complex, reinforcing the subliminal misandry which haunts all Anglo-American men. Here is Lawrence, one of my most informative correspondents:

Like I said, every man in the Anglosphere is a target of this machine, but wealthy American and Canadian men are the hardest hit, because the US legal system gives family court judges wide latitude, which really can't be appealed, to place arbitrarily high demands on the incomes of men who have been wealthy at any point. This is why Robin Williams committed suicide. At one point he was a very wealthy Hollywood A-lister. But after his two divorces, he was no longer pulling in that kind of money. The family courts didn't care. They said he once made big money, and in the fantasy unicorn filled land of US family courts, that meant he could just click his feet together and make the same money again. So they made Robin pay out the nose for alimony. By this time he was sick with Parkinson's Disease he couldn't make anywhere close to that amount of money, and his lawyer was warning him that prison time was likely coming. So he committed suicide (Appendix Q, p.291).

It is no surprise that the United States is the stronghold of such spectacles, partly due to its puritan heritage but also because of its litigious legal tradition and the entrenched nature of its misandrist feminism. Consequently, the American institutions of state take particular delight in bringing down successful American men and confiscating their wealth. Here is Brock, one of my American expatriate correspondents, on the institutional misandry which uniquely besets solvent, successful men in North America:

Many of my old work partners stayed in the US or Canada and got married. Huge, huge mistake. The ones who got divorced got wiped out, lost their homes and their hard-won assets, barely get to see their kids. Most are paying out the nose for alimony for ungrateful bitch exes who pluck their hard earned bank accounts dry. Child support is brutal and it's true, it doesn't support the kids, it's basically a scam and racket for the ex-wives to live high on the hog, plus the courts, judges, state treasuries that also get fat with a percentage of the child support and alimony money. Even my old partners who've stayed married in America are miserable, they live in constant fear of losing everything if the wives just decide to file for divorce on a whim, the husbands have all the responsibility and yet none of the power or benefits (Appendix P, pp.281).

Obviously, this legal racket focuses on successful men because they simply have most to offer the prison-divorce complex. However, ruining high-status males also reinforces the reflexive misandry embedded in American culture at every level; it is a misandrist variant of 'Tall Poppy Syndrome', a kind of gynocentric *schadenfreude*. Whenever the fate of broken idols like Robin Williams is paraded across the media, fear of female censure is reinforced in every North American man's mind, heart and soul. And because misandry is the Anglosphere's default condition, memes like #metoo replicate like cancer cells in the shelter of its nurturing embrace. Sexual False Consciousness – the illusion of male sexual freedom - is also maintained by this relentless misandry. Admitting mass sexual disenfranchisement necessarily involves acknowledging female hyper-hypergamy and other eugenic tendencies – and such criticism is not permitted in the gynocentric Anglosphere, where women can do no wrong. Despite feminist fantasies of corrupt, powerful 'patriarchs' oppressing women with impunity, Lawrence describes a completely different reality from his experience in the US prison system:

This is why you truly cannot risk marriage or child-rearing in the US or the English language nations just like Legal Eagle was warning. Above all if you're wealthy and have a lot to lose. Like Legal Eagle also said, prenuptial agreements don't really help because they're not designed to, the Anglosphere needs you as a slave that the vultures in power can get rich pickings off of. And the numbers back it up. In many of the American prisons I got assigned to, outside of the drug offenders-- another nonviolent noncriminal group wrongly incarcerated at outrageous rates— MORE THAN HALF of our inmates were men incarcerated for falling behind on child support or alimony, or hit with questionable domestic abuse or sexual misconduct allegations (Appendix Q, p.289).

While institutional misandry oppresses all men in the Anglosphere, a specific colonial version afflicts all men of colour living in the Anglo-American countries. Obviously, the massive over-representation of blacks in the American prison-industrial complex is an undeniable manifestation of this, together with the murderous conduct of the American police towards black crime suspects. As we have seen, Anglo-American puritanism served a pragmatic colonial agenda designed to limit the reproductive fecundity of 'subject' peoples. In simple terms, keeping their numbers low reduced the threat of revolt or insurrection. However, black males were the primary targets of this puritanical fixation because of their physical prowess and sexual virility; lynching, with its prurient focus on castration, is the most obvious and perverse expression of this misandrist campaign.

A general observation about Anglo-American culture is that, as my correspondent Lawrence observed, it has never truly acknowledged or come to terms with its past. It is like a neurotic that steadfastly refuses therapy. The unravelling of its accreted issues over the past few decades has a strong psychotic flavour: mass child abuse in the UK; political corruption, racist policing and misandrist jurisprudence in the US, Canada and other countries. The colonial legacy also continues to taint Anglo feminism, as we have seen. Although it draws ideological energy and support from the residual conflict created by oppressive colonialism, it also incorporates many colonial perspectives. As always, misandrist Anglo-feminists *reflect* the presiding culture despite their rhetorical opposition to it. Their true views can be seen in Reclaim the Night marches though African-American districts, covertly implying that all black males are bestial rapists and 'uppity' slaves. Such well-attested racist and elitist currents underlying American feminism are best explained by its origins in a post-colonial society. It also best explains why the United States - with its overmastering need to regulate the reproductive fecundity of slaves, convicts, indentured servants and Native Americans and even immigrants - should be the most misandrist, sex-negative and feminist of all Anglo nations.

Missing Pretty White (Anglo) Girl or Missing White (Anglo) Woman Syndrome is another troubling Anglo-colonial symptom, reflecting the distinctive exaltation young white women receive merely by virtue of race and gender in all Anglosphere countries. The Anglo 'mainstream' media invariably construct endangered young women as valuable 'front page' victims, while covertly dismissing all other groups as disposable. If the white women are also pretty, virginal and affluent, the media affords them semi-divine status. This disturbing Anglo-American archetype combines racism, puritanism and misandry in a single media package extolled across the Anglosphere whenever such a female is threatened, kidnapped or murdered. As with misandrist 'Tall Poppy Syndrome', these hegemonic layers interleave to ostracize and devalue all Anglo-American men, especially men of colour. The ongoing presence of Missing White Woman Syndrome in the pan-Anglosphere media utterly refutes its multicultural, 'liberated' rhetoric. In its most extreme form PWGS intimates that males, non-whites and even sexualized females have no right to exist, unworthy of comment or sympathy when they are killed or go missing.

The privileged treatment white women receive across the Anglosphere is now so obvious as to be acknowledged even by some feminists and cultural Marxists. However equality is defined, men are treated as third class citizens in every Anglosphere country. The whole culture exists to serve white, Anglo-American women who are viewed as faultless deities and the existential benchmark to which all others must aspire. This gynocentric agenda is absolutely dominant in the lamestream Anglo-American media, where straight men are routinely depicted as criminals, abusers or dangerous malcontents. Outside of professional sports, the heterosexual male viewpoint has been largely banished from the media. Gone are the days of Walter Kronkite: newsreaders, talk-show hosts and even weather reporters are now typically female, usually heavily sexualized and indoctrinated by sex-negative misandrist feminism.

In the Anglosphere, only female sexuality matters: straight males are tacitly viewed as destructive interlopers and their sexuality vilified. Female wants and requirements transcend all other considerations; in sum, society exists to serve *them*. The 'Soyboy', 'cuck', 'White Knight' or 'male feminist' is a disturbing response to this systemic oppression. These sad individuals have completely internalized the Anglosphere's misandrist narrative, idealising women and shunning all semblance of a healthy masculine identity. However, these men still rank very low compared to gay and transsexual males in the Anglosphere's misandrist caste-system. In a puritanical society with a reflexive revulsion of the male sex, women are invariably at the top and heterosexual men at the bottom. In between are various types of pseudo-female, who are now the official 'spokespeople' for masculinity:

Rulers: White, Anglo-American Women
Sub-Rulers: Non-Anglo Women
Administrators and Apologists: Gay and Transsexual 'Men'
Slaves: Cucks / White Knights
Outcasts: Heterosexual Men

So total is this gynocentric fixation that the new role models for 'men' are either psychologically castrated, whining Anglocucks or the new breed of transsexual 'hyper-cucks'. Authentic heterosexual men are ostracised from public discourse in the Anglo-American world: of course, this is why the manosphere has expanded to fill the gap. This was never more obvious than in the wake of the Alek Minassian massacre, where 'lamestream' media discussion was dominated by absurd cucks such as Mack Limoureux and David Futrelle, deluded Baby Boomer women and lesbian deviants (like the fabled 'Alana' who supposedly founded the 'incel' movement in 1993). The few 'males' consulted were transsexuals who 'ascended' to surrogate female status in the Anglosphere's gender-caste system.

Transsexualism is the ultimate expression of Anglo-American misandry. Subjecting oneself to hormone treatments and debilitating surgeries is now extolled as the highest aspiration for men in the Anglosphere. A man who chooses this course will receive support from the medical profession, from the mainstream media, from politicians, lawmakers, the cultural establishment and society at large. However, no corresponding help or approval is given to unemployed blue collar men, suicidal opoid addicts or male victims of domestic abuse, false-rape accusations or no-fault divorce. Why is this? Simple: because the latter are unambiguously male while the transsexual male is at least striving for female identity. In the Anglosphere, even a deformed facsimile of a human female commands infinitely more support and respect than a genuine male, however needy or desperate. In sum, our situation has degraded far beyond the old MRA demands for 'genuine equality' or 'restoring patriarchy' to defending male existence at the most primary level. The fraudulent misrepresentation of AIDs as a heterosexual disease in order to secure public funding is another manifestation of this 'homocratic' programme. No comparable efforts are made to combat the male scourges of suicide or opoid addiction.

While the burgeoning Anglo-American LGBTXYZ agenda presents itself as a revolutionary challenge to the existing social order, reproductive sterility and gender confusion are really conforming to the Anglosphere's traditional agenda and dancing to its tune. Anglo feminists hate sex with all the vehemence of a New England spinster; meanwhile, the non-binary coalition hate heterosexual freedom with all the zeal of an Alabama slave-master. Seldom in history was any 'dissident' movement more deluded about its true origins or motivations. Let us conclude this illuminating discussion with another quote from Richard Scarecrow's seminal essay on Anglo-American misandry:

What can be done to combat the hate - well - nothing. Myself, I fail to care for women (except immediate family). I do not need to care about a murdered woman who made a bad mating choice and ended up dead for it. I do not need to care when a woman gets arrested for hitting a police officer because she is used to hitting men and suffering no consequences. I do not need to feel any compassion for these people - they are a cancer in society. They make bad mating choices and end up dead, single whatever - Why should I care - I don't. Do I mock them - ABSOLUTELY! Is it because they are "having sex with everybody but me"? NOPE! Their bad choices in mating leads their predicament - a predicament I have to pay higher taxes for - be it for abortions - insurance - higher taxes - welfare for single moms etc... I end up paying for their careless behaviour all while I am the enemy to them (a white heterosexual male) (Scarecrow, 2017).

Well said, Scarecrow - for that is the bare bones of it. But something positive can be done about the all-pervasive misandry: we can leave the Anglosphere.

6.3. Tech-Nomadism

The minimalist lifestyle is one of the most interesting concepts explored by the dissident manosphere – reducing living expenses to a bare minimum opens up enormous opportunities for men dissatisfied with Anglo-American life. From a recreational standpoint, the money saved by minimalist living can fund stimulating jaunts to man-friendly societies. And with persistence the awakened man can ultimately relocate for good, as so many of us wish to do. There to taste soft, laughing lips and loving smiles on golden foreign shores…

While there are some interesting minimalist books and videos available, it must be said that far more inspiring models of applied minimalism can be found in the pages of history. For example, Genghis Khan conquered the largest land empire ever known. His army achieved this using extreme minimalism augmented by mobility and firepower. Each Mongol warrior was a one man army: he carried sixty arrows, a sword, his bow and even a needle and thread. He could live off mare's milk and horse blood if no food was available, obviating the need for a costly supply train. And anything else he required could be acquired on the march by raid and rapine. Genghis Khan himself despised the hoarding of wealth or possessions, finding pleasure in only sex and conquest: one in every two hundred men alive today is his descendant, an astonishing genetic achievement.

The legendary General Subotai, one of Genghis Khan's Four Dogs of War, was the ultimate embodiment of nomadic minimalism. His final campaign against Europe in 1241 involved marching thousands of miles before outwitting and destroying Europe's finest warriors in a brilliant sequence of battles using rockets, creeping barrages and smoke screens – none of which the West had seen before (Gabriel, 2006). Subotai had been commanding troops since his teens and most of his officers had campaigned with him in many lands. The renowned Hungarian cavalry were crushed at Mohi on the Sajo River after decisive European defeats at Legnica and Transylvania. Only the death of the Great Khan Ogedei prevented the total subjugation of Europe at Subotai's hands. Like his master Genghis Khan, the great general was buried in an unmarked grave now lost to history. For what mattered to these men was a glorious life, not raising futile monuments over rotting bones. Although derided as unlettered and barbaric, the Mongols had a tragic self-awareness far beyond that of their 'sophisticated' neighbours; for ultimately, everything is pointless in the face of eternity.

Yes, the modern world is corrupt and insipid; but if he chooses, a man can walk in the footsteps of ancient heroes. And since the rise of the Internet, nomadic minimalism has become a perfect lifestyle for the awakened man. Today, all anyone needs for survival is a phone/tablet/laptop linked to the Internet, an online bank account, a place to crash (any motel will do) and a motor vehicle. Whores and food can be ordered as necessity requires. Thus equipped, the modern tech-nomad has all the far-ranging mobility of his Mongol forebears. Liberated from place and circumstance, he spits on the sheeple and their sedentary lifestyle as the Mongols despised their 'civilized' neighbours. And having no ties or responsibilities makes him impossible to coerce or corral, as modern authorities are finding to their cost. The instantaneous nature of the Internet allows him to move money, search out opportunities and communicate with the flick of a finger. He is the supreme minimalist, completely impervious to marketing, advertising and other consumerist brainwashing.

However, the Mongols offer lessons beyond radical minimalism. Their empire incorporated nations from the eastern Mediterranean to the Pacific, yet ruled them all effectively. This short-lived 'Pax Mongolica' linked east and west for the first time ever; some even call it the world's first global civilization. And it was largely achieved by developing a flexible, internationalist outlook. Learning to think beyond one's birth country and indeed, the Anglosphere itself, is vitally important for the awakened man. The Anglo-American Matrix insinuates that nothing of note exists beyond its confines – or worse, that only Anglosphere countries have legal protections for their citizens (when the US locks up a huge percentage of its male population). Foreign travel quickly breaks down these lame assumptions; and bilingualism allows one to think outside the Matrix and build a lifestyle beyond it.

Beyond that, clear similarities between thirteenth century Asia and the contemporary Anglosphere make the Mongol revolution a valid lifestyle model for awakened men. Both regions were/are ruled by weary, discredited elites ripe for overthrow. Both cultures were/are brittle, defined by alienated citizens, exalted women and low trust relationships. Both regions were/are living on past glories, folk memories of a lost golden age which can never return. These weaknesses make the contemporary Anglosphere ideal for exploitation using nomadism, minimalism and other Mongol methods. Like the vast Khwaresmian Empire shattered by Genghis Khan and Subotai, it is a lumbering giant easy to outwit.

6.4. The Five Pillars of Anglosphere Dysfunction

The Anglosphere's misandrist agenda can be reduced to five broad conceptual fields or 'pillars'. These interact in various ways and all are present in the Anglosphere nations, to a greater or lesser degree.

The first pillar is social isolation. In the Anglosphere, the individual develops in relative isolation and is expected to be self-motivated, socially combative and emotionally repressed from early childhood. Heartless schools and educational institutions take on many of the socialization duties normally provided by the (now defunct) nuclear family, which is why so many Anglo-Americans are damaged and enraged. Because they grow up in relative isolation, they are far more reliant on the mainstream media for identity formation than children in comparable societies. This explains why a massive proportion of Anglo-Americans suffer symptoms of Borderline Personality Disorder, harbouring fantastical expectations culled from movies and TV shows. Cultural dissidents like Winston Wu and Steve Hoca talk at length about the friendlier, more sociable attitudes that prevail outside the United States, even in countries with relatively low standards of living (Wu, 2014; Hoca, 2017). They also talk about the obsessive focus on work that mars American social life (work does not have to eclipse everything else, as prosperous Scandinavian societies demonstrate). One of my expatriate correspondents explains why the Anglo-American cult of isolation reflexively inhibits the creation of healthy relationships:

The last point, and sort of a follow-up on the previous one about what makes the non-Anglosphere more suited for men and families than the Anglosphere, it's the safety-net traditions here. Now, again I know Americans get confused about this because they're so used to calling this "socialism" and looking at French social programs in just left leaning or right leaning terms. But the French social assistance programs are more properly seen as ways of making sure society stays harmonious, and this extends to things like family courts and divorce courts.

Part of why US family law is so stressful, and divorce court judgments are so harsh and devastating for men, is that there just aren't good safety nets in the US and Anglosphere, so Americans are always at each other's throats trying to extract money anyway they can. It's like a state of constant downward mobility and anxiety, and this contributes both to the tendency for Americans to divorce, and the grasping and nastiness of divorce itself there. In Europe, people in general are just less stressed and happier because people aren't constantly stressing about going broke from hospital bills or college costs the way Americans are. This also reduces the divorce rate and stops the ugly side that Americans show when divorce hits (Appendix Q, p.309).

Anglo-American culture is defined above all by its rapacious materialism, which is the second pillar of dysfunction. According to the French psychoanalyst Jacques Lacan, human personality is essential a void 'created' by external associations in early childhood. Because of dysfunctional child rearing by narcissistic, self-absorbed parents, Anglo-American self-identity is consequently far more shaped by material objects than most. This explains the voidlike sterility of Anglo culture, and its overriding fixation on material goods as 'food' for the needful self. In fact, the Borderline Personality Disorder so rampant among Anglo-American women is perfectly adapted (some would say designed) to feed the rapacious Matrix and its consumerist hamster wheel. In particular, the United States is a gynocentric brothel wherein men acquire material junk to get sex from empty, frigid women in a culture which deliberately raises the scarcity value of sex to inhuman levels. The demerits of such a society for men are self-evident, and explain the existential disaffection so common among Anglo-American males. One of my learned correspondents describes the discordant reality of Anglo-American social relations:

Hinting at this before, but something else that makes the Anglo brand of feminism such a wrecker for men and society, is the Anglo obsession with money and profits over people, and the stupid worshipping of big business and corporations. This may sound money (sic) coming from me because I'm a business owner, a hard-core capitalist and was considered right of center when I was in the US. But these ideology driven lines in the sand confuse more than they reveal because they're too damn broad.

Yes, I am a capitalist and fully support free markets for most things in society. But the problem is, too much of what the US and Anglosphere calls "free market capitalism" isn't really capitalism at all, it's more like lazy cronyist style fake capitalism. This in reality is more like socialism for the oligarchs and super rich buddies of people in power, like the third world corruption that rules shitholes like Mexico (yes, I said it) where a few families hold 90% of the wealth and brutally oppress the masses, extracting their wealth for themselves (Appendix Q, p.306).

The third pillar of Anglo-American dysfunction is the class system. Britain and the United States both have relatively low rates of social mobility compared to other industrialized democracies. Both countries are run by impermeable, self-contained socio-economic elites who attend private schools and frankly know little about mainstream experience or opinion. This is why Anglosphere populations are increasingly alienated from politics and think they have no control over their own lives. We have moved beyond a situation where people vote for competing parties to one where they are voting against the political class itself. Of course, people are free to enjoy the fruits of their own labour and pass these advantages on to their families (or whoever they see fit). However, in the Anglosphere this has led to the formation of political dynasties and an inflexible Deep State which are essentially undemocratic and do not serve the interests of the majority. Weird trends in Anglo-American foreign policy (for example Britain giving foreign aid to counties with space programmes or hopeless American attempts to democratize Islamic nations) originate in the detached and eccentric nature of the Anglo-American elite. Not all Anglosphere countries are thus defined; Canada and Australia are among the most classless countries in the world. However, these countries are increasingly ruled by idiomatic elites and will soon resemble their older cousins.

One of the most disturbing manifestations of Anglo-American class distinction is an ever-expanding criminalised underclass. This underclass is defined by gender, not just socio-economic status and low trust values, its male members frequently trapped in the prison-industrial complex. One of my correspondents, a former corrections officer called Lawrence, writes:

Chew on this stat for a moment, the United States of America has by a long shot the highest incarceration rate in the world, about 4 percent of the world population but getting close to 30 percent of its prisoners, with about 1% of our population in prison in any given year and, depending on the study, up to a fifth or even a fourth—that's 20 to 25 percent—of the US population being jailed for one reason or another at some point as either an adult or a juvenile, in most cases for charges that turn out to be trumped up or (as with child support) involve the hazy concept of "contempt". (And crazy enough, sometimes the Americans in jail are the "lucky ones", the USA also has the highest rate of citizens being shot by our own cops for complete misunderstandings or trivialities, and whites face just as much danger as minorities for that these days). And the US imprisonment rate is still rising. In fact, the United States with 320 million people has more prison inmates than China and India put together, even though these 2 countries have 2.5 billion people between them! The reason is obvious: Money. There really is a prison-industrial complex in the USA, I know because I was a part of it. And it really does make big money for a lot of people in control of it. It's the modern day update of the old plantation slave labor system (Appendix Q, p.287).

The fourth factor is, of course, residual Puritanism. Although religion is not the force it once was, the distinctive Puritanism of the Anglo-Saxon countries persists as secular Puritanism or repressive political correctness. This is the definitive core of Anglo-American feminism and explains the institutional misandry which dominates the modern Anglosphere. The Sixties Sexual Revolution was a brief lived anomaly and misandrist feminism has largely restored Victorian morality to every public arena: a man risks imprisonment for even talking to a woman in many places. Prostitution remains illegal in Britain and North America, and men who pay for sex are still morally and legally criminalized. Most males outside the top 20% in terms of looks, money and status will experience long periods of celibacy if they do not marry young (and even if they do). The 'lamestream' media still tries to peddle the myth of the sexualized Anglo-American woman; however, this narrative is created and maintained by sex-obsessed gay men and bears little resemblance to reality. In sum, Anglo feminism is now the major issue confronting males across the Anglosphere. Originally created to defend women's 'rights', Anglo feminism has morphed into a puritanical Gorgon obsessed with stigmatizing heterosexual sex, excluding fathers from their children, pathologizing masculinity, promoting transexuality, driving men from higher education and… well, you know the score by now. One of my well-travelled correspondents explains the difference between Anglo-feminism feminism and its non-Anglo counterparts:

So what about the feminists in Norway, Sweden, Germany, Denmark and Finland which had feminist traditions even before North America? It really is a totally different form of feminism. The feminists up there in Nordic-land and Germany can be shrill and loopy in their own way, yes. But up there, the feminism isn't misandrist, and they aren't obsessed with this "evil oppressive patriarchy" the way Anglosphere feminists are. For the Nordic feminists, it's more about true independence, sexual freedom and yes, actual egalitarianism. They hate the #metoo thing up there because they think it makes women look weak. They hate alimony for the same reason, in fact of all ironies, it was Nordic and German feminists who led the push decades ago to abolish alimony and restrict child support. And even to help institute paternity leave as well as maternity leave to encourage fathers to be with their young kids. It sounds crazy to us in the Anglosphere because "feminism" here is something so much nastier and misandrist by definition, but the feminists up in Nordic-land in Germany in general aren't misandrist and in fact do a lot of things that are very husband and father-friendly. Yes, they can irritate sometimes with their own "you go girl" talk and be a little standoff-ish at times, but to a surprising extent, most of them are actually reasonable, and mainly focused on making sure that girls and women have opportunities to explore and be creative— without doing this at the expense of boys and men (Appendix Q, p.302).

The fifth pillar is Anglo-American common law. This is the secret gate through which militant feminism alters society without even cursory reference to democratic processes. Since common law is more malleable and open to interpretation than the civil law which prevails in Scandinavia and Continental Europe, Anglo-American Judges adjust their judgements to satisfy the prevailing whims of the culture rather than sticking to legal precedent. Obviously, the Secular Puritanism characteristic of Anglo culture will strongly influence their decisions in favour of women in almost all circumstances. The fact that Anglo-American Judges hail from elite backgrounds with uncommon attachment to secular Puritanism only strengthens this reflexive judicial bias. Above all, the soulless materialism which drives Anglo-Saxon culture has made the divorce courts a rich feeding-ground for greedy lawyers, while feminist pressure groups exploit the malleable nature of common law to continually expand the range of anti-male Divorce outcomes. Common law is in truth the true nexus of dysfunction in the Anglosphere: the arena where class distinction, Puritanism and Materialism converge to make life unliveable for a huge number of men. One of my correspondents with extensive legal experience describes the situation in detail:

All incentives of Anglo family law and the associated Anglo culture now point in the direction of encouraging broken families, there's simply too much money to be made from divorce to discourage it, and too many ideological scores to be satisfied with it. Already we can see a polar opposite in comparison to the globe outside the Anglo world, where societies have intelligently walled off divorce as a profit-making center, removed incentives for it and—through culture, civil law and other factors—removed the ideological as well as the financial drive to promote divorce and the financial ruination that accompanies it in the Anglo world. In short you can be the perfect husband (or wife, in some cases): a high earner, good parent, helping around the house, and the chances are, it's still going to fall apart for you. Because that is what the American family law system is now designed to do to you and your family: to make it fall apart, for both ideologic and profit-driven reasons (Appendix S, p.322).

Together, these five factors cohere to make romantic life extremely difficult for most Anglo-American males. For example, class is closely linked to both materialism and sexual repression in the Anglo countries. The hyper-hypergamy of Anglo-American women – the assumption that they are divine angels too good for any man – obviously springs from this warped association. Opponents of the Manosphere ridicule its denizens as marginalised eccentrics – keyboard warriors and alienated deplorables. However, the Manosphere draws inspiration from lived experience in the Anglosphere and its five pillars of dysfunction. And its message has spread because of 'truth marketing': the experience of daily life in this culture simply supports its general arguments.

6.5. The Minimalist Lifestyle: Opting out of Consumerism

The success of Ghengiz Khan's Mongol armies demonstrated that those who would travel far must also travel light. Since most men reading these words yearn to depart the Anglosphere, the need to travel with minimal baggage, expenses or supplies becomes an important consideration. As a great traveller of all continents (except Antarctica), I have reams of valuable advice to share about minimalism, nomadism and adventuring in foreign lands. Further, I have gleaned much priceless knowledge from others immersed in this exciting lifestyle.

First, let me say that becoming a minimalism nomad involves more than just following a set of rubrics. In truth, you must redefine yourself. One of the primal lines sundering humanity is the nomad-sedentary divide. Think about it: relations between these two human types have never been good. The Holocaust was primarily directed against perceived nomads, namely gypsies and Jews. Moreover, sedentary peoples have harboured the same distrust of the traveller throughout history. Similarly, the nomadic Mongols viewed their settled neighbours as worms toiling in the mud. Rogan P Taylor's remarkable book The Death and Resurrection Show (1985) explores the reasons for this mutual distrust at great length.

While settled people have generally dominated since the late Medieval era, this has not always been the case. And with the rise of new technologies which permit the instant transmission of ideas and resources, the nomad is once more on the rise.

However, technology alone is insufficient to flourish as a nomad. To be blunt, it is a more demanding lifestyle than that of the landsman. Jews and gypsies are sturdy, resilient peoples for good reason: they have to be. The antagonism of settled peoples towards nomads always contains an element of envy; not just for their exciting lives, but also their abilities. The resourcefulness demanded by a nomadic lifestyle selects only the strongest and most intelligent; consider how Jews and gypsies are renowned for being tough and adaptable, masters of magic and sleight-of-hand. The Mongols and Vikings were also nomadic, and both were exceptional peoples. In short, the nomadic lifestyle is natural selection with the heat settings on maximum; the sickly and slow-witted cannot endure it. Village idiots are a feature of sedentary life, never the travelling carnival.

In an era when the nomad is more likely to be highly skilled and educated than most people, these observations are never more valid. Rigid identification with a given country or regions is now a marker of low intelligence and education, in fact; and with good reason. Indeed, my whole Thesis could be read as a repudiation of sexual localism in favour of sexual globalism. Slim, kind and trustworthy women are out there; but only for men with the guts and verve to flee the Anglosphere and claim them.

On lesson from history is that ruling elites are often the descendants of conquering nomads; for example, the Mughals of India or the Russ of Russia. With the most intelligent and able men now fleeing the Anglosphere in favour or a nomadic lifestyle, we are seeing the reversal of this process for the first time in history. The unique conditions of the modern Anglosphere, which penalizes men for being successful and competent, have deliberately ejected able men from settled society into pre-modern nomadism. Jesse, one of my American correspondents, writes:

It's scary to even ponder this but in my humble experience, hard as is to believe, the divorce court nightmares in the US have been getting even worse in past 5 years. I myself am on the expat trail on or before 2020, have a long-term contract so split my engineering consultation between Brazil and Chile and man, have to say, from what the poor American guys around me have been going through, it won't be a moment too soon when I leave.

The cautionary tales in my case were 2 guys I never would have thought would face the nightmare of a family court in America. These are the guys who would thumb their noses at MGTOW types, I wouldn't call them white knights, it's just that they had good, loyal religious wives and their marriages seemed solid.

Until they weren't.

One guy, Mormon, engineer like myself, had his own business making good money, 4 kids and the white picket fence. The kind of family you never thought would fall apart. But damn, when the wife filed for divorce, it all went straight to hell for the poor husband. His business kept away from home all the time and the sweet loyal wife began to stray, I mean I get ti she's human, happens even to the Mormons but what I don't get, why do the divorce courts slam the poor guy so hard? I mean, he lost EVERYTHING even though he had supposedly the best lawyers west of the Rockies. His home-- gone. Lost custody of the kids. Lost one of his cars. Lost hundreds of thousands in savings he had saved up for retirement. Alimony. And OMG, the child support. Pure hell for a guy, Over $100,000 every year plus the alimony (Appendix R, p.312).

That the Anglosphere has reversed the basic processes of civilization is remarkable in itself, but not surprising; gynocratic Anglo matriarchy is the antithesis of civilization, and must ultimately crush it. Unlike traditionalist MRAs, I do not seek to challenge or reverse this process. My goal is to guide men towards the best lives possible in these difficult circumstances, not waste words trying to alter the circumstances themselves. If able men must become nomads to achieve their personal life-goals, so be it; let them become the best nomads they can be. In these dark days, men need practical solutions that really work for them, not futile pipe-dreams and false promises.

Without further ado, here are my best tips for living cheaply yet effectively. Many of these can be applied in everyday life, not just on your travels.

Man can survive on milk and sunlight. He might not be running marathons, but he can survive. Milk is cheap and sunlight is free, so make sure you get plenty of both.

Eat porridge for breakfast. Its health benefits are endless: the humble oat raises testosterone levels, scours arteries, lowers cholesterol and even improves cognitive function. It is dirt cheap and can be acquired in almost any country. Go for organic rolled oats whenever possible. To spice it up, add a sprinkle of coffee grains and stir them in. The slow energy release of porridge is also ideal for the traveller living on a budget.

Green tea is indispensible to the minimalist traveller. It is bursting with antioxidants which promote cell health and fight the ageing process. It acts as an appetite suppressant and bacterial mouthwash, added boons for the traveller. From a practical standpoint, green teabags are feather-light and easy to carry. From tent to hotel room, green tea is the wanderer's friend. And it requires only hot water and a cup for preparation.

Massage your scalp vigorously every morning. Lean down over the edge of your bed, clutch your hair with both hands and massage it hard for three or four minutes. You should feel your whole scalp sliding back and forth during this process, and the hair tingling as hot blood stimulates the roots. I started doing this in my early twenties and retain all my hair – not to mention its colour. This activity also improves cognitive function.

Shun autistics. A major problem with the pan-Anglosphere men's movement is its colonization by autistic losers of the 'angry incel' type. Failing to understand or acknowledge their own issues, many of these critters believe they will get women and sex if only they leave the Anglosphere. However, nothing could be further from the truth: plane spotters will be incel wherever they are. My thesis is only relevant to neurotypical males who have genuine problems with Anglo-American culture; the kind of men who can get women but do not want the Anglo-American kind. Learn to spot autistics on your jaunts, and shun them completely. Hint: most of them are obsessed by weather, hats and time zones. Avoid.

Learn to dance well. Much of the incel problem in the West has arisen because most men cannot dance. Women love dancing, and for this reason most dancing clubs, groups and societies boast a surfeit of women. Dancing develops ease in touching and holding the female body, something of great value to inhibited men. It also engenders physical fitness and prowess, not to mention a positive mental 'frame'. At first, it might seem daunting or even ridiculous for the intellectual male type; however, dancing is the royal road to free pussy in almost every country outside the Islamic world (and even a few within it). From the minimalist standpoint, dancing is a cheap pastime requiring little outlay. It also requires little language, ideal for the wandering nomad.

Smash new foreign languages this way: learn the populist variant of any language first. Linguists estimate that the 'public code' used by the working class of any nation uses only 300 to 1000 words. Once these words have been mastered, you will be a functional member of any given society – at least in linguistic terms. Public code contains the main pronouns, core 'doing' verbs and principal conjunctives. Once these are mastered, the rest is easy. Treat learning a new language as a game, like children do, and you cannot go wrong. Above all, take every opportunity to go abroad and immerse yourself in the language as spoken by native speakers. Here is how my correspondent 'Phil' went about it:

Obviously if you're very high-skilled it's easier to get a work visa sponsored by a company, and obviously engaging or marrying a local girl, or just having an ancestor somewhere with ethnic roots in the country you want to go to. But you don't really need any of that. The way My gf and I both did it, we signed up for courses at the unis, first in Germany for me, and then did internships and made contacts while doing language classes. I studied regular business administration at a public university in the US, nothing special, but I got into Europe just taking higher level classes and took it from there. (Appendix E, p.237).

For quick and cheap mobility abroad, the bicycle, motor-scooter or motor-bike will suffice. All three modes of transport offer similar benefits to the Mongol horse: they are quick, reliable and versatile. Also note that many European countries are far more bike-orientated than the Anglosphere countries, with designated cycling lanes and bicycles cheap and easy to hire.

Broadband should be available and accessible wherever you go. For a minimalist tech-nomad, quick and easy digital communication is vital on the road. Make an Internet connection your chief priority in any land you occupy. With the Internet in place, finance, knowledge and security automatically follow.

The Spaniards have a wonderful saying: 'Garlic is worth ten mothers'. And indeed, the near-mystical health properties of garlic have been well demonstrated by western scientists. Four cloves a day will boost your immune system, lower cholesterol and strengthen your heart. Folk wisdom also stresses its value as a male aphrodisiac. Like green tea, garlic is cheap and widely available (wild garlic can often be found by the roadside). Simply squeeze fresh garlic mulch into soups, stews or any other food, eat hearty and enjoy the benefits.

Finally, be prepared to spend a little more to avoid staying in or near underclass areas. Ninety percent of xenophobic hostility comes from the underclass of any nation. This is as true of Venice or Moscow as it is of Chicago or Melbourne. Remember, you are an Anglo foreigner in a world which distrusts you. As a rough but effective guide to any district in any country, the underclass is generally shorter and uglier than other social classes. They also have louder voices and tend to shout a lot, expectorate and urinate in public. Many harbour scowls or taciturn stares and smile only with cruelty. Watch out for obvious signs of inbreeding such as squints, crooked teeth and cauliflower ears. Lots of youths in a given area also indicate underclass infestation: they simply have far more children than other people (after all, what else is there for them to do but breed like rats). Complete losers in every respect, the underclass is always looking to 'get one over' on other people. If trouble erupts, flee if you can; if you cannot, have at the blackguards and go down fighting for Queen and country.

Try beachcombing, especially in affluent tourist areas. More often than not you will find discarded coins, lost jewellery and a host of other valuables. I know a fellow who sustains long visits to Mediterranean Islands on the proceeds of beachcombing alone.

Equipped with these cheap but potent assets and nuggets of priceless knowledge, a minimalist nomad should be able to survive in almost any situation. Nomadism is more demanding then sedentary life, and you will need every edge to flourish in the lands of your desire. Nomadism is extremely unforgiving of infirmity and ill-health, hence the fortifying nature of my recommendations. The more you integrate minimalism into your lifestyle and experience its myriad benefits, the sedentary buffoons of 'mainstream' Anglo-American society will seem ever more weak and ridiculous. In no time the Anglosphere will be a distant shadow, your new life bright in front of you.

Part Seven

Building a New Life

**How to Break from Anglosphere Culture
and Begin your New, Liberated Life Abroad**

7.0 Introduction

And so we get to the hub of the argument: departing the Anglosphere. These chapters are designed to help awakened Anglo-American men make the leap successfully. They might even be considered 'reconnaissance' for your successful expedition. There is one important caveat to consider before embarking on this section, however. Make sure you are not autistic or mentally ill, or moving countries will not benefit you. All of these suggestions are for neurotypical men of normal weight and appearance who are genuinely struggling with misandrist Anglosphere culture. Moving to foreign shores will not help men with poor hygiene, who are overweight or who suffer from Autistic Spectrum Disorders. Such males should stay where they are and save their money.

7.1. Overcoming Sexual False Consciousness

The mainstream media are struggling. More and more newspapers close down by the month, or are given away for free. Viewing figures for terrestrial television fall year on year. Over the past ten years alone, dozens of UK lifestyle magazines have either retreated to the Internet or closed down altogether. The rise of outsider political candidates such as Trump or Sanders suggests that representative democracy (a fancy way of saying trans-generational Power Elite dominion) is giving way to the real thing. Still, even in its present reduced condition, the legacy media plays a vital role in deluding the masses into giving their consent to the social order.

Nowhere is this clearer than in the sexual arena. The legacy media are strongly committed to presenting sexual life in Anglosphere nations as a smorgasbord of priapic vitality. A programme broadcast on UK television – The Secret World of Tinder (2014) – was a perfect example of this agenda. In sum, the documentary claimed that Brits in London are having lots more sex because of Tinder. It dealt with the sex lives of seven people:

- A homosexual male
- A homosexual deviant male
- A lesbian with children
- 2 Heterosexual males
- 2 Heterosexual females

While the footage presented to us displayed predictable Anglo patterns of rampant compensatory deviance and heterosexual repression, this truth was carefully filtered to give the viewer a misleading impression of heterosexual plenitude and prowess. And this is how Anglo-American nations maintain the delusion of widespread sexual freedom.

According to the Anglobitch Thesis, the culture of pro-feminist heterosexual repression in Anglosphere countries informally promotes a compensatory culture of male sexual deviance. Meanwhile, heterosexual men are kept continually thirsty (and compliant) by limited sexual access to women, a state of affairs decisively maintained by misandrist feminism (strongly opposed to prostitution and other forms of recreational sex) but also embedded in the residual Anglo-Saxon culture, which is characterized by centuries of puritanical repression.

The people featured in the show were living evidence of this. The male sexual deviant was indeed making full use of Tinder to hook up with other men interested in role-playing as puppies, as was the 'conventional' male homosexual. Of course, this ease of sexual access explains why so many Western males are drawn to homosexuality: it permits them to have far more sexual partners (and more varied erotic experiences) than a nominally hetero orientation. The mainstream media's fixation with gays also helps to present Anglo societies as redoubts of liberation – after all, they really are having far more sex than most people. The woman told the interviewer she was endlessly hooking up with a string of partners and, since she was the mother of two children, we assumed she was referring to males. However, it soon transpired that she only had one partner, another woman, and everything she had previously said about her rampant hetero sex life was blatantly false.

The two heterosexual males were full of tall tales about their sexual escapades. One – a particularly ugly knave – claimed to be enjoying sex with eight women a week via Tinder. Smelling Anglo bullshit, and seeing no evidence for these thunderous claims, I waited avidly for the predictable revelation of his real sexual status. This turned out to be a conventional date with a middle-aged four, to whom he was clearly committed. So much for his 'eight women a week' – sexual self-delusion at its worst.

The final heterosexual male (a rather better-looking guy than the bullshitter) had an unsuccessful date with an entitled, uptight female. Predictably, no sex emerged from this encounter. Game over.

In short, the reality we observed differed vastly from the agenda projected – that 'everyone' was enjoying vast amounts of recreational sex via Tinder. Of, course, some people were having lots of recreational sex – in classic Anglo fashion, the male homosexuals. In sum, the documentary amply demonstrated the essential truth of the Thesis, in every respect. Aside from the deviants, there was no evidence of widespread sexual liberation anywhere.

However, the producers were careful to project the illusion of universal sexual liberation despite the contradictory evidence before our eyes. And this is how Sexual False Consciousness works: a sub-textual assumption of liberation is maintained at all times, even in the face of alternative evidence. SFC is like Hitler's 'Big Lie' or the Emperor's New Clothes: the more often it is told, the more likely people are to believe it. Proof or verification matter little; mass subordination to the shared fantasy is all. Indeed, all the Anglosphere nations operate an informal system of 'sexual reality shaming' wherein anyone daring to break ranks from SFC to discuss sexual reality is ridiculed or labelled a deviant. For example, Elliot Rodger's flatmates ridiculed him for admitting his Incel status; however, as Asian-American geeks they were almost certainly hardcore Incels themselves.

However, the 'lamestream' media's carefully-maintained façade is beginning to crack. The rise of the manosphere is beginning to undercut the delusions which sustain the Anglosphere. This can be readily observed in the sharp decline of the media channels which sell Sexual False Consciousness to the masses – newspapers, rock music and men's magazines like GQ and Playboy. Of course, the instant availability of online porn has hastened their decline; but online porn is far more honest than these ailing media institutions. For in their heyday, these seductive fabricators promoted the absurd fiction that famous models and actresses were sexually available to the average Joe. All utter nonsense, of course – but prior to the Internet, the mainstream media could tell the masses anything and get away with it. Now, a whole climate of online opinion has made it plain even to the stupidest man that models and actresses only want males of the highest status and view 'ordinary Joes' as disposable trash. Hell, even ugly Anglosphere women consider the bottom 80% of men as disposable trash, let alone models and actresses!

In short, sexual reality can no longer be denied. Before the emergence of the Red Pill, the sexual delusions promoted by the mainstream media are under unprecedented attack. The Anglosphere nations are not the sexual, social and economic utopias the mainstream media claim them to be; and the Manosphere is spreading this realization as never before.

It is said that the Samurai refreshed themselves every morning with the thought of death. Similarly, the awakened man striving to escape the misandrist Anglosphere should anoint himself with grim truth every morning. Let him repeat this mantra ten times: *I am not sleeping with models every night…*

Although there are important differences, the Red Pill mindset has much more in common with eastern religions than it does with Christianity. Like a Buddhist or Hindu, the Red Pilled man awakens from bondage in stages, discarding ever more Blue Pill delusions in order to reach his full awakening. Christianity, with its infantile promise of instant salvation, is the complete opposite of this focused elevation.

Blue Pill delusions can easily 'stand in' for the 'fetters' of Buddhism. Among these (in no particular order) would be the idea that Anglosphere countries are inherently superior; that all men are advantaged and all women oppressed; that relationships with Anglo-American women are 'redemptive'; that moving abroad and starting a new life is impossible; or that true liberation can ever be found within the Anglosphere. The most obstinate Blue Pill fetter is Sexual False Consciousness, which I will address later.

An even better spiritual analogy for the Red Pill path is Alchemical Gnosis, a distinctively western approach to achieving psychological wholeness (Ribi, 2013). The three stages of alchemical gnosis, the *nigredo, albedo* and *rubedo*, are described thus:

Nigredo – the preparatory stage, the encounter with the self.
Albedo – the marginal or luminal state.
Rubedo – the reddening, uniting the spiritual and the physical in a new mode of consciousness.

If we apply these stages to a dissident male taking the Red Pill, they redefine the experience in spiritual terms:

Nigredo means 'darkening', and this appropriately describes the 'Red Pill rage' that overcomes many men in the initial stage of their awakening. They realize everything they were ever told was a pack of lies, that women are not perfect angels handing out sexual redemption and that the culture they live in is essentially misandrist.

In Red Pill terms, **Albedo** involves transcending Red Pill rage and gaining a better understanding of one's deepest goals and ambitions. This might involve seeking out a foreign relationship or resolving not to die on Anglosphere soil, in the coils of the Matrix; it will be different for different individuals.

Rubedo means 'reddening' (appropriately enough, for the final stage of Red Pill enlightenment), the final unification of consciousness. In this state one recognises the various Blue Pill delusions that rule Western society (especially the Anglosphere), the most powerful of which is sexual false consciousness. Once this final hurdle is overcome, the acolyte becomes a Red Pill adept and ready to depart the Anglo-Feminist Matrix without a moment's regret.

As has already been said, Sexual False Consciousness in the last and most difficult obstacle to overcome on a man's path to Red Pill enlightenment. Overcoming it involves mastering two levels of delusion: the extrinsic and the intrinsic. The extrinsic aspect incorporates a man's model of the external world; the intrinsic involves his self-knowledge and understanding. While certain strategies are specific to either level, some can be applied to both. Remaining emotionally detached from Anglo-American women is one of these. Also, exclude all Blue Pilled clowns from your life since they will only bind you to the Matrix by their bad example. As soon as Blue Pill drivel starts falling from the lips of friends, shun them immediately. No other course is possible.

The extrinsic aspect is easier to master, especially since the decline of mainstream media. Once, the selfless female angels projected by television, rock music and lifestyle magazines were unassailable icons, offering romantic redemption to lovelorn males the world over. Only since the Internet have these gender-deities been effectively challenged – back then, anyone daring to question the assumption that all women are perfect goddesses was labelled insane, stupid or jaundiced (even now, it is hard to challenge these lame rubrics in public). This fake consensus imposed restrictive sexual narratives on the male population, punishing any who dared to 'break ranks' and discuss women honestly. In its heyday, even 'rebellious' youth culture extolled these gynocentric delusions with Stalinist zeal. For example, rock music projected sexualized women as the norm, without any reference to the frigid and sterile reality. The manosphere allows men to question these myths as never before, however. This is why the Anglo-feminist Matrix is so bent on shutting it down – either neo-masculine, MGTOW or TFL (True Forced Loneliness, a state of unwilling singleness).

As for intrinsic SFC, far more effort is needed to escape it. The final push to freedom proceeds by being totally honest about your sexual situation: become a Red Pill Buddha, completely honest about the sexual aridity of the Anglosphere. Accept that Anglo-American women are typically entitled, snotty and riddled with personality disorders. And accept that nothing will ever change in the Anglosphere, international nexus of gynocentric entitlement. And this is how to finally eliminate SFC from your personality code: total, ground zero honesty, 'keeping it real' 24 hours a day.

Internalizing this truth is the purest expression of Red Pill wisdom. And twenty-year old ass on sun kissed beaches will be your just reward.

7.2. Awakened Men Don't Owe Everyone the Truth

If you had a hot share tip for the NYSE or FTSE, would you wander the streets offering it to everyone? If you were scientist and had just discovered some Nobel Prize winning law, would you start telling the local bums in the subway about it? If you were a freelance engineer, would you give your latest invention to someone who might patent it? If you discovered a secret island full of comely women offering free sex, would you share its location with anyone but trusted friends? Of course not; important knowledge should only be shared with those who can appreciate it – and, more important, people who will not compromise it. Similarly, we awakened men are not obliged to share our truths about Anglo-American women, minimalist living (or anything else) with the broad masses of humanity.

If we consider powerful people like the Rothschilds, it becomes immediately apparent that they possess knowledge of finance that most people do not possess; and more, that this esoteric knowledge is the source of their power. While there is a deeply-ingrained Western instinct to resent those who hoard knowledge, it must be conceded that secrecy can be a highly effective life-strategy. In ancient Greece, for example, the various Pankration moves were jealously guarded by clans and families: in a fight, why risk being killed by one's own techniques? Similarly, duelling masters in Renaissance Europe only imparted their lethal fencing moves to the wealthiest clients. In Maritime England, sailors would only share the secret of a knot if their student first swore an oath of secrecy. In feudal Japan, the secrets of Ninjutsu were never divulged to anyone outside a tiny circle of adepts. Even today lawyers only dispense their expertise in exchange for lucrative fees, never for free. Above all, the story of Jesus shows the danger of freely imparting esoteric knowledge to the broad masses – betrayal by a fickle mob, followed by torture and execution.

The last example is the most powerful of all. Whatever the objective 'truth' of Christianity, it is a forest of instruction for the awakened man. The Average Frustrated Chump is an AFC because that is his natural state, more often than not; the condition he deserves. Like the mob which betrayed Jesus, he will not thank the man who attempts to alleviate his misery and ignorance. Ultimately, such a poltroon has no wish to be reminded of his misery and no desire to change it; he prefers to wallow unchallenged in his Never-Never Land of self-delusion and sexual false consciousness. In short, he is beyond redemption.

The astute reader can sense where this is going. There is a certain current in the Anglo-American Manosphere which tries to rouse 'all men' to resist their benighted state: a kind of gendered communism, if you will. For the reasons outlined above, I despise this tendency. The average Anglo-American male is a deluded White Knight chump who wants to be 'saved' by an Anglobitch; he truly believes that the 'sacrament' of poor-quality sex with an ugly, overweight woman will redeem all his misfortunes and transform his life. Why should such an oaf be 'rescued' from himself? Why offer him options, therapy or counselling? Why not let him simply pay the price for his own stupidity?

W B Yeats, in his poem 'To a wealthy man who promised a second subscription to the Dublin Municipal Gallery if it were proved the people wanted pictures', illustrates the correct attitude of the awakened man to mass opinion:

What cared Duke Ercole, that bid
His mummers to the market place,
What th' onion-sellers thought or did
So that his Plautus set the pace
For the Italian comedies?
And Guidobaldo, when he made
That grammar school of courtesies
Where wit and beauty learned their trade
Upon Urbino's windy hill,
Had sent no runners to and fro
That he might learn the shepherds' will.
And when they drove out Cosimo,
Indifferent how the rancour ran,
He gave the hours they had set free
To Michelozzo's latest plan
For the San Marco Library,
Whence turbulent Italy should draw
Delight in Art whose end is peace,

In logic and in natural law
By sucking at the dugs of Greece.

Similarly, we awakened men should remain resolutely indifferent to the plight of divorced White Knights, AFCs and other Blue-Pilled Anglo-American males. They are weak-minded onion-sellers, nothing more. Indeed, we should take a certain perverse pleasure in their various predicaments – a man should pay for the choices he makes. By extension, we should deliberately keep our valuable knowledge from them – for that knowledge gives us a decisive edge. Besides, courting the average Anglo male will only sully our riches: as Nietzsche said, 'Life is a well of delight; but where the rabble also drink, there all fountains are poisoned'.

For example, the fact that women outside the Anglosphere are generally thinner, more pleasant and attractive than their Anglo-American counterparts should only be shared with awakened men on fora like this: men self-selected for self-awareness and intelligence. Proclaiming these facts from the rooftops will only lead to an exodus of frustrated White Knights and ugly incels to our chosen lands, poisoning their wells of pleasure. The Caribbean, Latin America, Eastern and Southern Europe: these are erotic playgrounds for men who truly deserve them, not drooling neckbeards seeking 'traditional' wives to take back to Idaho. At its worse, drawing public attention to our message might lead to legal persecution for 'hate speech' or some other absurd charge. It is far wiser to keep 'this thing of ours' an elusive sanctum for men who can truly profit by it.

The Savage Pilgrimage, Pan-Anglosphere Dissidence, The Savage Lifestyle – call it what you will – has more in common with some eastern philosophies than contemporary western thought. Properly pursued, it presumes a certain disinterest in the 'plight' of the unenlightened even as it shuns commitment to people, possessions and institutions. The existential chains of Anglo-American civilization – marriage, children, careers, houses and material goods – are consciously discarded for a life of maximized experience. The journey becomes the goal, not arrival; the present moment is all; and personal experience supplants received opinion as the touchstone of decision. By definition, only an elite minority of self-aware and intelligent males can understand such concepts; while saving (or trying to save) the sheeple is fraught with thankless peril.

You owe them nothing, least of all truth. Be water, my friends.

7.3. Your Savage Pilgrimage

The overriding focus of our work is not merely escape from Anglo-American misandry; but rather, pilgrimage towards a better, more fulfilled and adventurous life. But we are not alone in this quest for a more fulfilling, man-friendly existence. There are many precedents in America's illustrious cultural history, and their inspiration has a surprising origin.

Jon Krakauer's fascinating book Into the Wild (1996) concerns an affluent youth named Christopher McCandless who dropped out of conventional society before dying of starvation (or food poisoning) in the Alaskan wilderness. Although his short but adventurous life ended in 1992, the bus where he died is still a place of pilgrimage. Sean Penn's film (2007) subsequently cemented McCandless' place in modern American culture as an icon of dissidence and restless alienation from the established order.

However, McCandless is not such an idiomatic figure. A distinctive strand of transcendental alienation has always defined the American male. It is present in the Hudson Valley School of painting, in leather-stocking epics, in Westerns, in the novels of Henry Miller and Jack Kerouac, in the memoirs of Jack London and Henry Thoreau, not just the lives of Christopher McCandless. While there is a disturbing strand in Anglo-American culture leading inexorably to feminism, machine values and secular Puritanism, there are alternative ideals or memes within the culture from which awakened men can also take inspiration.

The Masculine Quest is undoubtedly the most potent of these; and the one most at odds with secular Puritanism. But where did this distinctive American meme originate? If Anglo-Saxon commercial Puritanism were the sole ingredient in American culture, such dissidence would simply not exist. Fortunately, Anglo-American matriarchy, secular Puritanism and crabbed legalism are not the sole ingredients of American culture, as we shall see.

In his tremendous book, Albion's Seed: Four British Folkways in America (1992), David Hackett Fischer identifies four different strands in American culture: Scots-Irish 'backwoods' culture, southern Cavalier culture, Yankee industrial-commercial culture and Puritan New England culture. These all have distinct origins in Britain: the Scottish Borders, Southern England, the East Midlands and East-Anglia, respectively. And they all persist in modern America, however distorted by time and circumstance. Backwoods culture still defines rural American life, and its participants are Hillary's 'deplorables'; Cavalier culture still dominates Southern middle-class life; industrial-commercial culture rules Wall Street, Silicon Valley and the Pacific North West; while Puritan culture dominates law, academia and government.

Obviously, the Puritan-Industrial strains stand together, as do the Backwoods-Cavalier strains; and these pairs are mutually antagonistic. While the Backwoods-Cavalier strands are transcendental, hedonistic and masculine, the Puritan-Commercial strands embody all the crabbed, mechanistic, matriarchal, legalistic, repressive drivel we loathe with boundless fury.

Sadly, the Puritan-Industrial strand has now achieved almost complete dominance in the United States. Southern defeat in the Civil War was the beginning of this Yankee stranglehold, which their political dominion has only strengthened (Check out Clyde Wilson's The Yankee Problem: An American Dilemma (2016) for a scathing study of this ongoing programme). In fact, misandrist Anglo feminism is really just one part of a transplanted Yankee Puritanism with distinct origins in Eastern England (East Anglia). The puritanical tyrants Oliver Cromwell and Margaret Thatcher both came from this region of England, interestingly enough; which was a distinct kingdom as long as 1500 years ago.

In simple terms, the awakened American male's 'Masculine Quest' expresses a desire to escape the dominant Anglo-Saxon Puritan-Commercial culture. Indeed, the pan-Anglosphere men's movement as a whole can be viewed in these terms. The Quest is really just part of an ancient but ongoing struggle for male freedom from the oppressive binds of ancient cultural memes originating in the British Isles. The Matrix and the Quest, the Blue Pill and the Red; in most respects, these conflicts fit neatly into the Backwoods-Cavalier/Commercial-Puritan dichotomy explored above. Obviously, the virgin beauty of the vast American landscape has lent the American dissident's Masculine Quest a lyrical quality that British resistance to Puritan-Industrial oppression lacks completely. While the British stage the Mutiny on the Bounty to escape repression and the lash, the American male retreats into the wilderness, travels to Europe or pens On the Road – in short, does lyrical things.

American men still have an optimism that other men lack. Aldous Huxley suggested this was partly a product of social selection: the most spirited, hopeful and adventurous left Europe to find freedom in America. Exploration of the wilderness by fearless pioneers only heightened this daring spirit: And for all its faults, American liberty still inspires the world. However, the pioneering spirit now only exists among America's dissidents fleeing the Puritan-Industrial Matrix in pursuit of personal fulfilment.

The current debate over gun ownership is always couched in political, legal or criminal terms. From my perspective, the issue is a spiritual or cultural one: for the gun is simultaneously an American symbol of wilderness, freedom and virility. Abolishing the American's right to bear arms would instantly abolish Backwoods-Cavalier America and its unique, questing transcendentalism… which is, of course, why America's secular puritans and their feminist allies are so obsessed by restricting access to firearms.

The dissident man's conceptual toolkit is only enriched by knowing the true origins of the cultural memes he confronts on a daily basis. When the awakened man knows where he stands in the wider scheme of history and culture, it gives his life epic *gravitas* and decisive purpose.

7.4. Become an Internationalist

For men – and especially successful, educated and prosperous men - it is increasingly obvious that the best thing about the Anglosphere is the road out of it. It is plainly an evil empire intent on spreading its unique brand of gynocentric misandry and secular puritanism around the globe. Moreover, it is a uniquely hostile environment for men. This applies not only to punitive divorce laws and the associated prison-industrial complex, but education, the media and the general ambiance of the culture.

As we saw in Part 3, the Anglosphere's distinctive common law is intimately associated with gynocentric Anglo-feminism. Now we are addressing the need to depart the Anglosphere, it makes obvious sense to identify those nations and regions which are common law jurisdictions, and those which are defined by civil law. Although some jurisdictions contain elements of both (Scotland being one curious example), most fall into one definition or the other. Therefore, consider the charts on the next few pages very carefully. The first shows all the major Civil Law nations of the world while the second shows all the nations and territories which are Common Law jurisdictions.

It will be noted that the civil law nations are clustered in South and Central America, non-Anglo Europe and South-East Asia – all areas extolled by my expatriate correspondents. Meanwhile, the common law nations are predictably either Anglosphere nations or territories formerly ruled by them. It might be simplistic to say that awakened men should simply decamp to civil law nations but my correspondents' extensive legal commentary indicates this is the safer course for those who want to marry and start families. There might be curious exceptions such as Quebec in Canada (based on French civil law), Louisiana in the United States (based on French and Spanish civil law) and Scotland in the UK (based on a blend of common and civil law), but the reflexive identification of common law with the Anglosphere remains largely valid.

Figure 1: Civil Law Nations

Albania	Ivory Coast Cote d'Ivoire	Equatorial Guinea	Luxembourg	Serbia
Angola	Cambodia	Ethiopia	Mauritius	Slovakia
Argentina	Cape Verde	Gabon	Mexico	Slovenia
Andorra	Central African Republic	Guinea	Mongolia	South Korea
Armenia	Chile	Guinea-Bissau	Montenegro	Spain
Aruba	Colombia	Georgia	Mozambique	Suriname
Austria	Costa Rica	Germany	Netherlands	Sweden
Azerbaijan	Croatia	Greece	Nepal	Switzerland
Belarus	Cuba	Guatemala	Norway	East Timor
Belgium	Curaçao	Haiti	Panama	Turkey
Benin	Czech Republic	Honduras	Paraguay	Ukraine
Bolivia	Denmark	Hungary	Peru	United States – Louisiana only
Bosnia and Herzegovina	Dominican Republic	Iceland	Poland	Sweden
Brazil	Ecuador	India	Portugal	Switzerland
Bulgaria	El Salvador	Italy	Taiwan	Uruguay
Burkina Faso	Estonia	Japan	Romania	Uzbekistan
Burundi	Finland	Latvia	Russia	Vietnam
Chad	France	Lebanon	Rwanda	Venezuela
China	Egypt	Lithuania	São Tomé and Príncipe	

Figure 2: Common Law Nations

American Samoa	Based on law of the United States	Hong Kong	Principally based on English common law
Antigua and Barbuda	Based on English common law	India	Based on English common law, except in Goa, Daman and Diu and Dadra and Nagar Haveli which follow a civil law system based on the Portuguese civil Law
Australia	Based on English common law	Republic of Ireland	Based on Irish law before 1922, which was itself based on English common law
The Bahamas	Based on English common law	Israel	Based on English common law incorporating civil law and fragments of Halakha and Sharia for family law cases
Bangladesh	Based on English common law, with family law heavily based on Shar'iah law.	Jamaica	Based on English common law
Barbados	Based on English common law	Kiribati	Based on English common law
Belize	Based on English common law	Liberia	Based on Anglo-American and customary law
Bhutan	Based on English common law, with Indian influence.	Marshall Islands	Based on law of the United States
British Virgin Islands	Based on English common law	Myanmar	Based on English common law
Canada	Based on English common law, except in Quebec	Nauru	Based on English common law
Cayman Islands	Based on English common law	Nepal	Based on English common law
Cyprus	Based on English common law, with civil law influences	New Zealand	Based on English common law
Dominica Dominica	Based on English common law	Northern Ireland	Based on English common law

England and Wales	Based on English common law	**Palau**	Based on law of the United States
United Kingdom (UK)	Primarily common law, with early Roman and some modern continental European influences	**Pakistan**	Based on English common law with some provisions of Islamic law
Fiji	Based on English common law	**Saint Kitts and Nevis**	Based on English common law
Ghana	Based on English common law	**Saint Vincent and the Grenadines**	Based on English common law
Gibraltar	Based on English common law	**Singapore**	Based on English common law with some provisions of Islamic law
Grenada	Based on English common law	**Tonga**	Based on English common law
Hong Kong	Principally based on English common law	**Trinidad and Tobago**	Based on English common law
India	Based on English common law, except in Goa, Daman and Diu and Dadra and Nagar Haveli which follow a civil law system based on the Portuguese Civil Law	**Tuvalu**	Based on English common law
Republic of Ireland	Based on Irish law before 1922, which was itself based on English common law	**United States of America**	Federal courts and 49 states use the legal system based on English common law, which has diverged somewhat since the mid-nineteenth century in that they look to each other's cases for guidance on issues of first impression and rarely, if ever, look at contemporary cases on the same issue in the UK or the Commonwealth. Law in the state of Louisiana is based on French and Spanish civil law

As has been made perfectly apparent, no sane or rational man would consider marrying or starting a family in any common law country. The comprehensive infiltration of common law by feminist agendas has reduced all Anglo-American law to a mere tool of misandrist feminism. Not even a pre-nuptial agreement bestowed under common law confers the same protection offered by civil law. That said, it is probably best to marry in a non-western country if one has to marry at all.

Most of my readers are successful men, since these have most to lose by divorce or other types of relationship breakdown. To this demographic, the world law map is an invaluable tool which allows them to marry and form a cogent family while minimizing the financial risks associated with common law divorce.

While the civil law nations are far from perfect, they still offer successful men more legal and economic protection than the common law Anglosphere. In his eloquent response to an anti-Western Muslim, a commentator called Gearman explains this position in more detail:

Your posts are a prime exhibit of the binary, rigid, closed-minded, unrealistic thinking that blinds far too many MGTOW's and makes you miserable, since you're missing a really important nuance of the real world that Rookh and the others here are waking you up to. You couldn't be more wrong about the non-Anglo West especially France, Germany and continent of Europe, it's miles ahead of the Anglosphere in every way, and much more family-friendly and fairer to men and fatherhood. To you, everywhere in the West and even most of the rest of the world is "bad" if it has even a little bit of feminism to it, and even then a vague, undefined sort of feminism that you can't even provide details on (since you obviously haven't even been to these places).

Again, you're stuck in that kind of damaging, extreme "either-or" thinking that's also peculiar to the Anglosphere, and it will make you miserable and fail at everything you do, wherever you are— you have to break out of that superficiality and do deeper analysis. What Rookh and everyone else is making clear here, it's not feminism alone that's so damaging and wrecking to the lives and livelihoods of modern men, and to women and families, but the combination of a particular type of feminism—the adversarial driven "us against them" third and fourth-wave of the Anglo world— combined with Anglo Puritanism, cultural Marxism, the common law tradition (which makes divorce and the "metoo" witch hunt profitable to the extremists pushing it), the cuck chivalry white knights who enable "have your cake and eat it too" hypocrisy of Anglo feminists (claim to be strong and independent but need permanent alimony after a divorce) and the crony corporate capitalism of the Anglo world which sees politically incorrect men as easy targets to vulture off of. All of these things are unique to the Anglosphere, and they're what makes Anglosphere feminism uniquely toxic (Appendix I1, p.246).

Like the Victorian amoralist Ragnar Redbeard (2015), my perspective applies rigorous pragmatism to immediate and pressing problems. Most of my readers want safer marriages to pleasant and attractive women without having to convert to Islam or live in a mud hut, as Legal Eagle ably explains:

The only other possibility I can think of is this is your twisted way of trying to tell people here that the Muslim world is the only alternative to the Anglosphere. Sorry, but no thanks. People here are explicitly looking for expat options in the West or other First-World nations, yes mostly Europe but also Latin America and Asia, in part because like others have been telling you here, there's not a single stable, technologically advanced Muslim nation and Muslim culture is way too disposed against science, technology and modernity in general.

Plus the Muslim world has an even uglier version of the very Anglo puritanical elements we're trying to avoid and have caused a lot of this mess in the Anglosphere. And like someone said, now the Muslim world is also falling apart culturally and seeing it's own version of feminism arise, which is more like the poisonous feminism of the Anglosphere instead of the healthier, balanced version of the non-Anglosphere.

Sorry, but no thanks. For our purposes here the best expat options by far are still in the West or Asia or Latin America, just outside the Anglosphere. If you want to evangelize and tell people to join the Islamic world, go do it somewhere else. You are adding nothing productive here (Appendix J1, pp.250-251).

Even for male types who seek a less traditional relationship, the civil law countries are certainly less infected by misandrist feminism at a general level. It is notable that the western civil law countries also generally have a much more rational attitude on key lifestyle issues, such as prostitution. Aside from the Scandinavian countries, they also retain selective state secondary education – a vital consideration for men wishing to start new families. It is no surprise that the most dysfunctional state schools in the developed world exist in the Anglosphere, with crisis levels of illiteracy and student misbehaviour almost the norm.

For those men who wish to leave the Anglosphere for better sexual options abroad, make sure the country you are moving to is a civil law country rather than a common law one. A law professor who posted an extensive essay on my blog lays out the hard facts below:

The essence of what Mr. Kshatriya and the Blog contributors have discovered here is correct: that is that the Anglo common law system confers enormous power to the judiciary in notable contrast to civil law systems, which are governed more by statutes and broader democratic and popular will. This is what the common law, in both its pre and post-20th century forms, means at its heart: the judges' cumulative decisions and opinions create concrete, enforceable mandates of law in conjunction with, and often beyond anything contained in statutes and written constitutions. There was a time early in my career when I would have touted the advantages of the common law, at least for certain areas such as property negotiations and riparian rights (water management). But after learning and comparing the common and civil law systems, and in particular seeing how the divorce process has otherwise devastated the finances and emotional state of my once prosperous and happy son, I have come to conclude that there are certain areas where the modern form of the common law has become dangerous, family law being the most prominent.

And unfortunately as I will explain below, the dysfunction and corruption of Anglo-American common law in the divorce court context has reached dangerous proportions with no effective remedy to correct it. This, in practice, is at the foundation of why expatriation from the Anglo world has become unavoidable for marriage and family formation. As I indicated at the start, more broadly there is no realistic prospect in the short or long term of reforming the structures, cultural influences and legal decision-making patterns that have forged modern Anglo-Saxon family law. Not even a Constitutional Amendment, or any other sort of reform driven by popular impulses or collective action. Here is why.

The essence and power of the common law foundation of Anglo family law, in key regards, transcend even the U.S. Constitution itself (and its counterparts across the traditionally English-speaking nation states). You'd have to reform the basic substance and modern interpretations of the common law to achieve substantive change in the dreadful career, finance and family-wrecking dark heart of Anglo family law.

No statutory change or act transformed into a law, whether by a legislative body or a referendum, could repeal or reform it because the essence of common law resides in the collective thought and inclinations of judges, who are empowered to effectively make the law quite unlike magistrates in civil law societies and, in some areas, can operate effectively unconstrained by popular will or democratic wishes.

And there is the essential argument against common law, in a nutshell. Although his argument carries most weight in relation to the United States, the other English Speaking nations are also defined by common law. Here is the learned Professor again:

In fact I should stress here, I do not have a problem with judges using their reflection and sense of individual judgment to consider individual circumstances and special cases. I do not agree with statutory "3 strikes" laws that make punitive demands devoid of considering circumstances. But such fairness and rationality are not what modern Anglo common law instills in family court judges. The power of conflict theory and cultural marxism in Anglo legal scholarship means the weight of precedent creates an anti-family, anti-male and anti- "good man and woman" standard de facto for both statutes and case law. It is thus that the decision process for divorce cases in any Anglo country will almost always follow the perverse demands of the cultural marxist orthodoxy.

Result? The latitude of judges in common law systems, together with the conflict-theory basis of their doctrines, makes their power to impute financial obligations on financially successful spouses, particularly ex-husbands and fathers, dangerous in any real world context. Yet, as if the irony couldn't get any more bitter, even the minority of statute-driven family courts in the Anglo world are still stacked against you. In such cases, even the small potential relief of having a more reasonable family court judge, not steeped in the family-wrecking doctrines of concept theory, is almost always nullified by the statutory demands of custody assignment, child support and spousal maintenance. To contrast, judges in the civil law world do retain power to apply rationality and humane judgment on a case by case basis. Civil law does not mean judges have their hands tied, it simply means that they cannot, and thus have no incentive, to legislate from the bench. Court decisions do not become citable precedents in case law. Thus it is that legal decision-making is based on the more democratic and rational foundation of carefully considered statutory law with input from the people, as opposed to judicial elites in the Anglo world who have their legal thought shaped by the radical, irrational, misandrist and anti-Western conflict ideologies that mold them in law school.

The very fact that judges' decisions in civil law countries do not figure into the weight of precedent—with judges having no power to "make law" through case law—thus means that judges in Europe, South America, most of Asia and the rest of the civil law world are freed up to be more humane and more reasonably consider realities as they are on the ground in family law cases. By way of hard contrast, and as you have correctly realized Mr. Kshatriya, the very power that divorce court and general family court judges in the United States and Anglo common law world possess, in fact makes divorce law and family law judges a kind of priestly, undemocratic elite in the Anglo world. They need not be rational or respond to realities as they are on the ground, and their power to make law means they can indulge the radical ideologies and orthodoxies of "right thought" and political correctness in law school to create heavily misandrist and anti-family law through their written opinions. This is why the takeover of academia by the Frankfurt-School and its anti-Western, anti-family ideologies of conflict theory and cultural marxism are so dangerous. Again as you have observed, the common law of the Anglo world gives them the power to translate their radical ideologies into concrete law-making and case precedents that are doing more damage to family formation in the Anglo world than any other factor (Appendix S, pp.332-334).

The foregoing passage explains why any sensible man in the Anglosphere has to broaden his perspective in political, legal and social terms, especially where this relates to key lifestyle choices such as marriage or starting a family. The alternative is like putting a pistol with all its chambers loaded to one's temple and pulling the trigger. Judges in the Anglo-American world have far too much discretionary power which – given the misandrist and counter-traditional nature of Anglosphere culture – is heavily loaded against men, husbands and fathers in all divorce courts. Indeed, the rampant bias against men in the Anglo-American legal system generally doubtless owes much to this priestly autonomy.

Having made one's decision to depart and chosen a suitable country to relocate to, the awakened man should make a few reconnaissance trips to learn the language, culture and customs. About five extended trips in the space of a year should be sufficient. Then, with the knowledge, money and passion in place, he can make the leap.

7.5. Make the Leap

Making the leap outside the Anglosphere country of your birth can be a difficult task. A thousand forces anchor you to that land, binding you in a cocoon of apathy. For this reason, the descendants of recent immigrants find emigration much easier than Anglo-American natives. This chapter is therefore most relevant to Anglo-Americans, who will require the specific techniques I have developed in order to escape their birth culture and realize their dreams.

First of all, you need to develop an alienated, dissident mindset and maintain it all times. The psychological concept of 'frame' is all-important, here. Although it has been appropriated by pick-up artists, creating and nurturing a success-orientated mindset has value in a wide range of contexts. For example, the boxer Sugar Ray Leonard described a winner's mindset as a place where doubt and fear were barred entry at the border. Moral issues aside, cult leaders such as Charles Manson, Jim Jones or David Koresh were adept at presenting a flawless persona to their followers. Whatever their personal doubts or insecurities, maintaining this 'frame' of inspirational leadership gave them godlike influence over others. Similarly, dictators such as Hitler or Stalin carefully cultivated public 'frames' of strength and decisiveness, thereby securing mass obedience to their plans. Never mind that Hitler was an ailing drug addict or Stalin a slow-witted sociopath: the masses saw only their flawless 'frames' and responded accordingly.

Successful expatriation necessarily involves cultivating and maintaining a strong 'frame' or mindset which excludes all doubt or reticence. The emigrant must learn to despise those aspects of his own culture which are misandrist, sex-negative and deluded, even while he builds a potent mental image of the land he desires. Together, these become his 'Emigrant Frame': the rugged psychic structure which sustains him through moments of doubt and uncertainty. Remember that the media, education and most individuals in the Anglosphere are programmed to promote the delusion that life in Anglo-American countries is more or less perfect, and that cultural dissent is an 'illness'. Moreover, more of your significant others will have also internalized this agenda.

Hence resistance to your goals from friends, family and the surrounding culture will be considerable and only maintaining a strong frame will keep you on track. A certain degree of social withdrawal might be necessary: simply exclude anyone who derides your masterplan. Similarly, cultivate friendships and associations men who share your goals and values. Try to travel outside the Anglosphere whenever possible, being sure to savour the sexual freedoms on offer. Obviously, countries with legal and guilt-free prostitution such as Germany, Holland and Thailand are perfect for this. Such adventures will not only harden your resolve; they will strengthen your inner frame sufficiently to 'make the leap' and move abroad.

Ultimately, the aim is to jettison your Anglo mental baggage and truly think like a foreigner. The messages I have been promoting for over a decade must be implicitly accepted in their entirety, igniting your desire to escape the five pillars of Anglosphere dysfunction and realize your dreams.

Many perils await you reach your destination. Only creating and maintaining a strong mental frame will get you there; an impregnable inner structure wrought of relentless willpower, sure knowledge and blazing desire. With such a frame in place, almost anything is possible. Consider how cult leader Jim Jones compelled hundreds of his followers to relocate to Guyana, then kill themselves at his command: without strong frame, such things could never have happened. Similarly, consider how Stalin modernised his country in a few years, transforming an agrarian backwater into a modern, industrialized nation: only by imposing his personal frame on every sphere of Russian life were such goals realized. Similarly, would Adolf Hitler have risen from obscurity to become Chancellor of Germany without first cultivating a frame of boundless self-belief?

Ethical problems aside, cult leaders and dictators offer some of the best models of frame maintenance in history. Against all odds, these men dragged whole communities and nations with them on journeys to the unknown. But on a more mundane level, top investors like John Templeton or Warren Buffet accumulated vast fortunes by maintaining frame amidst fluctuating markets and economic conditions. Instead of following the herd into loss or penury, they shunned popular sentiment and flourished accordingly.

So let the man who would leave the Anglosphere erect his mental frame on rugged foundations. This book and Havok (2009), my first work, will serve him well in this regard. Also, he can draw inspiration from writers like Rampago Furioso, who have been strongly influenced by my message. Once your frame is in place, nurture it with exotic experience among the liberated peoples of the Earth. These might be in Continental Europe, Scandinavia, South America, Africa or the Far East. Soon, you will be so alienated from the misandrist, repressive Anglosphere and its dysfunctional laws, values and institutions that departure becomes inevitable. And having departed, your new frame will become the foundation of your new life.

An important corollary to dissidence and strong psychic frame is specificity. Travel widely but once you find the country of your desire, direct all your financial, mental and spiritual energies into relocating there. Without that high degree of specificity and focus, your expatriation efforts will most likely dissipate. Further, narrowing your focus will allow you to precisely determine whether relocation to your desired country is viable and realistic. You have to make sure that it has professional opportunities, political stability, a decent standard of living and will treat you in a reasonable manner. 'Pie in the sky' pipe dreams of ideal love will not suffice because the world outside the Anglosphere contains a wide range of different languages, religions and value systems. Here is Gearman, one of my correspondents, on the crucial importance of specificity in successful expatriation:

Just to elaborate, for people in the Anglosphere making concrete decisions about becoming expats, they don't get to choose some "pie in the sky" fantasy like what you have in mind, they have to choose specific countries. That's why specifics like the details above matter. And if you'll bother to pay attention, you'll see that the specifics of the non-Anglo West make them very appealing to us. In actual practice we look for first world countries with a high standard of living, where we can get a good job in our fields, but without the toxic feminism of the Anglosphere. And the non-Anglo West meets all our requirements for that. Yes, even Scandinavia does, even more so elsewhere in Europe, as well as Brazil and much of Latin America, China, Korea, Japan, even Russia and much of eastern Europe. All of these countries to varying extents have systems that are a result of the Enlightenment (Appendix I2, pp.253-254).

However, all the hard work and research will be worth it in the long run. Here is an intoxicating draught of inspiration from another of my correspondents:

Just to give you sense of how cool it is here and in Germany compared to the misery and drudgery of the Anglosphere toil, I love my gf now, but in keeping with Belgian and German custom, she's totally cool with me checking out other girls occasionally. She's even cool with me banging another hottie from time to time, just so long as it turns me on enough that I get aroused around her and she stays the top girl. To Americans it seems like it's an "open relationship" with Belgian girls on the side, but that's not how they see it here, the Europeans as a whole just see it is people being sexual as they normally are. My gf now even goes to strip clubs with me from time to time- and she's the one who picks them out! And nobody finds it unusual. I get 6 week's vacation, similar to what I got in Germany, I play a ton of sports but never have to worry about nutso medical bills if I get banged up, I make a lot of money in my job and they encourage starting a new business here, the food and wine are great, people are friendly and not at each other's necks attacking like in the US. My taxes are maybe a little higher than they were back in Florida for me but not that much higher and I get so much more for it here. (My taxes in Germany were even a little lower but I still got the health care and vacation bennies, plus free Master's classes.) And when my gf and I settle down and have kids, she'll have many months to stay home and stay with them and still be able to return to her job if she wants later on. I will never go back to North America now (Appendix E, pp.236-237).

With inspiration like that, what are you waiting for?

Part Eight

Distant Shores

Complete this Section yourself, at your Leisure…

Epilogue

This work is a mystery, born of mysteries. From its conception, the unseen hand of providence has guided my pen; and it is still with me, guiding it now. It marked me with a sigil of power, from outside the world; for I am the shepherd chosen to lead men from the Anglosphere to greener pastures. Note how each section bears a Golden Triangle; when you make this symbol your Frame of Mind, strong and perfect, no harm shall come to you. In your chosen land, far from the Five Pillars, display this sign that all may know you. It is yours, for all posterity; perfection for nothing, from the realm of hidden things.

This is not a conclusion, but a beginning. These eight sections stand strong against the Five Pillars of Anglo dysfunction, for all time to come. Anglo-American men, look long and hard at the wisdom gathered in these pages; and you will find an ocean of thought, endless in its scope, power and application.

Rookh Kshatriya,

Lake Windermere, 2019

References

Bibliography

Brown, Derren (2007): Tricks of the Mind, Channel 4 Books, UK.

Chomsky, Noam and Herman, Edward S. (1995): Manufacturing Consent: The Political Economy of the Mass Media, Vintage, UK.

Clark, Gregory (2015): The Son Also Rises: Surnames and the History of Social Mobility, Princeton University Press, US.

Clinton, Hillary (2014): Hard Choices, Simon and Schuster, US.

Davis-Hanson, Victor (2002), Why the West Has Won: Carnage and Culture from Salamis to Vietnam, Faber and Faber, UK.

Fischer, David Hackett (1992): Albion's Seed: Four British Folkways in America, OUP, US.

Gabriel, Richard A. (2006): Subotai the Valiant: Ghengis Khan's Greatest General, University of Oklahoma Press, US.

Krakauer, Jon (1996): Into the Wild, Villard, US.

Kshatriya, Rookh (2009): Havok, Authorhouse, UK.
.
Medved, Michael, (1993): Hollywood vs. America: The Explosive Bestseller that Shows How and Why the Entertainment Industry Has Broken Faith With Its Audience, Harper Perennial, UK.

Ollivier, Debra (2009): What French Women Know: About Love, Sex and Other Matters of the Heart and Mind, Piatkus, UK.

Orwell, George (1933): Down and Out in Paris and London, Gollancz, UK.

Orwell, George (1936): Keep the Aspidistra Flying, Gollancz, UK.

Redbeard, Ragnar (2015): Might is Right or Survival of the Fittest, Haole Library, US.

Ribi, Alfred (2013): The Search for Roots: C G Jung and the Tradition of Gnosis, Gnosis Archive Books, US.

Rosso, George A. (1994): Blake's Prophetic Workshop: A Study of the "Four Zoas", Bucknell University Press, US.

Shaxson, Nicholas (2012): Treasure Islands: Tax Havens and the Men who Stole the World, Vintage, UK.

Taylor, Rogan P. (1983): The Death and Resurrection Show: From Shaman to Superstar, Frederick Muller, UK.

Unwin, Joseph (1934): Sex and Culture: Oxford University Press, UK.

Ware, Vron (2015): Beyond the Pale: White Women, Racism, and History, Verso, US.

Wilson, Clyde (2016): The Yankee Problem: An American Dilemma, Shotwell Publishing, US.

Wilson, Colin and Seaman, Donald (1990): The Serial Killers: Study in the Psychology of Violence, W.H. Allen / Virgin Books, UK.

Media

Ford, John (1956): *The Searchers,* Warner Brothers, US.

Penn, Sean (2007): Into the Wild, Paramount Vintage, US.

Wachowski, Lana and Wachowski, Lilly (1999): The Matrix, Warner Brothers, US.

The Secret World of Tinder, Channel 4, UK: Broadcast 14th May, 2014

Internet

Christ, Antje and Dorholt, Dorothe (27 Feb 2019): "A lack of women in Asia - DW Documentary". Available at:

https://www.youtube.com/watch?v=0uj6bDqAVJA [Accessed 12 Mar. 2019].

Crawford, Bridget (Aug. 1, 2017): "Call for Authors – Feminist Judgments: Rewritten Torts Opinions". Available at: http://www.feministlawprofessors.com/2017/08/call-for-authors-feminist-judgments-rewritten-torts-opinions [Accessed 12 Mar. 2019].

Davies, Nick (Oct. 20, 2009): "Inquiry fails to find single trafficker who forced anybody into prostitution". Available at: https://www.theguardian.com/uk/2009/oct/20/government-trafficking-enquiry-fails [Accessed 12 Mar. 2019].

Farber, Madeline (May 24, 2017): "Women's Student Debt Crisis in the United States". Available at: http://fortune.com/2017/05/24/women-student-loan-debt-study/ [Accessed 12 Mar. 2019].

Furioso, Relampago (June 13, 2016): "Why MGTOW is so Important". Available at: https://relampagofurioso.com/2016/06/13/why-mgtow-is-so-important/ [Accessed 12 Mar. 2019].

Furioso, Rampago (May 4, 2018): "Your Life is Your Life – Go All the Way". Available at: https://relampagofurioso.com/2018/05/04/your-life-is-your-life-go-all-the-way/ [Accessed 12 Mar. 2019].

Hoca, Steve (1 Jan. 2017): "The Structural Barriers Behind Human Social Interaction". Available at: https://www.youtube.com/watch?v=h97l6CZx3b0 [Accessed 12 Mar. 2019].

Krumholz, Michael (Nov. 16, 2016): "Cuba Dave found guilty of promoting sex tourism, faces five more years in prison". Available at: http://www.ticotimes.net/2016/11/16/cuba-dave-verdict [Accessed 12 Mar. 2019].

O'Donnell , Jayne (Mar. 5, 2019): "U.S. deaths from alcohol, drugs and suicide hit highest level since record-keeping began". Available at: https://eu.usatoday.com/story/news/health/2019/03/05/suicide-alcohol-drug-deaths-centers-disease-control-well-being-trust/3033124002/ [Accessed 12 Mar. 2019].

Paton, Graeme (June 11, 2008): "Intelligent people 'less likely to believe in God". Available at: https://www.telegraph.co.uk/news/uknews/2111174/Intelligent-people-less-likely-to-believe-in-God.html [Accessed 12 Mar. 2019].

Rico, (Aug. 20, 2017): "David Strecker, Aka Cuba Dave Acquitted". Available at: https://qcostarica.com/david-strecker-aka-cuba-dave-acquitted [Accessed 12 Mar. 2019].

Scarecrow, R. (2017): "Too Far, Too Few, Too Little, Too Late". Available at: http://men-factor.blogspot.com/2017/03/ [Accessed 12 Mar. 2019].

Wilson, Rebecca (Nov. 16, 2017): "Only 52% of Graduates get Graduate-Level Jobs, CIPD Reveals". Available at: https://www.recruitment-international.co.uk/blog/2017/11/only-52-percent-of-graduates-get-graduate-level-jobs-cipd-reveals [Accessed 12 Mar. 2019].

Wu, Winston (2 Oct. 2016): "Why LOCATION is the key to changing your life, not thoughts or attitude - Self-help Secret". Available at: https://www.youtube.com/watch?v=JkQStiHJBw8 [Accessed 12 Mar. 2019].

Wu, Winston and Stark, Robert (May 22, 2014): "Robert Stark Interviews Winston Wu about American Culture". Available at: Starktruthradio, https://www.starktruthradio.com/?p=136 [Accessed 12 Mar. 2019].

Yale University (2019): "Yale Journal of Law & Feminism". Available at: https://law.yale.edu/student-life/student-journals-and-publications/yale-journal-law-feminism [Accessed 12 Mar. 2019].

Appendices

All thanks to my various correspondents for the wonderful commentary gathered in these Appendices. These comments are the true backbone of this book and far outweigh my other references in originality, scope and importance. Each comment is time and date-stamped, with the commenter's name denoting its authorship.

Appendix A: North Wind 10 January 2018 at 23:49

Great content and advice Rookh, I'm an int'l contractor and in the military before that, worked in dozens of countries, and years ago independently came to the same conclusions as you. The Anglosphere and its Stalinist family courts, divorce laws and alimony and child support slavery, based in puritanical Anglo culture and its cuck chivalry tradition combined with cultural Marxism, are uniquely disastrous for civilization and have made marriage and the family untenable in the English-speaking world. As you have, I've rejected the parallel but too often misguided claims of at least some corners of the MRA and MGTOW movements; sure they get some of the truth, but many draw incorrect or overgeneralized conclusions when they paint with broad brush and lambast "the West" instead of just "the Anglosphere" where the truly suicidal family law and divorce court practices are in place. It is still important for men to engage women and raise families, and civilization, including Western civilization, must be preserved.

But this must happen outside the Anglosphere, which is on a one-way course to civilizational suicide thanks to the madness of its misandry, crushingly oppressive marriage and divorce laws and the deeply rooted political correctness that makes it impossible to reform them. It isn't just the indentured servitude and neo-slavery of unchecked child and spousal support obligations forced onto American and Anglosphere men. As we're also seeing with the #metoo and #timesup media frenzy now, it's the way Anglosphere

Puritanism and dumb white knight chivalry give the most selfish, emotionally unstable women absolute power to ruin the livelihoods of productive men and businesses with inflated or wholly unfounded allegations. The solution is not complete disengagement from starting families or completely "leaving the West" as some MGTOW's push for, it is ditching specifically the US or other Anglo countries to move to a place outside the Anglosphere and starting families there, especially in the European mainland and other parts of the non-Anglo West. Contrary to at least some MGTOW lore, which has been sadly polluted and distracted by the misinformed anti-Europeanism of neocon and even Breitbart style "conservatism", 90% of the West is far more commonsensical and supportive of fathers and productive spouses than any of the suicidal nation-states of the Anglosphere. Not perfect, but reasonable enough that it's worth it to be a father and start families there.

Yes, there is a good deal of foolish PC, feminism and maddening short-sighted policy and culture infecting the non-Anglosphere nations of the West, too. But the vulture-like and predatory style of divorce, the rent seeking and extreme high risk to men's finances, well being and very freedom, is unique to the Anglosphere and especially the United States and Canada, where destitution and prison terms face even high-earning divorced men. There's a ton of good articles on why this is, and you've cited many of them. But the heart of it is the combination of legal precedent in Anglo common-law, plus lingering cultural precedents like Puritanism and the extreme cuck-ish nature of Anglo chivalry, have been absolutely toxic and suicidal for the Anglosphere when joined at the hip to feminism and cultural Marxism.

This is how and why even other Western countries with a lot of the same stupidity with feminism and cultural Marxism, like in Scandinavia, are in heavy contrast to the Anglosphere, surprisingly father-friendly and protective of the assets of a productive working man, forbidding alimony and being commonsensical with limited child support. They're civil-law countries, and without the self-destructive cognitive dissonance of Anglo Puritanism and cuck chivalry, their social democracy systems and welfare states actually provide a much fairer and more rational environment for both spouses and children. These policies in the non-Anglosphere world remove the asinine profit incentive and high stakes profiteering in US family courts, not only reducing the divorce rate but making sure men don't get "taken to the cleaners" in divorce as is routine in the US and Anglosphere.

Sweden stands out for this. Even with its own dumb forays into cultural Marxism, Sweden is one of the most pro-husband and pro-father countries in the Western world, with paternity leave, near forbidding of alimony in practice and none of this permanent spousal support BS like in the US. There's also capped child support, tradition on shared custody and a requirement that any women initiating divorce have to go out and earn a living. Yes Sweden has feminism, but in the absence of Anglo cuck chivalry and Puritanism, divorcing women don't get the "have your cake and eat it too" bullshit of the Anglosphere where they suddenly become needy dependents after divorce. In Sweden, the feminist credo of being an independent woman means what it sounds like, women after a divorce have to step up and work, without using the ex-husband as a meal-ticket. It's similar or even better in the rest of Scandinavia, the Catholic countries of the Mediterranean and South America, the German and centrally European countries and especially eastern Europe.

In fact, my absolutely favorite places to get posted for contracts are in France and central and eastern Europe. The ladies there not only hot but sweet and chill about simply being sexy, even though they can be assertive and independent minded they don't buy into the stupid misandry of the Anglosphere with its #metoo and "take the deadbeat Dad to the cleaners" mind-set. And they're earnest about starting and maintaining families. Just look at the way Catharine Deneuve and other French women stood up and spoke out against the #metoo Salem witch hunt in the US and Britain recently, going so far as to write a major piece in the French Monde newspaper to support the importance of men being able to hit on women without getting tagged for harassment. This is what too many MGTOW's and self-claimed "conservatives" don't get when they blindly trash Sweden and lambast "the West" in general, it's the Anglosphere, not the rest of the West, which has made both the process and aftermath of divorce so toxic for men or anyone who works and saves for a living, made marriage itself toxic and draining for men while making the workplace itself toxic for even the most innocent male to female interactions.

Some of these self-claimed conservatives will whine about how ditching the Anglosphere means the Muslims, Africans and Latinos will take over, but at this point it doesn't matter, and it's too late to stop it anyway. Anglo civilization has slit it's own throat with this insane Puritanism and misandry. Winston Churchill was sadly deluded with all his triumphalism in the history of English speaking peoples, the civilization may have been sustainable back then before feminism and cultural Marxism infected the media and universities of the Anglosphere. But in combo with the cuck chivalry and Puritanism of the Anglo world, made worse by the profiteering of the common-law system, it means the ugliest decline and fall, and for the Anglo world it'll be a lot worse than what the Romans saw. The birth rate and marriage rates of the Anglo populations in the Anglosphere keeps plunging farther and farther as the misandry of family courts and the overall culture continues to take it's toll, so much so that Anglo families can survive only in the non-Anglo world now.

Nothing will save the Anglo countries in their current form. The coming demographic dispossession of the Anglosphere will be painful, probably means a lot of nasty civil wars and society upheavals in the near future. But the crisis and complete re-set may be the only thing to save at least a portion of the Anglosphere by forcing it to look squarely at the suicidal madness of what's become Anglo culture.

Appendix B: Anonymous 12 January 2018 at 20:47

Couldn't have said it better, both you and North Wind get it! Forgive me for going on in detail myself but given the thought and intelligence you guys have put into your own insights here, I felt obligated to give an extended response myself.

I'm one of the "exiles" from the failing and falling down Anglosphere, moved from the US to southwestern France over a decade ago and it's been a blessing in every dimension: career, love life, family, life quality, health, education, food. Everything. I was part of a big movement of Americans and Canadians who made our exit right around the start of the great Recession. The Silicon Valley press never had a precise name for us, but most of us made our fortunes in the software industry, saw writing on the wall and cashed in our stock options before the big crash of the S&P and Nasdaq in 2008.

But after dodging one bullet, we were left pondering why we should risk everything again in the even more dangerous and unpredictable world of US divorce courts. Many of us had seen multimillionaire colleagues reduced to poverty and misery in US family courts after their wives sued for divorce. And slowly but surely we realized the problem was more than a few isolated cases or soothing marriage counselor platitudes. It was in the broader American, and more generally Anglophone culture itself. And in the brainlessness of the courts that give carte blanche to the most parasitic women to leech off their spouses who contribute to society. Around the same time we realized our skills were in demand internationally, and with Web design and software engineering jobs becoming portable thanks to remote platforms, it made sense for us to pack up and move. Most of us still wanted to start families and raise kids, but we realize we'd be putting our fortunes and hard work at risk by doing this in the US. Like you said, prenups don't give you any real protection in Ameican family courts. Only being out of the jurisdiction of these kangaroo courts entirely can do that.

Our friends and colleagues who lost everything were typical of the hypocrisy that's infected all US family law. The men were "working too hard", you see, not enough time for the wife and kids even though the men's hard-earned paychecks were supporting these selfish bitches' ability to shop themselves silly and whine and moan in the first place! American and Anglo grown women with kids are still basically whiny little girls this way, they're never satisfied with their lot no matter how much their husbands slave away for them, even if they work 80 hour weeks in some struggling software company to give them a life of luxury. This is where the Anglosphere goes full stupid. Almost any other country would realize the wives complaints have no basis, that they're acting like spoiled brats and tell them to shove it. But US family courts thanks to feminism, the politically correct "mainstream media" and the collusion of moron white knight cucks, instead indulges this female infantilism from coddled, spoiled brat wives with no appreciation for things like hard work, sacrifice and patience.

Thus the ongoing merry go round of inanity with "community property" awarded to wife too lazy to get off her own ass to work, on top of alimony, full custody and extortionate child support. If that wasn't retarded enough, now the #metoo bandwagon means the same spoiled brat women can pull the same kind of extortionate shit even with men who aren't their spouses in the US and rest of the Anglosphere. Just make a random accusation about made-up shit over a trivial "clumsy courtship" from 20 years ago and voila, a ruined man and a big payout for the attention-seeking whore. All fully encouraged by the Anglosphere and it's white knight cuck army. (Quebec is better but Anglo Canada is even worse, it's now so bad there that a defendant in sexual assault and misconduct cases can't even submit exonerating text messages to show their innocence!)

I get why some men go MGTOW, if they're stuck in the Anglosphere that may be their only alternative. But far better is to do what their ancestors did but in reverse, leave the North American cultural swamp and migrate out of the country, head back to Europe outside the British Isles. In my case I married a sweet French girl and have 2 lovely daughters and a son. Even if things go sour I know I'll keep the heart of what I've earned, child support would be capped, I'd still support my kids but in a way that's reasonable and above all, is for the kids only, not an end-run to indulge the ex-wife's profligacy. The same goes for my fellow colleagues in France and around the continent, even the ones who brought their American or Canadian wives-and-girlfriends with them. It really is true, if you absolutely insist on marrying an Anglo girl, don't to it in an Anglo land!

And best of all the chances of divorcing are a whole lot less since there aren't any lawyer leeches or judge vultures to profit from the divorce shitstorm like in the US. That's what the Napoleonic code and European law in general get you. And our family is stronger because of it. The French, Germans and most other Europeans are even cool with the open relationship and polyamory thing if that's your gig, and the families still do just fine. It's not our thing personally, but people are really about living and let live here. Another reason that the freedom from all the Anglo puritan horseshit is so refreshing.

One last point, don't listen to the morons who babble on about how "France is going majority Muslim!" These idiots are either deluded or full of shit, this kind of propaganda comes from the Gatestone Institute and other neocon rags trying to push the US into more wars in the Middle East, and they're terrified they'll lose their tax base for war if more Americans wise up and say adios to the Anglosphere and its bullshit. The France of 2018 doesn't give a shit about its former colonial empire, the immigrants now come from the old eastern bloc and ironically from North America while the Muslims are being shown the door. Macron's turned out to be a sly political fox, he pretended to be centrist but on culture and demographics he's more hard core conservative than Le Pen could have ever dreamed of being herself, and he's using clever measures to throw out the Muslims. For him it's more a matter of business and attracting tourists and workers to France, but whatever the reason, it works. Oh, and the taxes? I pay much less taxes in France than California or New York, both of which I used to work in. The numbskulls among the reflexive conservatives love to cite the claimed high taxes to Euro-bash. But when you put all the different American taxes on the ledger, including Medi/Soc Security, Americans pay more but get a lot less. There is no sensible reason not to come here, especially if you want to start a family, which we indeed still can and should.

Anglo Feminazis like Chanty Binx claim victimhood under the gender version of Marxism, but support ultra-Capitalist policies like a police state to protect mostly white upper class women. You never hear Chanty Binx complain about the plight of the poor and racialized Canadians and Americans, but focus on only white feminism and how to oppress everyone else's freedom of speech in the name of white feminist rhetoric.

"I get why some men go MGTOW, if they're stuck in the Anglo-sphere that may be their only alternative. But far better is to do what their ancestors did but in reverse, leave the North American cultural swamp and migrate out of the country, head back to Europe outside the British Isles"

It's getting worse for men to obtain residency and citizenship outside of their countries of birth and origin. With Trump promoting nationalism and causing an after-effect of Anti-American hatred, it will be extremely difficult for American (and to some extent Canadian) men to migrate to foreign countries unless he has family or connections to obtain citizenship.

At least 400 men in Toronto alone die every year from suicide, but you rarely hear this from your local news who encourage millions of men to enter a vortex of hell Canadian catchphrase "Come to Canada". Married men should not Come to Canada because Hell is waiting for them as soon as they land at Toronto.

Appendix C: George 15 January 2018 at 17:47

Altho Europe may not be happy about Trump's nationalism much, the Europeans and Euro authorities still don't look down on Americans or Canadians as a whole, especially when they want to leave America and come to work in Europe. If anything the opposite, they see all the worsening turmoil in America as an opportunity to recruit mostly skilled, hard working and capable immigrants who tehmselves usually have European ancestry.

I in fact help out with informal residency permit consultation for US and Canadian citizens looking to move to Scandinavia, Belgium and the Netherlands, and the big majority have had no trouble getting residency or citizenship, in the past year at least it's gotten easier. France for ex. is aggressively out recruiting skilled and trained Americans, Canadians and Brits to come there and paying them pretty well. Sweden where I currently work has a similar program as do the Netherlands and Belgium. Germany and Austria are also big supporters of the blue card program that brings in skilled workers. Even if your not super skilled, sign up for some classes, they let you work part time and save up, and you can use that as a bridge to pick up the language, always a huge plus and then find work to help settle down.

Picking up at least some of the language is also a plus to help dispel all the bad information and fake news about Europe that's all over the US and UK, including in MSM outlets. Like the OP was saying Breitbart does tell a lot of un PC truth but they've got a serious blindspot on Europe. Both Breitbart and liberal mainstream media like CNN, Time Magazine, Guardian and NBC ran some completely made up story about how Sweden had passed a law requiring a formal signed written contract to have consent for sex. Because I'd learned Swedish I instantly knew this whole claim was absolute bullshyte, turned out there were a couple Swedish tabloids that put up salacious stories about a proposed law in December that was focussed on protections in the adult film and other industries. And it didn't even take the form of a law, just proposals and increased protections.

So the US and British media completely mistranslated the story and then echoed each other to misreport it. This is "professional" journalism in the Anglo world for you, since most of their editors don't know Swedish or other languages they constantly report fake shyte about foreign countries. The Swedes maybe aren't quite as open about sexuality and frowning on the #me too crap as the French, Spaniards or Italians, but they and the other Scandinavians are practical people and mature about sex and sexual matters. All the more reason to learn the language here, it'll give you a leg up on coming here.

Appendix D: Ripper <u>17 January 2018 at 23:45</u>

Have to admit I'm taking a measure of perverse pleasure in the ludicrous extremes that the #metoo shitstorm is going with this Aziz Ansari mess. It's damn obvious that he had a bad date that didn't meet the girl's expectations, the kind of thing that happens to anyone and everyone at some point, from Joe Schmoe mechanic up to brad Pitt. And now because of this extreme stupidity and the blood stained minefield that Anglosphere dating has become, this blown out of proportion incident and the ones to come are going to single handedly bring down the Anglosphere. Destroy the Anglosphere, in fact, as in make it non-viable as a working society.

For women, now no man can possibly go and be "woke" enough to read her mind and all her nonverbal signals, so now every single man on a date is a rapist in the making. Every. single. one.

And of course now men are catching on to this utter no win situation in American dating and Anglosphere dating in general, and opting out. Completely. It is way to farking dangerous to even consider the madness of dating from now on. Ever.

So we've reached the point now where girls and women in the Anglosphere are condemned to a future of becoming celibate cat ladies. While men in the Anglosphere will indeed have no option but to go MGTOW, unless of course they move out of it like you guys are recommending. Notable that now, even dating or casual association at the workplace or socially is becoming far too dangerous for men in the Anglosphere. Ironically this will at least spare men the hazard of getting married in the Anglosphere with the, more probable than not, divorce and bankrupting alimony and child support to follow.

So the Anglosphere is officially dead. Or at least on its deathbed.

The Anglosphere is collapsing before our eyes. Stick a fork in it. Good riddance.

Any civilization so utterly dumb and self-destructive that it makes it impossible for men and women to have basic sexual relations and childbearing without a gazillion layers of bottled up social acrimony, mixed signals, mindreading and flaring resentments is too damn stupid, lame and pathetic to survive. You made some nice contributions to civilization at one point, Anglosphere, but now you've completely forfeited any right to survive with this absolute bullshit. You guys are right btw, the one solution for Anglosphere men at this point is taking off for distant shores and different cultures. Give me France any day with the majesty and nuance of a superhot bikini model like Laetitia Casta speaking out against the stupidity of this "movement", joined by her graceful, elegant sisters like Catherine Deneuve and the thousands of other French women who've called bullshit. Let's not jut talk about this here to our own choir, let's get onto other forums, Reddit and the chans, write letters to the editor or even newspaper and magazine articles- if you want to have a halfway normal love and working life these days, and real relationships as humans have had for millennia, you need to get out of the Anglosphere. There is no other way. This goes both for men and for the remaining sensible women in the Anglophere. Leave it. This is our era's "Go West, young man". We have to leave the civilizational shithole of the Anglosphere, there is no other way anymore.

To you American c***s and Anglosphere losers in general, the French are showing us what real women, with class and confidence, have understood for eons courtship, love and mating are a dance, a delicate and often misunderstood dance of seduction, and any civilization depends on it for its own survival. The puritanical and Victorian fainting couch f---witness of the Anglosphere was a poison pill for the civilization for the beginning, that seems to have been activated into a death blow for the Anglo world when added to fourth wave feminism, neo-

Leftism and the corporate "throw 'em under the bus" attitude of US and Anglosphere "money above people" corporations.

Anglo fools at one point thought their civilization was superior to the French, Germans, Spaniards, Italians and Portuguese. But now with all the Anglo men (and halfway reasonable women) realizing they can find a sane society only in places like France, Germany, Portugal, Italy, Spain and South America and Asia, the Anglosphere is going to see a massive, increasing exodus of millions of its people, leaving only the non-reproducing dregs behind. No sympathy from me, the Anglosphere has slit its own throat.

Appendix E: Phil <u>19 January 2018 at 20:46</u>

Another expat here, visiting the US again in the #metoo age of misery, can confirm everything above. As smart as you guys observations have been, I'm not even sure your observant words capture how beyond miserable the US and Anglo world is compared to not only Europe's mainland but also Russia, Brazil, Argentina, Chile, and most of East and Southeast Asia. I've seen it every time I return to the US, but now more than ever before, the contrast is extreme, the metoo mess is directly impacting completely normal, nice and good people in the worst possible way. In Belgium where I now work, and this goes equally for Germany where I was posted at 3 years ago, the culture is a world away from the non stop gloom of the US where I grew up. And the picture y'all posted at the top is so on-target! In Germany and Belgium you run into hot girls like that all the time, fit and trim, wearing thong bikinis out in public, strong and confident women but also sweet and sexy, genuine and happy to interact with men. Not to mention more true blondes than anywhere in the US but they're also intelligent enough to have a real conversation with. People are ambitious and motivated and they do work hard to advance their careers, but men and women know how to eat, dance, enjoy other's company. Oh, and to have sex like normal human beings. Belgian and German girls love for men to hit on them, yes they want you to take care of yourself, stay neat and in shape, be ambitious and have at least some game, and eventually you gotta pick up some of the language(s) (French and/or Flemish in Belgium depending, obviously German in Germany or east Belgium). But they don't expect you to read their minds and they don't call out harassment for flirting even at the workplace, heck if there's a hot girl on your project team both the men and the women in the office will be puzzled if you don't ask her out at least once. The pretty femmes even in the small towns in Wallonia (south part of Belgium where I am now), or western Germany (Nordrhein Westfalen for any y'all traveling this way), will just casually stroll out in a little string bikini onto the side streets on a warm Saturday, far from the beach, just for the sake of being sexy, nobody bats eyelashes.

And back in America? Oh, mon Dieu, quelle difference! Americans nowsadays are tight, anxious, looking over their shoulders, #metoo and the media lynch mob has everything to do with it. Men in America, and it seems like about everywhere in Anglosphere, can't date for fear of having any slight misconstruance or bad communication aired out as dirty laundry on Fabricatebook- oh, I mean "Facebook" or Twitter or the extreme feminist blogs the next day. Even normal women are constantly under pressure from their "feminist sisters" to "you go girl" and find any reason they can to make the men around them miserable. Both men and women in America are miserable at the work place, can't even look at each other without the spectre of harassment coming up. What's worse, the feminist radicals at Vox, Bustle, TheVerge, Ohnotheydidn't, Vulture and the shrill echo-chambers of the FBverse and Twitterverse are fanning the flames, to encourage women in North America to "name and shame" every single man they've had the slightest unpleasant encounter with over the past 2 decades, and any going forward. Sadly it seems like this is spreading to everywhere in the Anglosphere. And to Israel from what my friends down there are saying, seems like they're now an extension of the Anglosphere and they're getting a lot of our worst elements, turned up a bit to be even worse.

So, I guess here's the summary-line for you poor souls cursed with a Y chromosome living in the US or Canada, and it sounds like Israel or Britain too. In the #metoo era, your next date, work place interaction, water cooler conversation, any interaction private or public with a women even if it went well- it's now fair game to be "outed" with your name and pic attached, on social media, by these lynch mob witch hunts. That's seriously where the media and movement are going. I kid you not. And it's dangerous. In polls done of Millennials, almost 40 percent believe even a guy just winking or giving a compliment on appearance to a woman is now sexual harassment. Note the poll's of both sexes, and since men overwhelmingly disagree, that means a scary huge majority of young women think this. Plus, black and Latina women are actually more sensible when you break down the poll's tabs, they don't subscribe to the "everything a man does is harassment" line and a much smaller minority of them say this. So, when you break the poll numbers down, 80 percent of Millennial white girls in the United States and Canada are ready to spring sexual harassment charges on you if you just wink or them, hold a door for them or say they look nice. And even worse, to publicly humiliate you by name in social media and make you a pariah and unemployable. Stay away from Anglo girls if you're in the US, Canada or UK, you're inviting disaster!

Funnily enough, the girl I'm now dating steady with in Belgium is an Australian girl. But the thing is, she's been here a few years and "gone native" so culturally she's like the Belgians now and the Germans next door. And it's night and day. Just to give you sense of how cool it is here and in Germany compared to the misery and drudgery of the Anglosphere toil, I love my gf now, but in keeping with Belgian and German custom, she's totally cool with me checking out other girls occasionally. She's even cool with me banging another hottie from time to time, just so long as it turns me on enough that I get aroused around her and she stays the top girl. To Americans it seems like it's an "open relationship" with Belgian girls on the side, but that's not how they see it here, the Europeans as a whole just see it is people being sexual as they normally are. My gf now even goes to strip clubs with me from time to time- and she's the one who picks them out! And nobody finds it unusual. I get 6 week's vacation, similar to what I got in Germany, I play a ton of sports but never have to worry about nutso medical bills if I get banged up, I make a lot of money in my job and they encourage starting a new business here, the food and wine are great, people are friendly and not at each other's necks attacking like in the US. My taxes are maybe a little higher than they were back in Florida for me but not that much higher and I get so much more for it here. (My taxes in Germany were even a little lower but I still got the health care and vacation bennies, plus free Master's classes.) And when my gf and I settle down and have kids, she'll have many months to stay home and stay with them and still be able to return to her job if she wants later on. I will never go back to North America now. If there's one place in the Anglosphere I have a bit more respect for it's Australia, not just due to my gf but the Aussies seem a little more rational in general, I see that with my gf's friends when they come here. But depressingly I feel like the cultural obsessions of the US and North America have a way of infecting the whole Anglosphere so it sounds like all the metoo and general misandry misery of North America is heading for Australia soon too.

Should probably add, since a lot of you guys are probably wondering, I know a lot of you guys have talked about moving out to other countries, but I bet a lot of poor souls stuck in North America are wondering how you actually do that. It's not as hard as a lot of people say it is. Obviously if you're very high-skilled it's easier to get a work visa sponsored by a company, and obviously engaging or marrying a local girl, or just having an ancestor somewhere with ethnic roots in the country you want to go to. But you don't really need any of that. The way My gf and I both did it, we signed up for courses at the unis, first in Germany for me, and then did internships and made contacts while doing language classes. I studied regular business administration at a public university in the US, nothing special, but I got into Europe just taking higher level classes and took it from there. Another technique, express an interest in starting a business in many countries. Or just start out working in one of the old Iron Curtain eastern European countries, like even Lithuania or Estonia, Hungary, Bulgaria, doing anything, science work, English teaching, tutoring, whatever gets you started. As soon as you get a work or residency permit in any country, even if it's like Slovenia or east Poland, you're good to go form there to move to any other country in the EU.

And what I said above, all the invigorating and and healthy cultural elements of Belgium and Germany, and of France like the guys before pointing out? They apply to everywhere in Europe, at least aside from Britain. The Nordic countries and Holland really are awesome too, even though they have some of the stupid cultural flottsam from the Anglo countries they water ti way down and still have common sense, plus men and women are a whole lot more open and free around sexual matters, and they're just culturally stronger. Italy and the other Mediterranean countries are a whole lot like France, just with more distinctive cuisine and more sunshine, and improving economies to work in too. All good choices, you won't go wrong working and staying anywhere in the EU. Not hard, and it's well worth it!

Appendix F: Anonymous <u>19 January 2018 at 23:47</u>

Truer words rarely spoken, thanks also for the tips on actually getting to Europe. I'm off to Norway myself next year to start work with one of the oil firms there, though eventually planning to settle down in either Sweden or Finland. Tons of reasons, you all covered most, and indeed the Nordic countries are under rated as good destinations. Beneath the surface of their goofy social experiments they're solid places to raise families. That's ultimately why I'm leaving Texas and the US in general, I don't want my kids to be raised in such a toxic environment as North America is become.

I've also done some lurking on the fem-crazy Twitters and blogs, and indeed between having to vomit to get rid of the foul taste of their hatred for both real men and women, I got a taste of what the #timesup and #metoo zealots are planning next.

Now they're pushing for female prosecutors to indict Aziz Ansari formally on rape or sexual assault charges, to make an example of him. And apparently a number of women DA's and prosecutors are up with that, got to prove their cred with the metoo mob sisterhood.

And Ansari's just the start, he's the example to be set and from there, women will be able to retroactively withdraw consent in the United States and Canada after any sex act. No statute of limitations. So 20 years later a woman could regret a sex act with you, or just make it up, and then boom you get your ass hauled into court, wind up on the sex offender registry and publicly shamed and ruined.

Oh but wait, there's still more. Several contributors to the blogs working as prosecutors or trial lawyers are going to specialize in marital rape accusations. So now, for any reason, a date gone a little bad, a wife just wanting an excuse to smear her husband and get alimony, just a woman seeking attention which is extremely common, boom, there's a fast path to a rape indictment against an innocent man since consent can be arbitrarily and retroactively withdrawn.

Feminists in North America are now in the process of formally making sex equal rape, and the man has no defense. So I guess the fertility bearing rate of the Anglosphere is about to drop to 0.5. Oh, except for the Africans, Latino groups, native Americans and of course the Muslims, who ironically enough, actually will mass rape and then impose a real shari'a patriarchy on the stupid Anglobitches who no longer have the protection of the men or more rational women who've all left. North America is toast. Leave while you can.

Haha, looks like some of the w's on my rickety old keyboard got switched up with v's, just swap in w's and it'll read right. Though some of the v typo's make it read unintentionally funny, especially where the marriage part is concerned.

Appendix G: **James Bond** <u>21 January 2018 at 03:38</u>

Excellent observations. It's getting to the point in Anglo countries where it's dangerous for men to interact with women. No wonder why so many men are going MGTOW in the US, Canada, Australia and the UK.

Soon women in Anglo countries will be asking, "Where have all the good men gone?" The answer is they will have moved to non Anglo countries or have gone MGTOW.

Appendix H1- Anonymous <u>21 January 2018 at 07:29</u>

This is the most delusional collection of posts I ever seen. As an European born guy and blocked here in the "eurosphere" all the statements made here are, ALL, against reality. Europe is not the Philippines or the pre- Mohamed Bin Salman Saudi Arabia.
I don't even know if I will have the strenght to write everything because every single word is comfutable and overally it's an huge work. My english is bad? I can't give a fuck.

The North American Expat named Anonymous tell us how the family laws in the USA have been rigged by feminism and everything is against men. The fact is, the very same is in most part of europe, above all france, where it's illegal to make DNA tests to be sure that your divorced wife's child is your own. In Europe, with few exceptions, the family laws are wronged and unfair like in the USA. Why? Because they are copy-cats. The same about so called family violence, so called rape (regretted sexual intercourses, etc...), so called women's rights (like reserved working places), so called pedophilia (AOC is lower only on the papers), and everything else. Meanwhile right now we will have the very same american situation about the so called sexual harassment because of the #metoo peice of theatre.
In many countries, like France, approaching a gilr will soon be a crime, if you don't meet her standards. Scefically, France, a country without age of consent (!!! so you would think it's a good place for men, since AOC and marriageable age for post pubescent females is the indicator of the respect of men's right, the lower it is the more men's rights are respected), has already criminalized the purchase of sexual intercourse from whores. French female policy makers stated that they are fed enough of men and unwanted attention. So, even withouth AOC, France is a shithole place for men. But, tell me you moron, in which way a country ruled by a cuck, who is a victim of real pedophilia because he is being molested by the teacher he married since when he was 15, can be better than US or Canada? Do you think it's natural to be married

242

with a mummy 26 years your senior? In which way such a guy could improve men's condition?

About the muslims, what you say about cucked Macron is true and you should be sad of that, but you as american moron who enjoys bomibng muslims, don't understand that Isalm is the last line of defence of men's rights.

So, North American Expat named Anonymous, don't teach us about how much europe and france are wondeful, just because your frog wife is still not annoyed by you. Give time to time, and she will steal everything from you. To me, you look like more to a guy who, 10 years ago, left the sinking ship because his common skills would have been soon replaced by a typical BODAWAY without even leaving India to move in the silicon valley. So you found refuge in a backwarded european country (aka france) in which the eagle in your passport is enough to get a well payed job. Well done, but don't say bullshit about the feminist europe, please.

• The Ripper tells us that: "Give me France any day"
Well, I already wrote about France, but, man, I tell you, Mrs Casta is facing a bad backlash for her words. She was hated 20 years agou because she was too much sexy being so young, beautiful and big tits; now they have a political reason to hate her more. The same faith for based mommy Catherine Deneuve. You don't have idea when the feminist machine catch on you with all its force.

The fact that a few real women tell the truth, doesn't mean that the mayority agrees.

Go east, man. (note: the soviet version of feminism was not hatred on men...).

You would think that it's over, that the sitaution couldn't get worse, right? No, we have the Expat Phil that starts on digging shit.
Europe mainland? srsly?
France is described up.
Sweden is the feminists' hornets' nest, they were the first to cimininalize the customer of whores and right now the govt is

making casual sex a crime unless you sign a contract with the girl/woman. The cuck governor of sweden is proud of such a new law.

Norway? Ask Eivind Berge.

Italian courts believe to every possible shit the females say, so the last one is that a pair of cops have been accused of rape by 2 american (!!!) girls even if the messages on phones state differently; they will lose the uniform and risk jail (not that I have any simpathy for the pigs...). If they catch you cheating on your wife, the court will make you lose everything.

In Greece there is the witch hunt against men who buy sex from refugees females.

German women balme the misconduct of muslim men against white men patriarchy. Reseved train wagons, reserved swimming pools, free sexual harassment compliants to the cops in the case you don't meet the girl's standards, and so on... Many of them treat you like a sexual object, it happened me with a girl, for whom I was just her fetish; and some turned muslim (like that very same girl I dealt with, and) like the 16 yo girl named Malvina who appeared in KIKA, dating a muslim guy (alt rightists made up a shitstorm because the guy looks "too old for her"... just to keep up with the AOC theme and the cultural imperialism of the USA and UK).

Do you really like to be surrounded by bikini girls whose ass and tits will never been yours? Are you a masochist? That's why I support a forced modest dress code, even more in feminist countries of the west.

Should I go further?

LatinoAmerica? again, srsly? Have you ever considered the helluva bunch of feminist new laws passed everywhere? From Venezuela to Colombia? (so you can't balme communism). And right now that we have the worst pope ever? The black pope bergoglio? a men hater feminist scumbag like never before. Today he advocated for even stricter feminist laws for fight what they call "femicide".

So, if you are a fit, good looking anglo male cunt, don't teach us about how wonderful european women are, because if you can interest to a german or a french girl, you can interest to a texan girl from a conservative rural area too.

Also, pay attention on writing to take care of yourself, because I got the interest of that german girl for something that is the opposite of being fit. It's all about her own standards, brothers. Fat or fit, tall or short, etc... and if she changes her mind, just start on preying your gods, because it will be rape, even years later.

I only agree with you Phil, about the Israel and the Jewish conspirancy. Israeli men are in deep shit like the rest of us, and I don't give a shit if the israeli women at the end want to settle and have kids to fuck up arabs in the numbers because it's a patriotic duty (and that's true, so you have many ppl messing about the jewish conspiracy). They are over 30 years old creeps in the last 3 days of fertility, looking nasty.

James Bond, the best MGTOW is Expat MGTOW (that indeed is not real MGTOW if you still date or are interested in girls, that is something natural and normal), but only in countries where feminism is still not strong, or your assets are enough to make you to have a safe life (examples: philippines and surroundings). Check out the videos of MGTOW Expat, Kris Cantu and friends. But Europe is not an option (at least western europe and places like poland or latvia).

Finally, remember, you all angloamerican patriotic male cunts: this situation it's all your and your own fault only. It started after the 9/11 with the collusion between feminism and imperialism against muslims. If you ever served into an armed force of USA, UK and NATO, you are the source of the problem.

Why in most part of muslim countries men didn't commit suicide before the imposition of feminism by the west via the bombs?

Allah Hafiz, brothers.

Appendix I1: Gearman 21 January 2018 at 19:27

Anon,

Your posts are a prime exhibit of the binary, rigid, closed-minded, unrealistic thinking that blinds far too many MGTOW's and makes you miserable, since you're missing a really important nuance of the real world that Rookh and the others here are waking you up to. You couldn't be more wrong about the non-Anglo West especially France, Germany and continent of Europe, it's miles ahead of the Anglosphere in every way, and much more family-friendly and fairer to men and fatherhood. To you, everywhere in the West and even most of the rest of the world is "bad" if it has even a little bit of feminism to it, and even then a vague, undefined sort of feminism that you can't even provide details on (since you obviously haven't even been to these places).

Again, you're stuck in that kind of damaging, extreme "either-or" thinking that's also peculiar to the Anglosphere, and it will make you miserable and fail at everything you do, wherever you are—you have to break out of that superficiality and do deeper analysis. What Rookh and everyone else is making clear here, it's not feminism alone that's so damaging and wrecking to the lives and livelihoods of modern men, and to women and families, but the combination of a particular type of feminism—the adversarial driven "us against them" third and fourth-wave of the Anglo world— combined with Anglo Puritanism, cultural Marxism, the common law tradition (which makes divorce and the "metoo" witch hunt profitable to the extremists pushing it), the cuck chivalry white knights who enable "have your cake and eat it too" hypocrisy of Anglo feminists (claim to be strong and independent but need permanent alimony after a divorce) and the crony corporate capitalism of the Anglo world which sees politically incorrect men as easy targets to vulture off of. All of these things are unique to the Anglosphere, and they're what makes Anglosphere feminism uniquely toxic.

What stands out most about your posts is their vagueness, the way you decry "feminism" in the non-Anglo West in general but fail to note precisely why it's upsetting. This marks you as a kind of autistic type who would be miserable wherever you go. As a contrast, look at the specifics everyone else is providing on why Anglosphere feminism in particular is toxic, and why it leads to SPECIFIC POLICIES that make families and normal interaction with females impossible in the Anglosphere. Divorce, for example: the permanent alimony, extreme excessive child support without caps (to fund the ex-wife's excesses not the kids), the stupid "spousal support to keep up previous lifestyle" standard, going to prison if you can't pay alimony or child support, the "deadbeat Dad" meme, Dads consistently losing custody, super-expensive divorces, and an insane high rate of divorce (more than half and rising of marriages). ALL THESE MISERIES ARE VIRTUALLY UNIQUE TO THE ANGLOSPHERE! That's what you don't get. Even though divorce happens in the non-Anglosphere West, it's much less common, it's far less expensive, it doesn't involve the financial wrecking ball of the Anglo West, joint-sharing custody, capped child support (a "playboy principle" that prevents a gold-digging ex-wife from any "profit" from divorce), no slagging on men after divorce, mediation, much more amicable. When divorce happens outside the Anglosphere, it's a minor blip rather than the complete devastation that couples in the Anglosphere routinely experience. And that's because the non-Anglo West has avoided the very division-promoting and hypocritical style of feminism of the Anglosphere.

Appendix H2: Anonymous 21 January 2018 at 07:34

Gearman, you must be the typical angloamerican miserable loser moron I described before. You write about things you absolutely don't know.

I can't be wrong about places in which I live my daily life. Oppositely, you are completely wrong about place you never visited beside when you were dressing your uniform of vile imperialist bitch.

You and the other angloamerican morons who wrote here before have a wrong idea of europe due to the privileges that the angloamerican passports give you, since you don't even try to understand what is going on here.

You write about that imaginery thing you call "cultural marxism", but you never read a Marx's single line in your whole life.

"Cultural marxism" simply doesn't exist; and if you believe that you are delusional like those who think that SJWs are commies.

But what you patriotic miserable losers fail to understand is that the whole feminism thing was exported in the same way you exported democracy. Europe is passing everywhere specific gender laws to protect, give privileges to females at expenses of men, and I'm not about the family laws that allows females to financially rape their ex husbands, which are 30-40 years old. The aim is to install females in a position of untouchability and omnipotence. Stalking, sexual harassment, rape convictions without evidences, different penalties for same crimes, even no penalties at all, age of consent arbitally raised, harsher punitions than those written in the laws for crimes committed against females, etc...

And this shit is not an european "privilege" because YOU EXPORTED ALL THESE MISERIES OUTSIDE THE ANGLOSPHERE VIA SOFT POWER IN THE WEST AND BOMBS IN THE MIDDLE EAST! YES, YOU MALE ANGLOAMERICUNTS WHO THINK THAT YOUR DAUGHTER/MOTHER/SISTER ARE PRINCESSES AND NOT THE SLUTS THEY ARE!

Check the suicide rates, you miserable loser.

Appendix J1: Legal Eagle <u>22 January 2018 at 18:24</u>

Anonymous

It's getting hard to tell whether you're being deliberately annoying or you really are as obtuse as you sound. Or perhaps you're an agent provocateur and a Cultural Marxist in reality, coming onto these blogs to spread disinformation and discourage MGTOW's and expats. Having used to associate with types like you, I'm starting to suspect the latter, since your techniques and style of writing-is EXACTLY what we were taught to use in Agitprop for the new left. It's You are a textbook case of agitprop to try to hijack a movement: full of generalizations, lack of specifics, thorough obfuscations, ad hominem personal attacks on people offering reasoned, seasoned advice, extreme stances with no shades of gray, unbalanced pessimism, defeatism, outrageous claims.

Either you're a Cultural Marxist yourself in disguise, or you're a paid troll for the big corps that fear mass US expatriatiion or perhaps even on the payroll of anti-Western activists like Soros.

Nobody could be as obtuse, obnoxious, misinformed, dumb, arrogant, pessimistic and clueless as you AND be so urgent to spew your ignorance all over a board where people are making informed discussion. It just doesn't happen IRL. Anyone who's spent even a day in a country outside the Anglosphere knows it's radically different in other countries especially with the way they handle marriages and claimed harassment because the cultures, laws and policies are so different. People here are pointing this out not just through experience but through concrete references to laws, policies and customs that make them different. Yet your stock response basically boils down to, "Because I can find a single example of a feminist in a foreign country, that means all foreign countries are just like the Anglosphere with divorce and #metto".

Never mind the fact that (which is the only point that matters) such voices have no influence in making actual policy outside the Anglosphere because the overall culture in the non-Anglosphere, including in the West, is so different and does not allow career, finance and life-ruining divorce, alimony and harassment penalties like in the US. That is the ONLY THING THAT MATTERS in the real world, not your obsession with finding a single example of a feminist overseas who mimics the US insanity around #metoo and divorce policies. Stop and think and you'll realize this is WHY thousands of prominent women (and 99% of the population, both male and female) in the non-Anglo countries reject Anglosphere-style divorce and #metoo insanity.

Whatever your real intentions you are absolutely not an MGTOW like you claim you are, and you are adding nothing productive to a serious discussion.

The only other possibility I can think of is this is your twisted way of trying to tell people here that the Muslim world is the only alternative to the Anglosphere. Sorry, but no thanks. People here are explicitly looking for expat options in the West or other First-World nations, yes mostly Europe but also Latin America and Asia, in part because like others have been telling you here, there's not a single stable, technologically advanced Muslim nation and Muslim culture is way too disposed against science, technology and modernity in general.

Plus the Muslim world has an even uglier version of the very Anglo puritanical elements we're trying to avoid and have caused a lot of this mess in the Anglosphere. And like someone said, now the Muslim world is also falling apart culturally and seeing it's own version of feminism arise, which is more like the poisonous feminism of the Anglosphere instead of the healthier, balanced version of the non-Anglosphere.

Sorry, but no thanks. For our purposes here the best expat options by far are still in the West or Asia or Latin America, just outside the Anglosphere. If you want to evangelize and tell people to join the Islamic world, go do it somewhere else. You are adding nothing productive here.

Appendix H3: Anonymous <u>23 January 2018 at 05:15</u>

@Legal eagle
You are a complete loser and a moron, that's the reason you moved out, since your poor skills in law. You are so uncompetent that don't know the legal systems basics.
But, I tell you, fighting my facts with your low level slogans (that are the very same of gearman's...) won't help and makes you look like a typical feminist "activist".

Of course, if there will be a men's libe, it will be from Muslim world fighting against you vile american scumbags.

You --> in the Jahannam.

Appendix I2: Gearman 21 January 2018 at 19:30

You see? Specifics. In specific policy which is what actually affects people in the real world, the Anglosphere is concretely far worse for men and families in general. More specifics, as the same goes for the metoo hysteria. Once again, look at where metoo has caught on, and become an ever more massive wrecking ball that's making it impossible for men and women to have normal relationships, posing concrete danger for men's livelihoods and making "sexual harassment" and "sexual misconduct" a weapon that can be used anywhere, at anytime, in any workplace or for any reason, with an accuser having total power to ruin an accused without any evidence even for things that may (or may not) have happened decades ago.

Where is the #metoo McCarthyism taking place, anon? It's almost exclusive to the Anglosphere, and also to Israel (which has more or less become an extension of the Anglosphere in recent times). Where is #metoo being rejected, or at least diluted, mocked and shoved aside so much that it has little effect? In France, in Italy, in Austria and Germany, in eastern Europe, the Nordics, in Spain, in Portugal, in Greece, in China, in Japan, in Korea, in Thailand, in Vietnam, in Brazil, in Latin America. Even the Anglo MSM is constantly whining about how #metoo and #timesup "just isn't catching on" or "just won't translate" outside North America, the UK, Israel and the Anglosphere as a whole. There's a reason for that, again the toxic feminism of the Anglosphere is a world away from that in the non-Anglo West. You see? Specifics. This is what people in the real world care about, not the vague "everywhere if feminist" junk you're spouting.

Just to elaborate, for people in the Anglosphere making concrete decisions about becoming expats, they don't get to choose some "pie in the sky" fantasy like what you have in mind, they have to choose specific countries. That's why specifics like the details above matter. And if you'll bother to pay attention, you'll see that the specifics of the non-Anglo West make them very appealing to us. In actual practice we look for first world countries with a high standard of living, where we can get a good job in our fields, but without the toxic feminism of the Anglosphere. And the non-Anglo West meets all our requirements for that. Yes, even Scandinavia does, even more so elsewhere in Europe, as well as Brazil and much of Latin America, China, Korea, Japan, even Russia and much of eastern Europe. All of these countries to varying extents have systems that are a result of the Enlightenment.

And as a result of the way information spreads, and modern living standards have evolved, yes all of the countries in the non-Anglo West, South America, Russia and eastern Asia are going to have some degree of feminism in them and women wanting to be somewhat independent. But that in itself doesn't make them bad places, in fact if it encourages women to be truly independent and not try to leech off husbands during marriage or after a divorce, it boosts the living stands of men and fathers, and makes it safer and a more encouraging environment to start families. This is the "Sweden type paradox" a lot of expats are bringing up, even though feminism is strong up in the Nordics, it's not the toxic Anglosphere type up there because it's not hypocritical. Women who claim independence actually have to be that way, so there's no alimony, limited sort of child support and cultures that are quite favorable to fathers, paternity leave, and men's and father's rights. I also know plenty of Anglo men who've moved to Scandinavia for their jobs or to marry local girls there, and they're all very happy. Even the divorcees have emerged with no trouble at all, they're still able to raise their kids and start new families.

Appendix H3: Anonymous <u>22 January 2018 at 14:34</u>

Where is the #metoo McCarthyism ? Everywhere, idiot.
What about: #IchAuch the bitches from germany,
#BalanceTonPorc the bitches from france, #QuellaVoltaChe the
bitches from italy, #YoTambien the bitches from spain and
latinoamerica, #أنا_كمان in places like dubai, UEA and egipt (where
so called rape is punished with death penalty after that you
imperialst bitches overthrew Morsi and backed the terrorist Al
Sisi), ... only in the anglosphere? what the fuck are you taking
about?
In europe females are standing in grat masses against white men.
And I'm sure that they are the same in india, thailand, philippines...
But you can't be aware of this shit since you are into your self
rightious agloamerican bubble.
We have expats everywhere here, oh, no not here anymore cause
they r gone LOL! you miserable idiot. In europe you and ppl like
the angloamerican men who moved in scandinavia are fine (but
wait when their gf or wives get tired of them and you will see)
because of your passport, otherwise you would be treated as like
us or even worse because you are shit.
There is no such thing as "good grade of feminism", and mislims
know well. The problems start from the right to vote but the real
shit is due to the last 15 years work of angloamerican moronic
soldiers, the scum of humanity, imposing the feminist agenda after
the 9/11 whorldwide, and the pro west propaganda and soft powers
(feminist NGOs).
In place like philippnies, feminism is already there, but westies can
have good life if the have enough assets.

Appendix I3: Gearman <u>21 January 2018 at 19:39</u>

Men in the Anglosphere, as a major contrast, have tons of
responsibilities and no rights, and are openly scorned by the
culture, seen as little more than walking ATM's to tap by the
vultures of society, while women shun femininity while at the
same time demand that Anglo men shoulder both old
responsibilities of traditional men and an ever-growing and
impossible laundry list of impossible responsibilities of new
"woke" men, that's what the toxic feminism of the Anglosphere
has brought about. And the media, public officials and useless,
short term driven corporations pile on this tendency to make things
even more miserable for Anglo men, they're an easy target after all
to milk for their financial assets and what's become slave labor.
All this while men in the non-Anglo West, South America and
Asia get to enjoy first-world living standards, good jobs and
normal relationships with women and families. Again this is even
the case in the Nordic countries, even though a lot of MGTOW
and self-claiming "conservative" morons are always trying to take
jabs at Sweden and Scandinavia, in practice they only can ever
come up with stupid anecdotes, inaccurate statistics or weird-
sounding special case laws or practices that, upon deeper
examination, turn out to have been mistranslated or made up
completely.

On the things that really affect men in a country, like divorce laws
or the poisonous sexual harassment atmosphere made worse by
#metoo, they're suddenly silent, and that's because the Nordic
countries in practice are better than the Anglosphere in real world
areas. Even more so in France, Germany, Spain, the Netherlands,
Belgium, Italy, eastern Europe, Brazil and most of South America
and East and Southeast Asia. Women in those countries still
embrace femininity, both traditional and modern, and while they
do embrace a modern level of independence, they're also very
favorable to men, fathers and families, discouraging divorce,
making it unprofitable and in general, having a healthy, normal

and common sense view of male-female relations that's a world away from the mass hysteria of the Anglosphere.

It's odd you heap praise on the Muslim countries for "a total lack of feminism" which isn't even accurate, but in reality, expats from the Anglosphere can't go there in practice because most of the Muslim world is a basketcase, too backward technologically, politically unstable, too little science and tech, too culturally different. You don't solve one extreme (Anglosphere toxic feminism) with the opposite extreme of the intellectual closure of Islam and the Muslim world. And if that wasn't enough, the Muslim world is also very puritanical like the Anglosphere—a big root of the problems in both. Yet now the Muslim world, too, is experiencing fast falling birth rates and it's own form of feminism creeping in, which guess what, looks a lot like toxic Anglosphere feminism because it has the same puritanical roots. The Muslim world would give Anglo expats the worst of the both worlds, a lack of technology and first world standards, but also a lot of the crazy Puritanism and now even feminism that hits the Anglo world.

In fact here's another bit for you, the Muslims are now largely moving out of Europe on the continent and going to other places. Even at its worst the Muslim population in France was totally exaggerated, real studies with professionals show it's actually as low as around 3 percent in France and Germany, but now even they're moving out, in the past year alone there's been a mass Muslim exodus from France and mass Muslim emigration from Europe in general. And guess where they're moving to? Yes, most are moving back to Muslim countries in the Middle East. But a big minority are actually moving to the US, Britain, Canada and other Anglosphere countries. Why? The imams say it straight—the puritanical traditions of the Anglosphere are more palatable for Muslim Sharia law, but Muslims can never fit into the much freer, normal and healthier, non-Puritanical societies of France, Germany, Netherlands, Italy and the Nordics.

Appendix H4: Anonymous <u>22 January 2018 at 14:57</u>

Stop whining bitch, about how tough you have, because it isn't.
Despite the arbitrary and inhuman aoc laws, america is kinda
pretty fine for smart men, since they have the pre marital contracts,
that in europe are illegal almost everywhere.
You speack like a machine so that you look like a feminist
yourself: "cultural marxism" "toxic feminism" (like if there was a
non toxic feminism) and shit on.
You miserable tradretarded keep up with the family shit and the
divorce bullshits, but the truth is that not only in the EU divorces
are raging everywhere, but ppl don't even marry anymore! They
just live together but since the govts are at the feet of females, such
type of way of live are enough to make the man responsible for the
woman in most countries, so even if you don't marry her, you will
have to support her even after she cheat on you or left you. Even
worse if you have kids.
Those are one of the many specific policies the Angoamerican
bitches exported on here. Just a few years ago everything was
different.
Scandinavia is the worst of the worst: it is the laboratory of
feminism, where the most extreme things are tested at first. In
Sweden, very soon, if you (not you if you have an angloamerican
passport) get laid with a girl, you will be punishable for "rape" at
her will unless you sign a contract before.

"Even more so in France, Germany, Spain, the Netherlands,
Belgium, Italy, eastern Europe [...]. Women in those countries still
embrace femininity,"

you are such a miserable fool... "YUROP" IS NOT DIFFERENT
OR IS EVEN WORSE THAN ANGOLOAMERICA! Here
females are racing to act like men in every possible field, not only
work, but even in romance.
I do praise real muslim countries, since there is no place for
feminism in there.

So I'm not prasing places like Egipt, MBS's Saudi Arabia, UAE, Dubai,... but I do praise Talibans' Afghanistan (that had nothing to do with 9/11 and terrorism, despite the official propaganda), the new direction of Pakistan or the new direction of Erdogan's Turkey after the coup attempt.
Every anti american / anti west place is good, indeed.
Great Iran, from the shias side.
While I'm more for places like in south asia (thai, philippines, etc...) I do love that there are people fighting against the western disvalues.
If you think that dressing modeslty is puritanism, you are a clown.

Your studies about migrations are real like ronald mcdonald. I invite you to check the Landings in south italy an spain or the eastern europe route (that you don't even know because of your ignorance). And the best part is that feminists are welcoming them and many are even converting to date muslim men.

Appendix I4: Gearman <u>21 January 2018 at 19:41</u>

As for places like the Philippines, yes they're nice places and I wouldn't discourage Anglo men from moving there if they have the means. But at this point, it's very hard to get a good job there that pays enough to live well as one expects in a first world country. I'm sorry to be brutally honest, and I don't believe this is the case with all or even most MGTOW's, but extremist MGTOW's like you will always be miserable because you simply aren't realistic. You divide the world into extremes, wanting a fantasy of a first world country that has zero feminism and women without any independence or all. The world simply hasn't evolved this way, and your binary, extremist view of the world will make "all or nothing" MGTOW's like you unhappy everywhere because you fail to embrace good alternatives for raising families that are right before your eyes.

Even worse, you do major damage to MGTOW in general by getting sucked into these kinds of superficial "either-or" distortions of reality. You remind me of the extremists who shout, "Sweden must be unacceptable because it has a lot of feminism and socialist programs", but failing to actually think and analyze, and realize like above, that beyond all the left vs right pissing contests, the specific "way" that Sweden's policies take shape lead to an environment that's surprisingly father-friendly and family-friendly. Why? BECAUSE SWEDEN AVOIDS THE TOXIC DIVORCE AND #METOO HARASSMENT "GET THE DEADBEAT" ENVIRONMENT OF THE ANGLOSPHERE. (And again note, other non-Anglo Western countries like France, Germany, Spain, Netherlands and Italy are a good deal better than Sweden.) It isn't just us here.

Read the things that Roosh Valizadeh posts up or the forum commenters are posting up on Rooshv forums or Return of Kings, or at Chateau Heartiste. It's not some nebulous "Western feminist culture" that's the problem for men in English-speaking countries.

It's that the Anglosphere, and specifically the Anglosphere, has made it far too dangerous even for normies—perfectly normal men who want to be husbands and fathers—to marry, have kids or even enter into normal dating relationships with women. The cost-benefit calculation shows it's far, far too dangerous to consider marriage or childbearing when you have a greater than even chance of winding up in poverty or even prison from marriage or having a kid in the Anglosphere, or losing your hard won career, earnings, reputation and savings from sexual harassment hysteria, even from casual dating or work interactions, that's only going to get even worse and more oppressive in the next few years. That's because of specific marriage, divorce and harassment policies particular to the Anglosphere and Israel, and those are a direct result of the unique toxic feminism combined with Puritanism, cultural Marxism, opponent-driven court system and common law that's unique to the Anglosphere and Israel.

The difference on this site and with this thesis, is that Rookh and the commenters here actually provide a concrete solution that's practical and can be realized by men in the real world. Yes, a lot of MGTOW's will be fine with just celibacy and Internet porn, but many MGTOW's still want to have emotional and physical relationships with women, and to start families. It's just in the Anglosphere, for good reason, they see no solution. Rookh and the many informed expats here provide the solution—moving out of the Anglosphere—and ways to practically accomplish it. By offering nothing but pessimism, extremist distortions and "they're all the same" or "all Western women are bad" falsehoods and overgeneralizations, you not only provide bad information to men, you turn them off of MGTOW.

Bottom-line is, In practice, the non-Anglo West (that is the continent of Europe) plus Brazil, most of South America and the advanced countries of east Asia, all provide a reasonable compromise of conditions that make them not only livable but prosperous first world countries for Anglo men to become expats in, both modern but also without the toxic feminism and toxic, "at each other's throats all the time" culture of the Anglosphere and of North America in particular. It's specific policies, like rational divorce and marriage policies and lack of the #metoo hysteria, in the non-Anglo West, Brazil/South America and most of Asia that give proof of this. Like most of the other posters here I've worked all over the world (photography and mechanical engineering in my case, contracts wherever I'm needed), and we're posting here to share that perspective to help a lot of you guys, as we know you're fearful that you can never safely have loving relations with women. We're here to help you realize that there are great alternatives for us. It's just that they have to be pursued outside of the Anglosphere, and especially in the non-Anglo Western countries of the continent in Europe and in Brazil and the rest of South America.

Appendix K: Anonymous 21 January 2018 at 23:24

As an Australian MGTOW, I agree with all of you that the women of the Anglosphere are bad and the #meetoo movement has gone too far. In fact, #meetoo and #timesup has been a boon for MGTOW in recent times as more men in the Anglosphere begin to realise that dating, relationships and marriage are no longer an option and would lead to financial and legal misery if things go wrong for no apparent reason.

However, I take what you all said about life in Western Europe and Scandinavia being better than the Anglosphere with a pinch of salt as these parts of the world are equally as feminist and misandrist as the Anglosphere (If you want proof of how bad things are for men in Sweden, look up the Swedish documentary "The Gender War" by Evin Rubar). Also, keep in mind that things may be good now where you currently are, but they will change 10 years down the track as more countries in Latin America, Easter Europe, East Asia, South-East Asia will adopt the feminist policies of the Anglosphere, Western Europe and Scandinavia (I remember hearing about feminism spreading from the Anglosphere and into the rest of the world from watching a few of Turd Flinging Monkey's YouTube videos).

Appendix H5: Anonymous <u>22 January 2018 at 15:09</u>

"BECAUSE SWEDEN AVOIDS THE TOXIC DIVORCE AND
#METOO HARASSMENT "GET THE DEADBEAT"
ENVIRONMENT OF THE ANGLOSPHERE"
I wrote for the well of other because if I were writing back to you
it would be a time loss because you are a pure miserable idiot.
SWEDEN HAS DIVORCES AND EVEN MORE HAS NO
MARRIAGES ANYMORE! YOU LIVE IN A FANTASY
WORLD. If you stare at a girl you can be jailed, if you approach a
girl and offer her a dirnk but you are not in her standards you can
be jailed, if you cum into a girl and she changes her mind while
you are cumming, you WILL BE JAILED (ask the HERO
JULIAN ASSANGE).
Sweden is the worst place ever, unless you are a dark skinned
alchol drinker fake muslim tugh.
Sweden govt even pay for artificial insemination of the old cunts
"who need no men".
As opposit of you, roosh moved out and experienced how europe
is a shithole today. Have you ever watched or follwed him
recently? and what about the "not bang" book series? Roosh V2.0
is pretty black pill, from "the game man, the game" to "feminism".

Here I post just facts. Pure and simple. There are no good western
women. Period.
Even some (because they are still not to the level of the western
ones, lukily) non western women who are "imported" (bcoz for
feminists is human traffiking) on here, after that they integrate the
locals, became cunts like the locals. They get divorce to steal the
money and shit...

The rest is your delusional fantasy. I'm sorry to burst your bubble.

Appendix L: Michigan Mike <u>23 January 2018 at 18:10</u>

Anonymous, for your own good, stop posting all your autistic ramblings here and take a good, long break from the Internet. Seriously. I worked for many years in an autism clinic and it's clear as day to anyone in the field that you have serious mental health issues whether related to autism, Asperger's syndrome or elsewhere on the autism spectrum disorder (ASD). I'm trying to help you here because people on most other forums let alone IRL will be much harsher with you, for your own sake, stop, take a break and get some help.

Take a step back and look at your rambling, bloviating posts on this site alone, and you'll see you're doing what's called perseveration and a failure of reality testing. Your long, uninformative, vague and desperate posts seem like "doing something" in your own mind, but they only invite derision and ridicule both form lurkers and posters here b/c you are clearly uninformed on the topic, and ramble on and on to display that fact.

Again, friendly advice, the same I've given to 100's of others in your shoes:

1. Take a good, long hiatus from the Internet, at least a week.
2. Talk to people in real life, person-to-person. Socialize.
3. When you do get back online, think about what other people are interested in and police what you write to be relevant, topical and informed. If you'd humiliate yourself IRL, don't put it online either.
4. When evidence clearly goes against you, stop screaming about whatever's obsessing you.
5. Never, ever proselytize online, esp. for Islam. People in the West dislike Islam due to its backwardness, violence and failure to mature, and your desperate bloviations only make people hate it even more.

6. Above all, make sure what you write in the virtual world connects to the real world. Notice how other posters here are analytical, detailed and give info pertinent to real-world decisions, to effect of, "While non-Anglo Western and other modern nations may have feminists, in practice the differences in their core beliefs and lower impact mean that marrying, divorce, dating and workplace and other IRL interactions do not carry practical harm to men and families, making it safe and reasonable from cost-benefit standpoint to move and start families outside the Anglosphere. Whereas Anglosphere feminism is far more tangibly lethal with tangible and high risk of ruin and even prison from divorce, alimony, child support or dating or harassment allegatoins."

Do you see? Detailed, analytical information with real-world relevance, quite a contrast to your vague bloviations about "but other modern countries have feminism too!" which is like saying "look, the sky is blue!" It contributes nothing of value, and since you perseverate constantly on it, you only irritate people. Do yourself a favor and take a long break from your keyboard.

Appendix J2: Legal Eagle <u>22 January 2018 at 19:53</u>

Just wanted to tl-dr the informed points above to sum up in simple terms just WHY the Anglosphere is so measurably different and DANGEROUS for men compared to the non-Anglosphere (West and East) when it comes to marriage, divorce, simple dating, harassment and overall lifestyle and interpersonal relations. I'm an attorney specializing in family law, now working overseas myself with a basis to make the comparison, and this is really all you need to know about the real-life decisions you'll have to make in the Anglosphere versus outside of it:

--- Marriage and having kids are now fundamentally non-viable options in the Anglosphere because of one specific quirk above all in the way the Anglosphere handles divorce: You literally become a slave to the state upon marriage or having a kid in the Anglosphere because at that point, the state has the power to extract your assets without limit in the event of divorce, separation or abuse allegations. Again; ALL of your assets, your savings, earnings, even your work potential, before or after marriage, can be seized from you after you marry or have a child in the Anglosphere, because the US court and civil system gives women and family courts absolute discretion over all your assets and even future earning potential, WITHOUT LIMIT. Now with #metoo, a variant of the same unchecked power has also been placed into the hands of the state (courts), institutions and women with a chip on their shoulder, to bring about complete ruination and financial damage to a man even outside of marriage, due to any hazy allegation of "harassment". All of this is reinforced by the powerful Anglosphere cultural meme of "man = deadbeat".

--- Outside the Anglosphere, especially in old Orthodox and Catholic countries (Mediterranean, France, Latin America, central and East Europe) and most of Asia but yes, also in non-Anglo Protestant lands (Germany, the Benelux region, Scandinavia), the state has no such power over a man after marriage and having a child. Instead he retains full control over his assets, savings and future earnings, and all forms of support payments are strictly capped. By the same token fatherhood is also explicitly supported (hence sharing of custody, paternal support, mediation), and the #metoo hysterics are dampened both by cultural disapproval and by explicit laws and policies that forbid a woman from ruining man's career and reputation through simple allegations. (The defamation laws are also much tougher in the non-Anglosphere, and women making such accusations are harshly punished.)

That's it, the one reason above all why, as this Blog correctly makes clear, the Anglosphere is fundamentally more dangerous than the non-Anglosphere to basic rights especially for men, families and rational women. The state and a wife or ex-wife in the Anglosphere, or even a meddling busybody bureaucrat, has enormous and essentially unlimited power to drain and enslave a man financially. This is why you have to ditch the Anglosphere and set up elsewhere, and this is one area where the MGTOW's are exactly right Simply dating, associating with women and marrying in the Anglosphere literally and tangibly-- not in some abstract way-- expose even a highly skilled, wealthy, upper class men to real risk of improverishment, public humiliation and severe downward mobility in Anglosphere countries.

This is the difficult and painful message that my old law firm, when we were speaking honestly, would convey to clients looking for a "solution" to their concerns about asset exposure to marriage in the US and Canada. If you marry and or have a kid in the English-speaking world, from that point on you have a sword of damocles over your head. It's as simple as that, and again, the MGTOW's are right on here. In fact perversely it's even worse if you're a rich or upper-class man, all your assets, including anything you've inherited can be extracted from you under Anglosphere law. On contrary, this is what someone referred to by the "playboy principle" in the non-Anglosphere-- even very wealthy husbands can never be asked to pay beyond a statutory and low limit as support, which does indeed discourage gold-digging since the "lifestyle standard before divorce" is not a factor.

Just focus on this point and avoid all the distracting issues, because whatever other cultural factors you're considering, these are the ones that affect you directly as an individual, and put you at infinitely greater danger of destitution and disaster in the Anglosphere versus outside it.

And just to throw cold water on any assumptions that "there still must be a way to safely date and marry in the Anglosphere", I'm sorry, but there isn't. Like I said above, domestic and international family law is my legal specialty, what I've done every workday for the past couple decades. I've worked in dozens of US states, several Canadian provinces and then several law and legal translation offices overseas in Europe as well as (in 2016) in Cordoba, Argentina. My law partners and I have seen literally thousands of men in the US and Canada show up in our office, nervously asking about ways to protect their assets in the event of divorce, wondering about "the perfect prenup" or if marrying a religious girl in a religious ceremony, or a foreign girl protects them. (Short answer-- it doesn't, not if you're still living in North America or anywhere in the Anglosphere.) I'm sorry, but if you want to establish a meaningful relationship with a woman, have kids, start a family-- the things fundamental to any society for centuries-- there is now no alternative to becoming an expat outside the Anglo world. None.

The family law policies in the Anglosphere really have become THAT dangerous and perverse, and now with the #metoo hysterics and media push, it's only going to get even worse for men, families and reasonable women in the Anglosphere. I think other posts here have covered why, but if they haven't, here's the tl-dr: it's due to the particularities of Anglo common law (which is we learn from Day One in law school, is a whole different animal from civil statutory law), stare decisis and political/administrative inertia in

Anglo legal tradition (feminists claiming female independence while clinging to "helpless wife" assumptions used to justify long term alimony), the oppositional essence of US law, media and culture. And don't think the political system, elections or either US political party will give you relief. For ex., guess who shot down two major attempts at alimony reform in Florida and Alabama, both of which have esp. harsh alimony statutes that hit ex-husbands hard? The foolish pro-alimony white knights were none other than two "conservative" Republicans, Rick Scott and Roy Moore. (The real reason Roy Moore lost the Alabama Senate election is that he imposed permanent alimony payments on a major Alabama publisher who was understandably embittered-- the things you learn working in family law.)

If it wasn't clear already, pre-nups offer very limited protection that's all but useless amidst the full discretion of divorce court judges, esp. after kids are born but even before-- even my own ex-law firm partners virtually laugh when husbands request them now, they simply don't help. Not "marrying a good girl" or "marrying a Christian or religious girl". Here's a nasty stat for you: the biggest jump in divorce, esp. nasty expensive divorces, in past decade has been among Christian and esp. Mormon women (!). Not marrying a foreign woman in the US-- once under US law, she'll have the same power to ruin you as an American woman, and fall under the same poisonous "deadbeat man" Anglosphere cultural influences that push other "nice women of good character" to divorce in Anglo countries.

Since I guess concrete paths to expatriation are becoming a topic here, f.y.i. my ticket overseas was to do legal translation. This is not only one of the easiest but also most lucrative paths to expatriation and you can do it even before getting fluent in another language, since there's such heavy demand for translation of documents and policy reports from the US and UK into the major languages of other (esp. European) countries. And yes, I got started in Sweden before focusing more on Continental law and translation now. And yes, it is true. Although Scandinavia, Benelux and Germany do have more traits in common with the Anglosphere, they are indeed worlds better because they reject the fundamental principles that make marriage and divorce (and now, even dating and harassment) so dangerous to men in the Anglosphere. The only other non-Anglosphere countries that come close are actually Switzerland (which does have some nasty divorces of its own, but still nowhere near the same damage, level or frequency as the Anglosphere) and Israel (which is the only country as bad as the Anglosphere).

I grew up in a traditional religious family myself, my father and mother are among the fairly few American couples who not only stayed married but actually happily so. And even for me and my brothers, my parents have urged us to never get married in the US. They've soon too many friends and neighbors get ruined. Expatriation is the only option. Save your earnings, sell your assets while you can (esp. now that the equity and property markets are at such high) and use your savings to head out of the Anglosphere, A.S.A.P. People here have been giving some good options-- France, Mediterranean or other Catholic/Orthodox countries in southern/central/east Europe or Latin America, Russia/former USSR, non-Anglo Protestant (Germany/Benelux/Scandinavia), most of Asia. But anywhere else will spare you from the literal slavery and vulnerability to asset destitution that greets you upon marriage or childbearing in Anglosphere countries. Don't listen to any idiots who whine stupidly about how "France, Germany, the non-Anglosphere has feminists and #metoo too". Yes, and they also have no power to ruin you in marriage and divorce let alone dating overseas, because the structure of the laws is fundamentally different, the oppositional cutlural nature of the Anglosphere is absent, and the overall culture even in very modern non-Anglo countries like Japan, Korea, Scandinavia, Germany and France still emphasizes traditional feminine responsibilities while honoring the importance of fatherhood. The whiny feminists overseas are powerless there, drowned out by institutions and the 99% of people who value fairness and reason.

Appendix M: Warburton

A great deal of wisdom here LE, thank you for sharing. A couple add-ons to your great points, not only do crazy feminists, technocrats, and judges have the legal power to reduce men, families and rational women to destitution in the Anglosphere, they actually do. In terrifying numbers. The risk of financial calamity from marriage and divorce in the English-speaking world, and as you say now from just dating or workplace association, isn't just theoretical. It's real, and very frequent. More than three-fifths of American marriages collapse in divorce, and its' very ugly and expensive there and in Anglo-world in general. We're talking tens or millions of men and families, across the Anglosphere, brought to ruin and financial collapse by divorce or a miserable marriage even it stays together.

You covered most of these bases. I'd also add that divorce is a huge profit center, not just for the divorce lawyers, the courts, judges, even states make big money from divorce settlements. O worked as a paralegal for several years myself while taking night classes, and saw another ugly truth about why child support and spousal support demands in North America are out of control and, unlike outside-the-Anglosphere, have no limit: courts and states get a nice little cut of alimony and child support as "processing costs", at least in many states. So when states don't raise taxes explicitly to meet all their deficits, they go after husbands and fathers with a brutal "secret tax" in family courts to make up the difference.

Plus, a point to add to your great expat advice: Another way for Americans, to get to Europe at least, is to find someone in their family-trees who came from the Old Country. If you have a Greek, Swedish or Italian ancestor somewhere, you're golden, and this is the fastest way to get there. I'm off to Italy later this year myself, hired as a statistician. But my cousin is using her traced roots to get there right along with me next year, and with full citizenship. Use every advantage you can.

Appendix N – Billy <u>3 February 2018 at 04:40</u>

Well, I'm just an ordinary expat without any special expertise or law background, can't match the intellectual fire power of you guys here but can give my two cents here on why it's better for families, certainly men and fathers when you go outside of any English-speaking country.

Me, I'm just a hayseed outta Iowa, never even went to college but I made a pile of money working in the fracking industry up in the Dakotas and out west.

Well, right outta high school and a millionaire, muscled up working out in the field, you get a lotta female attention, I thought for a while about marrying a girl near where I was working.

But a relative, couple friends thankfully talked me out of it, warned me a lotta things you guys are saying here. Gold diggers preying on what I earned, going to jail from child support or checks to the ex wife. Even a nice girl getting turned to a ho and encouraged by all her friends and divorce court to go after a guy's money.

What the prison guard's been saying (see Appendix Q), it makes sense with what I was warned about. It's like once get hitched, have your first kiddo, now you got a whole posse of leeches egging the wife on to divorce you. Because it's like there's a bunch of leeches ready to get rich at your expense when you divorce. That's how it is in the US at least. And Canada.

So what I did, I started up in Norway with their petrochemicals operation, made a pile more money there, banged some hot Viking women. Sweet days. Hopped thru some more countries, but settled down in Austria, I mean the Alpine country where they speak German, not Australia.

Best choice I coulda ever made, Europe in general, Austria specifically. Haven't gone read all the comments, but I got the gist, and yeah it's true, you don't lose your shirt if you get divorced in the Euro counties. Yeah you do in the UK cause it's Anglo I suppose, saw that when I was up around the North Sea fields.

But yeah I knew some American guys who got hitched with some hot blonde Viking girls in Norway and Sweden, got rich, then some of them split up. But they kept the money they made, their houses, car, shared raising the kids. The wives never got alimony, they don't do child support it's just they both continue to raise the kids as they would otherwise cause they share the raising. But no jail, no community property, you keep what you earn, and the ex-wife, she earns her own money, up there the ladies demand it of themselves even beyond the law itself. If these guys had got divorced in America, they'd lose their shirt cause the exes could take everything. But not Norway and Sweden, not Europe.

And Austria now? Perfection. The laws, culture, ladies are hot, sexy, freaky but also traditional and feminine when you raise kids. A lady gets nothing if she divorces you so people stay married, or have a fling here and there but stay out of a family court. I played the field awhile, eventually tied the knot with a sweet Russian girl who came to Vienna, we're expecting our first later this year.

Appendix O - Ranger <u>5 February 2018 at 05:24</u>

Great to see your thoughts Billy, I must say it adds a bit of fun and perspective to have a blog discussion that can ponder such serious topics of law and society and then be just as comfortable talking about banging hot Euro ladies. Which let's face it, it's the cherry on top of being an expat.

I'm ex-military and like a lot of Americans was posted in Germany for years, so I did the side-by-side comparison. The summary in as few words: truth here from you guys, so much truth.

Some of my fellow grunts went back to the States and got married. Total mistake, total misery. Their wives slept around while they were deployed. All the frickin' time. Then they filed for divorce. And the wives got everything from a man who served his country getting shot at. She got the house. The car. The dog. She got his savings. A chunk of his pension. Alimony. Child support often more than the poor guy was making after returning to the home front, because divorce court judges are c*nts in the extreme and like you all said, can impute any BS amount to what the guy "should" be earning. And the worst? The man-hating she-beast feminists, joined by mangina and white knight assholes, cheer the gold-digging Anglobitches on in the USA for wrecking good men like this.

You wanna know the real reason why so many US vets commit suicide? No, it's not the wars in Iraq and Afghanistan or PTSD. It's that we get hit with divorce papers, lose our assets and our kids, then get spat on by a crazy feminist, man-hating society that cheers our ruin. WTF????

Now compare, me and my fellow grunts who stayed in Germany after discharge. Now I gotta say, I love South American girls. For me Colombia, Brazil, Panama, if I could somehow get posted there I'd be h happy happy camper.

But outside of that, German ladies rule. French girls are hot too, not hating, but the German girls got that special *something* something, especially once you pick up enough German you can hit on them in the native tongue.

On divorce here? Yeah it happens, but in Germany and Europe, it is true, divorce is just a bump in the road, nothing like the total wreckage you suffer in the US. They don't even really have family courts here, it's all a "mediate it and be done with it" thing. You don't lose your kids, you keep your house and car, you keep what you've earned and saved in your profession and your hard work. No alimony. CS is a max amount and you don't get gouged. So a girl can't gold-dig here, a lot more incentive to work things out if things get rough. I've known hundreds of American guys who came to Europe, got hitched, some got divorced. Not one single one got ruined. They don't want people to divorce here, so the laws make sure you can go without hassle.

But that's the beauty of it, all this makes divorce less likely. And like I said, the German girls have that something and it's less common. They can be independent-minded sure, career-oriented, but somehow when it comes to sex and being hot, they're so much more into it than any American girl I ever dated. Same with the other European girls, in fact even the other grunts who brought their American or Canadian gf's here, once they acculturate they change so much for the better. And the ladies love kids here. My wife and I have 3 and she still stays hot and fit.

Appendix P – Brock <u>22 February 2018 at 22:18</u>

Can totally confirm the good advice the expats have been giving here about not just the advantages, but the necessity for ambitious, wealthy, high skilled, professional, intelligent and/or aspiring or just commonsense men in the Anglosphere--or just women who see the increasing feminazism of Anglo countries to be crazy--to expatriate. There really isn't any other option.

I think most of the expat meetups are wrapping up now but we've had a lot of discussion and food-for-thought based on the things you and the bloggers were writing here, one of our presenters even put up a seminar on how the civil law in Europe, Asia and non-Anglo Americas is like the "ultimate prenup"! It really does protect you from damage from a divorce and it instantly squashes all the timesup and metoo hysteria that's overwhelming Canada, the United States and the Anglo world.

I can also speak from personal experience, some partners and I moved to Sweden over a decade ago, totally fortuitous work reasons, and those of us who got divorced lost nothing, we came out completely unharmed compared to our unfortunate brothers in the US.

It's not advertised a whole lot but Sweden is the high-tech mecca of the current century now. You can actually make comparable money as in Silicon Valley or Seattle in Sweden's tech start-ups and incubators, not only in Stockholm, yet for much more manageable cost of living than the Bay Area or Washington State, and you can get Swedish and EU citizenship if you stay at it. Plus lots of venture capital and state support, much better than the US or Canada. I actually worked at Microsoft for a while while several of my business partners worked or contracted with Google, FB, Oracle, Apple or other big or small tech firms, but when we set out to start our own companies, Sweden actually made some good offers. (Chile's another good place for that and now Germany,

France and even Holland are also inviting tech entrepreneurs with similar grants.)

None of us were thinking much about divorce or prenups at first, but after a while, several of us got married in Sweden. I got married to a gorgeous Swedish girl from Uppsala (university town), my main business partner to an American wife who came with him to Sweden.

I wound up having 3 kids and my partner 2 kids with his wife, and we both got divorced. The long hours took a toll, and my business partner had an affair after the stress got to be too much. We were nervous about it since we knew of cases of Americans back in the US being wiped out from divorce, paying out the nose for alimony 30 years later. And yes, we did know of 2 guys back in the US, both well-off, who wound up in prison when their job situations went bad and child support and alimony got to be too much! US family courts haven't the littlest clue about earning money and how people out in the real word do it, they just assume you can wake up and be a millionaire without trying, and then when you can't, they throw you into prison for it!

But in Sweden? Divorce is almost painless. They despise the very concept of alimony in Sweden and neither of us had to pay any of it, even though we made far more than our wives. Custodial assignment is generally joint, so there wasn't even an issue of child support at all-- my ex-wife and I both contribute to raising our kids. Both of our exes were immediately expected to look for work after the divorce and with some state help, they did find jobs, though we voluntarily chip in when needed for the kids (nothing state enforced). <u>We didn't lose our homes or our cars.</u>

And remember, this is Sweden, supposedly the world capital of feminism. No messy divorces here, no timesup or metoo hysteria, no ruined lives after marriage. Some anon commenters say feminism is a problem outside the Anglosphere, but it really isn't, the "feminism" in the Anglosphere is more like "feminazism", it's malicious, scornful, hate-filled, nasty, ugly and harsh. In Europe, Asia, the non-Anglo Americas, what passes for "feminism" is a whole different animal. It's not zero-sum or hate-filed or shrill like you see in the US. It's just more about spreading more opportunities. (IMHO it would be a whole lot better in fact for Africa and the Middle East to have more feminism, women there really are terribly oppressed, and the unsustainable birth rate and overpopulation in much of the 3rd world is due to too little of the right kind of feminism if anything).

Many of my old work partners stayed in the US or Canada and got married. Huge, huge mistake. The ones who got divorced got wiped out, lost their homes and their hard-won assets, barely get to see their kids. Most are paying out the nose for alimony for ungrateful bitch exes who pluck their hard earned bank accounts dry. Child support is brutal and it's true, it doesn't support the kids, it's basically a scam and racket for the ex-wives to live high on the hog, plus the courts, judges, state treasuries that also get fat with a percentage of the child support and alimony money. Even my old partners who've stayed married in America are miserable, they live in constant fear of losing everything if the wives just decide to file for divorce on a whim, the husbands have all the responsibility and yet none of the power or benefits. Even the wives and ex-wives are usually miserable, US feminazism has warped them and ruined true relationships and families. Nowsadays, no need to even marry to experience this misery, one false accusation by a female colleague at work in the US or in Canada and right there, your career is over, you won't get another job and then you'll have the joy of being sued for sexual misconduct, losing what meager remaining savings you have.

Tbh I feel like a guy has to be ignorant, a masochist, a cuck or just dumb to even think about getting married or having a kid in the Anglosphere. Especially the USA, Canada, Britain or South Africa. Just don't do it. I mean, sure, if you're dirt poor with no skills or prospects, then fine, get married because you have nothing to lose. (Even then I'd caution against it, your situation might change.) But if you have skills? A good job? Make good money? Have a car and nice house? Have some savings? A good education? Family money? Good work ethic? Entrepreneurial? Just want rationality and fairness in a marriage, and to be able to raise your kids? You'd have to be crazy to get married or start a family in the United States. Or Canada. Or anywhere else in the Anglosphere. You'd be putting everything you've earned on the line for no prospect of gain.

Work in the US or Anglosphere if you have to, but don't marry or have a kid, instead save your money, sell your assets and build a nest egg to expatriate. Or if you're already married, move out as soon as you can. Nowsadays, <u>I don't even think it's worth it to stay and work in the Anglosphere anymore</u>. You can make very good money, often better overseas, especially in Europe and Asia but even some parts of the non-Anglo Americas, depending on what you do.

All with much more reasonable cost of living instead of the bloated inflated prices of everything in the US nowsadays. With better women about anywhere you go, though yes if you bring an American girl here she'll tend to become less bitchy in big part because she can't get anything out of divorce, they don't have the circling vulture lawyers here because they don't have anything like the USA's divorce court here, or the profit motive connected to it. You get better health care too. And there's paid maternity and paternity leave plus 6 weeks vacation so you can be with your kids, but the taxes are around the same total amount as in the USA, because they don't just piss away all their tax dollars pretending to be imperialists, throwing trillions away in near east wars or giving trillions for Wall Street bankers with political connections to waste on hookers and crack. So whether you've saved up money or are starting your career or education, just move out of the Anglosphere. It's just not worth the devastating risk to your finances and well being to marry or have a kid in the US or UK, and you'll have a better quality of life in almost any industrialized first world country elsewhere, and even a lot of still not so advanced countries too, especially in the non-Anglo Americas!

BTW I hope some of you guys are able to write newspaper and magazine articles or even books or web guides on all the wisdom you've been putting up here since the expat meetups got going. All the info you've been putting up particularly on the civil law advantages of the countries not in the Anglosphere, especially the guys with law and law enforcement experience, just pure gold! I know guys in the US, Britain and Canada and South Africa especially are desperate for this kind of good info, since the MSM media is too politically correct to even get into this issue. This is bestseller material!

Appendix Q: Lawrence 30 January 2018 at 05:31

Applause for Legal Eagle's intelligent and historically informed perspective here. A US-based old buddy of mine got wind of this Blog and suggested I contrib my own frightening observations as a prison guard to add to what Legal Eagle said, 'cuz I've seen the neo-slavery impositions of the Anglosphere and specifically American "family law" system on American men, up close and personal, in their full brutality. Legal Eagle is dead right, the Anglosphere really is a uniquely dangerous death trap, in every way, for any man who dares to even attempt a relationship with women, and especially for those poor souls who become husbands or fathers particularly in the US. Expatriation, as he said, really is the only option now.

And I'll underline something else he said because everyone here needs to be well aware of this for your own protection, as someone who's seen too many wealthy and upstanding American men literally enslaved in US prisons after divorce: the greatest danger for men in the Anglosphere is actually for wealthy men and professional men (and oddly enough, for a growing share of non-feminist non-crazy women), above all those with fiscal discipline, lots of savings, investments, assets and earning potential. For most potential hazards, your wealth and assets protect you, but it's the opposite in the upside down world of Anglosphere family law. For wealthy and well-paid American men and their peers in the Anglosphere, marriage, having a kid and yes, now in #metoo world even striking up a conversation or hooking up with women paint a huge, ugly red bullseye on your back for the lunatic family court system in North America to come after you and profit at your expense. Not just to take your assets and impoverish you, which they absolutely do and which family law gives them full power to do, but also to toss you into prison. Yes, rich, upper-class and professional men not only robbed of their assets under full cover of law, but also thrown in jail, a tyrannical practice unique to the Anglosphere.

I know because I've seen this with my own eyes year after year with horrible repetition, and often for kids that weren't even from the imprisoned "father". Forgive the wall-of-text I'll be putting up here, but I feel like men in the Anglosphere, above all the USA don't understand the very real threat to their very livelihoods and even status of free citizens they're facing if they marry, have a kid or in today's #metoo inflamed world, even associate with women who can later hit them with harassment charges. I doubt that even Legal Eagle, despite his wisdom from practicing family law, could really see this at a gut level. The MGTOW's are correct in the corruption they've identified in the divorce court system, but even most of them don't see the horrible path this corrupt system eventually leads to. However, it is something you see as a prison guard with your jail cells filled with men who committed no crime, confined there because US, Canadian and British family courts have imposed impossible financial demands on them, literally making them slaves for the prison-industrial complex to profit off of. This is one of the ugliest sides of the society wide disaster that the Anglobitch culture has given rise to, and Rookh was well ahead of his time in putting many of the threads together. In my former line of work, I saw the horrible, kafka-esque end result of Anglo misandry and feminazi feminism: total impoverishing, a jail cell, literal slavery, even for wealthy and highly skilled men. In fact, ESPECIALLY for wealthy and highly skilled Anglo men, who are this corrupt machine's favorite targets in America and the Anglosphere.

Here's some background. Before I myself went the expat route a few years ago, I had a job for about 10 years as a corrections officer, building up some savings and then later as a flexible shift job while taking correspondence courses in computer graphic and Web design and finishing a Master's in database management. I really wasn't a traditional fit personality wise for a corrections officer, I've always been bookish and nerdy and not really into rapping knuckles. But my family has been in law enforcement for a few generations and prison guarding can be a decently paid gig. So I used the job not only to make money but also observe the US justice system up close, which I would later be able to generalize to much of the Anglosphere.

And here I have to warn you, if there is any job that will redpill you from your 1st month on the job into becoming an MGTOW, it's being a prison guard. Because you see the effects of the legal Weapon of Mass Destruction that is US divorce courts and family courts generally right up close. That's because the large, large majority of the prisoners we watch over in our jobs aren't violent, aren't dangerous, aren't even really criminal. They're either tossed in the slammer for the "crime" of minor drug possession (not dealing, just personal possession) or more and more, for contempt of court due to failure to make alimony or child support payments. And yes, this is a uniquely Anglosphere practice, mainly US, Canada and Britain. The rate of such imprisonments in France where I now live and work, and every other country in Europe? Or South America which follows French and Roman legal tradition? 0%. They simply don't do that to men here.

And yes it gets worse for anyone in the Anglosphere, like Legal Eagle said a terribly big fraction of the men in US or UK prisons for child or spousal support payments? They're wealthy and upper-class men, because their assets give the family kangaroo courts wide authority to impose outrageous and impossible payment demands on them. This is due to a family judge practice called "imputation", which essentially means the judge, completely ignorant of real economics of actual job and earning potential for a man hit with a divorce suit, can pull a random number out of her ass and tell the man, "this is what you should be earning". And this makes upper class and especially rich men particularly vulnerable to an enslavement by the family courts. While there are some idiot white knight male family court judges who do this, it's mainly naïve feminist female family court judges who see a man who's wealthy or has been at some point, and automatically assume the guy can grow money on trees. They're not only feminist idiots, they're ignorant about business, real hard work or what it actually takes to earn a lot of money, and how risky and uncertain, famine to feast a high-earning position or job is. So ironically it's the wealthier men who are hit the hardest by family court judgments since the judge can impute any ridiculous fantasy of what he "should" earn out of her ass, regardless of reality, and she'll always pick an outrageously high demand. Then with any dip in the man's fortunes or the broader economy, he of course can't make the impossible imputed payments, and then boom, it's off to jail for the "deadbeat" man even if he's been a model citizen. I saw this there in the prisons I worked at, day in, day out. And no, it's not a bug. It's a feature of the insane Anglosphere system. Why you ask?

Chew on this stat for a moment, the United States of America has by a long shot the highest incarceration rate in the world, about 4 percent of the world population but getting close to 30 percent of its prisoners, with about 1% of our population in prison in any given year and, depending on the study, up to a fifth or even a fourth—that's 20 to 25 percent—of the US population being jailed for one reason or another at some point as either an adult or a juvenile, in most cases for charges that turn out to be trumped up or (as with child support) involve the hazy concept of "contempt". (And crazy enough, sometimes the Americans in jail are the "lucky ones", the USA also has the highest rate of citizens being shot by our own cops for complete misunderstandings or trivialities, and whites face just as much danger as minorities for that these days). And the US imprisonment rate is still rising. In fact, the United States with 320 million people has more prison inmates than China and India put together, even though these 2 countries have 2.5 billion people between them! The reason is obvious: Money. There really is a prison-industrial complex in the USA, I know because I was a part of it. And it really does make big money for a lot of people in control of it. It's the modern day update of the old plantation slave labor system.

The catch of it is, to make money from a slave economy, you need lots and lots of slaves, and you don't want them to be too violent or dangerous either. But then how do you get normal, law-abiding men (and also many women) into the heavily profitable US prison slave system, when jail is only supposed to be for criminals or bad guys? The answer, you simply fill up the prisons with people, mainly men and preferably white men, who aren't actually criminals, but who can be tossed into jail for victimless "crimes" like drug possession. And for simply doing the thing that humans are biologically programmed for—having relationships with women and fathering children. So how to drive these decent law-abiding men into the slave plantations of US prisons? Simple. Create a vicious, misandrist culture in the USA, and the Anglosphere more generally where men and particularly white men are vilified, demonized and turned into objects of hatred and scorn, encourage women at every opportunity to divorce men and "sock it to 'em" in divorce court, and now with #metoo, encourage women all over the workplace, bars, gyms, wherever to start a massive witch hunt against men for simple flirtation or even looking at them, while lobbying to make the vaguely defined "sexual misconduct" charge (that is, it's whatever a feminazi decides it is) into a punishable offense. And there you have it, millions of American men and other Anglosphere men ripe for confinement in the lucrative slave complexes of the Anglosphere, which we call penitentiaries.

Because that's what the insane, bloodthirsty family court madness of the US Anglosphere is—an unholy alliance of profiteering interests that unites radical feminists and cultural Marxists, with government bureaucrats, with corporations and big business who want to make huge profits off slave labor, and with the mainstream media and social media that has created a politically incorrect object of hatred that's ripe for targeting and enslavement—the men of the Anglosphere, especially white men. (Notice how quick Mark Zuckerberg was to bow to radical feminist pressure in censoring "fake news" on Facebook—he wants to align social media as much as possible with the same misandrist hatred that rules the MSM and academia).

And above all, this Anglosphere and above US alliance of dirty interests targets wealthy white men and a few uppity Asian-American men for "diversity" (I've seen this too in the prisons), after all you guys have far more wealth and assets for the state and the gold-digging woman in family court to plunder, much more to drain you dry of before they toss you into prison where you can make a bunch of fat cats even more profit as a slave. Doesn't matter whether it's a public prison or a private prison, the US and Anglosphere war on husbands, fathers and men on general is all about the money, ultimately, and they need slaves to make the big money.

This is why you truly cannot risk marriage or child-rearing in the US or the English language nations just like Legal Eagle was warning. Above all if you're wealthy and have a lot to lose. Like Legal Eagle also said, prenuptial agreements don't really help because they're not designed to, the Anglosphere needs you as a slave that the vultures in power can get rich pickings off of. And the numbers back it up. In many of the American prisons I got assigned to, outside of the drug offenders-- another nonviolent noncriminal group wrongly incarcerated at outrageous rates— MORE THAN HALF of our inmates were men incarcerated for falling behind on child support or alimony, or hit with questionable domestic abuse or sexual misconduct allegations. (And to make this figure even more terrifying, as it should be if you're even considering marriage or child-rearing in the US, all this was BEFORE the #metoo craze which is going to send those numbers up even higher). The US really is a banana republic particularly in its prison-industrial complex, but without the nice weather, beaches, good food and sweet pretty ladies of the countries usually labeled banana republics.

I know I'm sounding grim with all this, but I'm trying to be honest about all this and give you all warnings of the real horrors you're exposing yourself to with marriage or child-bearing in the English-speaking world, and nowadays even with male-female associations, because courts in the Anglosphere from then on, into the indefinite future, have real power to take away your assets and literally enslave you as a prison inmate. To put this another way, what Legal Eagle was saying in his post, about how men in the Anglosphere become slaves as soon as they get married or have a kid—I'm not sure how much even he realized that this isn't just a metaphor. It literally is true, and once you've been cleaned out financially, you're ripe for the slave market of a US family court that will assign you to your slave plantation—an American prison.

At one point in my corrections officer job, the incarceration of men for child support and alimony arrears got so bad that a group of us prison guards came to the warden, complaining that we were being unethically ordered to guard men who really weren't a threat and who should have never been sent to jail. Once imprisoned, they usually lost their professional licenses, their driver's licenses, became unemployable so they just wound up back there again. The warden just shook his head, he knew how corrupt the system is, how the US family courts, media, politicians, universities, feminists and the prison execs all work hand in glove to profit off the US slave economy fueled by all the husbands and fathers tossed into prison. How it creates sick incentives that encourage divorce and profiteering. (This is another reason the US divorce rate is by far the highest all over the world, so much money is made from it). But the warden knew he was powerless to reform it. Just like we were as guards. The vultures of the Anglosphere want their prison slaves, and husbands and fathers are an easy target.

Like I said, every man in the Anglosphere is a target of this machine, but wealthy American and Canadian men are the hardest hit, because the US legal system gives family court judges wide latitude, which really can't be appealed, to place arbitrarily high demands on the incomes of men who have been wealthy at any point. This is why Robin Williams committed suicide. At one point he was a very wealthy Hollywood A-lister. But after his two divorces, he was no longer pulling in that kind of money. The family courts didn't care. They said he once made big money, and in the fantasy unicorn filled land of US family courts, that meant he could just click his feet together and make the same money again. So they made Robin pay out the nose for alimony. By this time he was sick with Parkinson's Disease he couldn't make anywhere close to that amount of money, and his lawyer was warning him that prison time was likely coming. So he committed suicide. Here's another famous case, a guy in New York with same sort of situation, once made a lot of money on Wall Street and became upper class, told to pay alimony every year after that at insane high levels, lost his job in recession== then off to prison when it became impossible.

https://www.bloomberg.com/news/articles/2013-08-26/jail-becomes-home-for-husband-stuck-with-lifetime-alimony

Brendan Fraser has been hit with a similar judgement, tens of millions of dollars in alimony.

Wealthy men across the US, Canada, UK and the Anglosphere generally are hit hard like this. And yes, a lot of them wind up in prison. The incarceration rate in Canada and the UK isn't quite as bad, but this happens there too because the misandrist structure of the laws and family courts is as bad as in the USA, and the legal systems share the same insane practice of imprisonment after court-ordered impoverishing of a man. I found this out ironically after I expatriated and was working as a Web and database planner, when my previous experience led prison systems in many countries to contract me to help with their intake software and legal briefing documents. This imprisonment of men for marriage or kids (or in these #metoo days, just for "harassment" that in reality is "any interaction with women") really is an Anglo phenomenon uniquely. Whatever stupid idiosyncrasies the rest of the West has with feminism, they don't throw men in prison for this.

The very worst case I saw as a prison guard was a surgeon, yes an American surgeon who was one of the most respectable guys I ever met, hard working, worked until 2 a.m. 6 days a week to save people's lives. With all the work hours, his wife got "lonely" and started sleeping around, eventually having 2 kids that weren't even his as he found out later. And then she filed for divorce so she could take the surgeon's money, blow it on cocaine and stupid luxuries for herself without doing any work herself (that's the real destination where the "child support" money goes) and sleep around with her favorite Chad of the week, all on her hard working surgeon ex-husband's money. She won an insanely high judgment in a US family court, millions of dollars in child support and "alimony" that the poor surgeon would have to pay. Since by the court's judgment, "she should be entitled to maintain the same standard of living after the divorce", even though this greedy gold-digging Anglobitch is the one who filed for the divorce to steal from her hard-working husband who was actually saving people's lives.

After a few years of doing this, and losing his house and his nice car, the poor surgeon threw out his back while helping a patient onto an operating table. He had to cut down his hours as a surgeon, and went to the divorce court asking for a reduction in the support demands, and ask that his lazy, spoiled brat bitch ex-wife get a damn job herself. But the court refused using the same delusion filled imputation bullshit they pull on other ex-husbands, claiming he could somehow make millions of extra dollars using his surgical wizard skills somehow. Which he couldn't do in reality with his injured back, something the family court judge couldn't or wouldn't even try to understand. So then now the alimony and child support were demanding 120% of his income. You see, the family court system will never let you off the treadmill once they target you, especially if you earn a lot of money. Eventually he drained his savings and retirement, couldn't make the payments at all—and he wound up in the prison where I was a corrections officer.

The corrupt American family court-media-feminist-academia cultural Marxist-big business-prison industrial complex had worked perfectly to ruin this poor man, and what a prize they had. A dedicated, hard working US surgeon, saving lives every day, drained of his money and reduced to poverty by a gold-digging, spoiled greedy bimbo who divorced him due to his very dedication, had kids with other men to force him to pay bullshit "child support" in addition to never-stopping alimony, his assets taken by his gold-digging ex wife and the state to grease their own corruption, the "child support" in actuality supporting the ex wife's corrupt, hedonistic lifestyle after divorce. And then the poor surgeon himself made a literal slave in a US prison, stripped of his license and made a perpetual debtor, worked to the bone but never allowed to profit from his own efforts or hard work. That really is how it works in the US family court and prison system. That poor surgeon was the worst case we ever saw, made us so mad we were talking about how we were going to "free the Bastille" and start a revolution ourselves to stop all the corruption, Robespierre style. And free all the innocent men, and even some women, who were imprisoned this way, to feed more slaves to the machine.

Because if you're an American man, particularly a rich, well to do, middle class or upper class man with skills, saved money, assets, wealth and a good job, that's what you really are. Fresh meat for the Anglosphere family court meat grinder machine. Like Legal Eagle said, you are literally a slave with marriage or child-bearing in the US or the greater Anglosphere, from that day on, the state and officials have full purview over all your assets and unlimited ability to seize them. Legal Eagle saw this from the legal debate and court side, I saw the horrible result from the prison side, where men were sent after all their assets had been stolen by the family courts and their only further "value" was as slaves to the prison-industrial complex. This shit's real, guys.

And now, in the ugly aftermath of #metto, #timesup and #nameandshamehim, you don't even have to get married or have a kid in the Anglosphere to become a slave. Any interaction with a women, even something as casual as a glance or an innocent conversation, opens you up to charges of harassment and sexual misconduct. And given that as much as half of young white women in America find even innocent male female interactions to be harassment, you're in great danger at any moment. Many harassment and misconduct changes now are being assembled by our corrupt legal-prison-industrial complex system to become prosecutable offenses. But even short of that, the witch-burning in social media means that any vague accusation, whether recent or months or years ago, will make you unemployable and a social pariah. You'll lose your health insurance and ability to earn a living, and then the state will have all kinds of additional ways to brand you a criminal and toss you in jail.

Now on to one more thing Legal Eagle talked about, which is precisely why the Anglosphere poses such a unique and lethal risk to men in general, and husbands and fathers specifically, while other countries including others in the West and Europe do not, despite the poisonous fumes of Anglosphere and especially American culture. I'm not an expert in legal history or common and civil law like Legal Eagle is with his attorney experience, but as a LEO (we corrections officers are classified as this just like police officers are) we do need to understand at least the essence of the law. Our job is to enforce it after all. I'll do like Legal Eagle and spell right out, best I can, just why the Anglosphere legal and culture tradition has turned into a monstrous machine so deadly for men, and for normal women who want to start a family, and why expatriation now is the only option.

As reminder I'm in France now, have been for years, and as a Web designer who's often called on to help with the software used for prison intakes and legal briefings for law enforcement personnel, I also get a lot of international contract experience. I don't want to claim the non-Anglo world is a paradise, yes we do have dumb, shrill and annoying feminists here too. But there really is a huge difference away from the Anglosphere because the feminists have nowhere the level of the power or cultural approval they do in the Anglosphere, and in France and throughout Europe, are shunned and ridiculed by even the mainstream media and society. The misandry is combatted in a lot of surprising ways, the safety nets are open to men as well as women here, the "sock it to him" attitude of the USA is throttled, people are cooler with nudity and sexuality so harassment isn't an issue. But it's really the legal structure that matters most in making things so lethal for Anglosphere men compared to the protections of the non-Anglo world ruled by civil law. Even if I don't know the fine legal points of common law against civil law like Legal Eagle, I can tell you pretty specifically how they're so different in practice, and why the civil law countries are a far better choice for Anglo men and sensible women, above all for professional and wealthy men, to expatriate to, settle down and have families.

a. Practically speaking, "common law" means Anglosphere law, while "civil law" which comes from Roman law, is continental law, used in Europe, in South America which is continental-based, eastern Europe, and apparently in a lot of Asia, which for some reason has copied a lot of civil law practices. (I'm a lot less familiar with Asia so I'll trust Legal Eagle's word on that). In the USA, Canada, UK and Anglosphere generally, common law in practice means judges have much more latitude to impose harsh and arbitrary penalties, which they'll often feel free to do if they're riding political currents and punishing a group that isn't "politically correct". This also creates a toxic legal atmosphere in the Anglosphere which attracts the most militantly feminist female lawyers to become family court judges in a sort of selection process. Like I said I don't know the fine points of common law like Legal Eagle, but I did see how it played out in practice in US family courts when we were briefed on the court proceedings for inmates who had been confined for nonpayment of child support or alimony.

And it was very clear from the transcripts that the PC memes of feminist "you go girl" culture and the spewings of cultural Marxist academic journals had found their way into the American family court judges' rulings, where the man was automatically assumed to be a deadbeat and loser deserving punishment. Yes, even lifesaving surgeons with back injuries were thrown into this pile, and while misandrist feminist judges were the usual culprits, there were plenty of stupid male white knight family judges doing the same bullshit. I've heard some people claim that Jewish family court judges male and female were particularly inclined to go the misandrist route, but tbh I'm not sure I really saw this, I think they were maybe overrepresented in general among the lawyers and judges, but plenty among both the stupid white knights and the hate-filled feminist judges ready to incarcerate some poor ex-husband for child support or alimony arrears, were old fashioned Anglo Protestants. Especially up in New England where I worked early in my career as a corrections officer. It's clearly something in Anglo culture that combines with Anglo common law to fuel this insanity in the judges, possibly the strange combination of cuck-like chivalry by some men and zero-sum radical feminist hatred, unique to the Anglosphere, that maybe one of the other commenters made a note of.

The lesson to draw here is that it's the "playing with fire" basis of Anglo common law that makes this possible in the Anglosphere, as I'll explain, civil law countries reign in judges and don't let them do this. The essence of common law in practical sense, is that the law is based not just on prior court precedent but also—and this is the main point—on "broad political currents" in society that the court supposedly interprets. Despite the US Constitution, which is essentially statutory law, the common law, which predates the Constitution itself, means family court judges in the US and general Anglosphere can "go with the PC cultural flow" which family courts in France, Germany, Norway, Brazil, Chile and the non-Anglosphere in general cannot do. And when rampant misandry and "sock it to 'em"—even against a lifesaving surgeon whose gold-digging wife had 2 kids with other men—is the cultural current, US and Anglosphere judges have latitude to "go with it" and formalize the misandry in their decisions.

The common law, I suspect, is also why the Anglosphere, and I guess Israel from what Legal Eagle is saying (haven't been there so can't say personally), is unique in the way judges and the state have full purview to review and seize all of a man's assets. The civil law of the continent in Europe makes that a no-go because judges are handcuffed legally, while the common law gives Anglosphere judges a lot more power over men's finances. Combine that with the selection for feminazi lawyers to become family court judges, steeped in the latest misandrist bile from the media and women's studies journals from academia, and boom, you have a formula for turning "sock it to him" into formal rulings by judges to seize all a man's assets. Especially a wealthy man, who's a juicy and favorite target for the unholy alliance of radical feminist Anglosphere family courts with the profiteering lawyers and prison-industrial complex, particularly in the United States.

This is the "laymen's term" explanation for what Legal Eagle was saying: Anglo common law means that practically, a family court judge in the US and Anglosphere is a little dictator with uncontrolled and unappealable power to make state pronouncements that a man must 'pay up" unrealistic amounts that add up to more than 100% of his assets and salary. And make him a pauper. There is no restriction on the delusional imputation that a family court judge can do with spousal support and child maintenance expectations for a man.

The judge in the Anglosphere can cite, as precedent, both previous decisions but even "flavor of the moment" social movements like #metoo and whatever misandrist junk is being spilled out in US university academic feminist journals, since an Anglosphere judge has so much latitude.

Not so in the non-Anglo world, especially in Europe and South America which is continent-influenced and where civil law rather than common law prevails. This is really where continental civil law from Europe shows its virtues—it's in its essence more rational than Anglo common law, and by its very nature it imposes strict limits on what a judge can do, and how much of a man's assets a judge, and thus the state, can review and effectively take control of. Again guys like Legal Eagle will know about this more than I would, but after being in France for a while and trying to master my French, I read a French language book that talked about how the Romans came up with law. They were almost scientific about it, a lot of philosophy and long term thinking, and that's the heart of civil law that dominates almost every country outside the Anglosphere. Above all the Romans were realistic about how human passions of the moment could corrupt the law courts, and they were very frank about how women in particular, would too often get caught up in what we now know as misandrist hate campaigns like #metoo and the "sock it to him" hatemongering of divorce courts. That's why civil law in effect protects men from harm and makes marriage and family formation possible outside the Anglosphere, and that's true even in countries that, like in Scandinavia, have opened themselves up too much to many of the stupidities of Anglo-American culture. Despite this, the civil law tradition even in Scandinavia shields men in actual practice, something they don't have in common law-dominated Anglo clountries.

In the practical terms of family courts themselves, family court judges in civil law countries are kept on a much tighter leash than common law Anglo countries, so the PC feminist "flavor of the moment" is irrelevant—the statutes are what matter, not vague prior "precedents" or media-driven memes like in the Anglosphere. That's why, like Legal Eagle said, child support in the non-Anglo world is strictly capped, why alimony is almost nonexistent. The non-Anglo world is much safer for men in general, especially for upper-class and wealthy men, because the caps are kept deliberately low by the civil law legislative process. This stupid Anglo standard, that after divorce "a woman should be entitled to maintain the same lifestyle as during marriage"? The non-Anglo countries call bullshit on that. By civil law codes, if a woman files for divorce, she then has to get off her ass and earn her money herself. And they HATE gold-diggers in Europe, which the civil law formalizes. It doesn't matter if the man has been a millionaire surgeon, like the poor unfortunate inmate I worked with, or a billionaire industrialist—a divorcing spouse is not entitled to his fortune, whether he made it before or during the marriage. She'll get only enough to provide basic support for herself and her kids given cost of living, and beyond that she has to work. A wealthy husband will customarily contribute more to help her get job prep at the start, and a husband who's having tough times or just lost his job will be given a break to get on his own feet.

Generally the civil law that Legal Eagle talks about, means that men in the non-Anglo world can marry, have kids, divorce if it comes to that, without putting their assets at risk. Because not only is there no alimony, but child support is kept low and works differently, as the woman filing for divorce is expected to work and do the supporting herself. Again this shows the rationality of the civil law which is developed by community leaders with long term thinking, as opposed to divorce law and family court judges with a feminist chip on their shoulder, swayed by the PC whims of the moment. The "playboy rule" that I and I think Legal Eagle are describing above, is done this way for a reason. It discourages divorce for one thing, so non-Anglo Europe and South America have much less of it than the Anglosphere. It also encourages shared custody, since a woman gets no advantage from profiteering through the child support bullshit which usually just supports a custodial parent's excessive lifestyle. It means men don't go to prison, since child support is low, it doesn't "rack up" and there's no alimony. It also means that lawyers, judges, states and the prisons don't get to be gluttonous greedy pigs like in the US, UK and Canada, since you can't profit from the divorce process, like I saw time and time again with all the poor ex-husbands sent to the prisons I was assigned to.

This in laymen's terms is what Legal Eagle was saying in his first point, the civil law of Europe, South America, east Europe, everywhere outside the Anglosphere is a far better protection of a man's assets, wealth and freedom than any prenup, because it totally changes the math and economics of divorce, takes away the incentive for it, prevents profiteering and makes custody shared. That's why, even if feminists and dumb Anglo culture get into non-Anglo countries, they're tightly shackled in what they can actually do. It really is true, I have seen this. Feminism and dumb Anglo-PCism are laughed at in France, Austria, Italy, Spain, Portugal, Holland, Belgium and east Europe, and whiny feminists especially here in France are vocally mocked and marginalized, but they do have some currency in Germany and Scandinavia, which makes them a little too vulnerable to stupid PC fads and feminist farts from the Anglosphere. (Although as I'll get to below, Nordic and German feminism really is a breed apart from misandrist Anglo feminism).

Yet despite this, the actual process of marrying and divorce in Germany and the Nordic countries has the same legal structure, with the same statutory protections as men enjoy in France and the Mediterranean, and it's because those countries also follow the civil law instead of the common law of the English-speaking countries. If the feminist harpies from the Anglosphere came to Germany or the Nordic countries, they could bleat all they want, but they have no power to ruin a man in a divorce as is routine in the Anglosphere. And so men in Germany and Scandinavia, especially upper class and wealthy men, have their assets walled off and protected from the state the same as we do in France. If a woman files for divorce in northern Europe as much as France or southern Europe, she doesn't get to do any gold-digging, and if she has a rich husband, she isn't entitled to his wealth. The statutory limit is deliberately kept low to discourage divorce and encourage custody sharing, and if she still goes ahead and files, she is responsible for getting off her ass and getting a job. No freebies on a husband's dime, whether he's rich or not so rich.

b. The different feminisms of the Anglosphere as opposed to the non-Anglosphere. I know Rookh was bringing this up as a main topic, and when it comes to things like sociology and cultural history I'm really not too familiar, so I can't really comment with the depth a lot of you guys have here. But I can say this from direct observation, the feminism of Scandinavia and Germany really is a world apart from the hate-filled, virulent misandrist madness of the Anglosphere, and ironically it further serves to help northern European men and protect them from divorce or #metoo-like harassment witch hunts. This isn't so easy to explain to people in the Anglosphere because the cultural framing of reference in Europe is so different, but I guess here's the essence of it.

Consider for a moment a European country infamous for its loud, obnoxious feminists, say Norway, Sweden or Finland. For the poor guys stuck in the Anglosphere, as I was until I expatriated, when we hear "feminists" even overseas, we instantly think of the vitriol-filled, openly misandirst American, Canadian or British harpies like Emily Lindin at Teen Vogue. For those who don't know, she was the disgusting bitch in the middle of the #metoo witch-hunting who wrote on Twitter a few months ago, ""if some innocent men's reputations have to take a hit in the process of undoing the patriarchy, that is a price I am absolutely willing to pay." This is the character of Anglosphere feminism: it's shrill, resentful, spiteful, malicious and clearly full of hatred, less concerned with helping women than with doing damage to Anglo men in any way possible. (If these crazy feminists really wanted to help women, they'd campaign against the oppression in Muslim countries like Saudi Arabia).

So what about the feminists in Norway, Sweden, Germany, Denmark and Finland which had feminist traditions even before North America? It really is a totally different form of feminism. The feminists up there in Nordic-land and Germany can be shrill and loopy in their own way, yes. But up there, the feminism isn't misandrist, and they aren't obsessed with this "evil oppressive patriarchy" the way Anglosphere feminists are. For the Nordic feminists, it's more about true independence, sexual freedom and yes, actual egalitarianism. They hate the #metoo thing up there because they think it makes women look weak. They hate alimony for the same reason, in fact of all ironies, it was Nordic and German feminists who led the push decades ago to abolish alimony and restrict child support. And even to help institute paternity leave as well as maternity leave to encourage fathers to be with their young kids. It sounds crazy to us in the Anglosphere because "feminism" here is something so much nastier and misandrist by definition, but the feminists up in Nordic-land in Germany in general aren't misandrist and in fact do a lot of things that are very husband and father-friendly. Yes, they can irritate sometimes with their own "you go girl" talk and be a little standoff-ish at times, but to a surprising extent, most of them are actually reasonable, and mainly focused on making sure that girls and women have opportunities to explore and be creative— without doing this at the expense of boys and men.

And you'll be relieved to know that despite the cultural excrement floating in from the Anglosphere, Anglo-style feminism really isn't catching on there. That's in part due to the fact that German and Nordic universities are structured so differently, they focus on gaining real skills and frown on Anglosphere bullshit like gender and women's studies programs that for the most part are just high tuition welfare for PC feminists and administrators. But it's also because the northern European feminists just plain don't like the Anglo style of feminism. (And like I said, the French, Austrians, southern and eastern Europeans just don't like feminism at all).

As to why this is, I have my own theory. I know a lot of you guys have talked about how the crazy Puritan tradition in the Anglosphere, or maybe the Victorian era, is responsible for making the Anglo version of feminism so toxic by making sex itself an item of scarcity that women gain power by making rare, and that pushes the societies to harmfully separate the genders from an early age so they don't understand each other. Now, I'll say I think there's something to this. Repressing male-female sexual interaction in the Victorian or Puritanical tradition does lead to a lot of societal perversions directly and indirectly. Directly, I feel like we saw this in the Victorian period, and today in Afghanistan with the sexually repressed Pashtun tribes that make young women unavailable for sex before marriage, resulting in men's schools and clubs plagued by homosexual weirdness. More importantly, I feel like this does contribute to the "men are evil" misandry of family courts and #metoo extremists since it paints any sexual association as evil, and since men in general are more associated with sexual interest towards women, it means that Anglo feminists frame their misandry with a lot of Puritanical shaming and disgust at sex itself.

And the different, more freewheeling attitudes of Europe towards sex and sexuality are truly a lot different, which probably steers the culture sharply away from Anglo-style feminism, even among the feminists there. Before my fiancée joined me in France—and I'll admit it here, even after we got married—one of the places I loved to go was up In NE Germany. Tbh German, Polish, Czech, Swedish and Finnish girls are sexy as hell in general, something about that Baltic area, and these gorgeous ladies never have hang-ups about being sexy, attracting men, even being nude or out in thongs in public. When you talk to them, many will say they're feminists, but their coziness and lack of frigidness around being sexual totally changes what feminism means to them. FWIW I see the same kind of thing down in South America when I've been there, particularly down in Brazil, which is the one country I would have chosen if I didn't wind up in Europe. Crazily hot women, independent, often say they're feminists but it all means something a world away from Anglo feminism. (In Brazil, when a girl says she's feminist what she really means is she likes to be the one in control in bed). So from that observation I think you guys are right, the way that Anglo feminists have been conditioned to view sex itself as dirty and nasty, a hang-up from our Puritan tradition, may contribute a lot to the nastiness and misandry of US and Anglo feminism.

Still, I think there's something else at work in the Anglosphere which has to do with Anglosphere history. Most countries in the Anglosphere were settled by invading British colonists who pushed out the natives and took slaves. That's the history of North America in essence. But this all changed in a nasty and bloody way for the Anglosphere that was very different from Latin America, where there wasn't the history of open and hateful group conflict like there was in America's civil war in later history. It just seems like the lines are more blurred in Latin American countries. So North America, in particular, has had this nasty history of rival ethnic and racial groups, displacing the natives and fighting bloody wars against each other, and never came to an understanding about it. And then cultural Marxism came, whipping up and playing on these conflicts as a wedge against the West, and it found its most fertile ground in the Anglosphere. The malicious Anglo feminists of US divorce courts and #metoo seem to borrow a lot of that group warfare language, and maybe that combined with the Puritanism has made the Anglo strain very ugly and hostile.

c. This one's simpler—the media culture of the Anglosphere is a world away from what we have in Europe, especially in France.

That's part of why #metoo never caught on in France, Italy or the rest of Europe outside the UK. We just don't have that kind of voyeuristic "gotcha" culture that plagues the Anglosphere. Some anonymous commenter was whining that Catherine Deneuve, Laetitia Casta, Brigitte Bardot and the other French women luminaries were harshly criticized in the media after they came out against #metoo. This guy obviously hasn't been to France and doesn't speak French, because he's totally wrong on this. Deneuve, Casta and Bardot all speak for the overwhelming majority opinion of both the French masses and the French elites, who find the #metoo stupidity and the misandry of US and Anglo family courts to be a laughing stock at the very least, and a threat to society that should be shunned. This view is shared by 96% of the French people, and the French media openly mock the few French feminists who try to imitate the Anglo feminists, and whose own attempt at #metoo here fell totally flat. Caroline de Haas in particular is roundly ridiculed by French women even more than men as being totally out of step with French culture and reality in general, and she wound up being a punchline humiliated by comedians all over the country after her lame response to Deneuve.

Notice for example the tears of the misandrist mainstream American and other Anglo media about how #metoo has failed completely in France. They know the media and culture of Europe spit on the Anglo delusions of cultural relevance in areas like this, and it burns them up inside.

https://www.theatlantic.com/international/archive/2018/01/france-me-too/550124/
https://www.newyorker.com/news/daily-comment/why-did-catherine-deneuve-and-other-prominent-frenchwomen-denounce-metoo
https://www.thewrap.com/catherine-deneuve-joins-100-frenchwomen-bashing-puritanical-metoo-witch-hunt/
https://www.nytimes.com/2017/12/16/world/europe/italy-sexual-

harassment.html
https://www.nytimes.com/2017/10/26/opinion/italian-feminism-asia-argento-weinstein.html

In fact it's gotten so hostile and humiliating for these Anglo feminist imitators that they're now set to leave France, setting up in, where else, the UK and Anglo provinces of Canada. In all their whining and butthurt, they say that the Anglo countries are more receptive to their shrill misandrist feminism, which itself is telling.

d. Hinting at this before, but something else that makes the Anglo brand of feminism such a wrecker for men and society, is the Anglo obsession with money and profits over people, and the stupid worshipping of big business and corporations. This may sound money coming from me because I'm a business owner, a hard-core capitalist and was considered right of center when I was in the US. But these ideology driven lines in the sand confuse more than they reveal because they're too damn broad. Yes, I am a capitalist and fully support free markets for most things in society. But the problem is, too much of what the US and Anglosphere calls "free market capitalism" isn't really capitalism at all, it's more like lazy cronyist style fake capitalism. This in reality is more like socialism for the oligarchs and super rich buddies of people in power, like the third world corruption that rules shitholes like Mexico (yes, I said it) where a few families hold 90% of the wealth and brutally oppress the masses, extracting their wealth for themselves.

This is what the US is becoming as it embraces this fake oligarch capitalism rather than true free market capitalism, and it's exactly what I saw working as a corrections officer with the prison-industrial complex in the United States. Like I said above it's a big part of why we have the world's highest rate of incarcerating in the US, the prisons here are in essence slave labor camps and plantations that constantly need fresh bodies and more slaves, and it's a big part of why the divorce court insanity is so awful in the

US and Anglosphere. For the Anglosphere, every part of the miserable divorce process, and now the #metoo screaming, is a chance to profit.

Family courts provide a lot of profit for the lawyers, judges and the states too like Warburton was showing. Gold-digging ex-wives get huge profits from alimony and child support just like the states. And then when the Anglo man's assets are drained dry, especially a wealthy Anglo man who's such a rich target, he's sent as a slave to the prison-industrial complex to extract his slave labor and further profit, both private and public prisons do this. Another reason the Anglosphere is so deadly for a man who wants to hold on to his wealth and start a family. It's just like healthcare and college in the Anglosphere, the marriage and divorce court system, and now the "harassment industry" after #metoo, is another place for the most corrupt oligarchs in the US to make big profits.

There's a term for what the Anglosphere has now that economists use, it's something like "rentist seeking". I'm not sure exactly and economics overall is one of my weak points from college. But whatever the term is, it has something to do with asshole oligarchs, profiteers and parasites in essence skimming off the wealth that real producers in society produce, like manufacturers or that surgeon who got sent to my prison after impossible child support and alimony demands. It's yet another reason to expatriate out of the Anglosphere, the culture no longer values real capitalism, it's more about profiteering and extracting money from people who do real work. Which is exactly what American family courts, and Anglosphere family courts generally are set up to do.

This is maybe another less noticed reason why the non-Anglosphere is much safer and more welcoming of men, and of women who want to start families, than the Anglosphere. Business and free market entrepreneurs are greatly valued in France and Europe, but they care about real capitalism here, not the cronyism that's become the big thing for the Anglosphere. This is another reason why the non-Anglo European and South American countries, and yes this includes Germany and Nordic-land, so strongly oppose the insanity of US divorce courts, discourage divorce and prohibit alimony. They just see this as part of the crazy profiteering and cronyism that's consuming the Anglosphere economies from the inside, parasitically. They hate the idea of divorce lawyers and ex-wives, let alone courts and prisons making profits off something so terrible as divorce. And they realize there are lots of things in society, like divorce and health care, where profiteering is a terrible thing. So they forbid it, and it's another reason divorce rates are so much lower in Europe, while divorces in general cause minimal damage to those involved in it.

On this topic I know Legal Eagle said Switzerland was a little different, and yes I have heard of the Swiss being unusual in the nasty, sometimes US-style divorces they have there. But as I understand it, that's because Switzerland is a bit of an oddball, the last country in Europe to given women voting rights while still having paternalistic "protections" for women that haven't caught up to the reality that women work these days. It's more of a legislation lag than anything else, and as Switzerland is a civil law country too, that's correcting itself. The Swiss absolutely do not profiteer from divorce the way Americans and other Anglosphere countries do, the Swiss are sharp eyed capitalists in the traditional sense.

And another reason why the Europeans and South Americans hate Anglo profiteering creeping into very inappropriate places, like divorce and family courts—when people aren't valued, eventually the society changes out the people and the demographics change. This is a big reason why the US is already a majority non-white country in its school-age population, with the rest of the Anglosphere following suit. Corporations in the US don't want to train or support American workers, they want bigger profits fast, and the best way to do that is to import surplus labor through mass immigration to depress wages. Short term profit, long term disaster and civil conflict. France has a totally different perspective. I know the US media likes to go nuts over all the trouble French Muslims supposedly cause, but in reality they're only around 3 percent of the population and actually dropping as Muslims and Africans leave what's becoming a very culturally strict society now, which I think someone else mentioned. The same goes for the Swedes, Dutch, Germans, Italians all of which are much tougher on immigration than Trump could ever dream to be. By refusing mass immigration this means they have to invest more in their own people and not profiteer off them. Which means none of this parasitic bullshit the US loves to pull in things like family courts and healthcare.

e. The last point, and sort of a follow-up on the previous one about what makes the non-Anglosphere more suited for men and families than the Anglosphere, it's the safety-net traditions here. Now, again I know Americans get confused about this because they're so used to calling this "socialism" and looking at French social programs in just left leaning or right leaning terms. But the French social assistance programs are more properly seen as ways of making sure society stays harmonious, and this extends to things like family courts and divorce courts.

Part of why US family law is so stressful, and divorce court judgments are so harsh and devastating for men, is that there just aren't good safety nets in the US and Anglosphere, so Americans are always at each other's throats trying to extract money anyway they can. It's like a state of constant downward mobility and anxiety, and this contributes both to the tendency for Americans to divorce, and the grasping and nastiness of divorce itself there. In Europe, people in general are just less stressed and happier because people aren't constantly stressing about going broke from hospital bills or college costs the way Americans are. This also reduces the divorce rate and stops the ugly side that Americans show when divorce hits.

One thing I haven't mentioned yet, is that my wife is actually American herself, and she moved to France with me. There have been a number of expat conferences in the US recently drawing American expats in, across the world, to spread their wisdom to other Americans thinking about expatriating. (A lot of people at my conference are aware of Rookh's site, so I'd say there are at least thousands of men lurking specifically to find about expatriating from the misandrist mess the US and Canada have become). Anyway, one of the guys I talked to in the US conference talked about how he and his wife in Washington State nearly divorced after the costs of their first child, who needed specialized care, nearly made them insolvent.

This kind of ridiculous economic stress from healthcare, daycare, college tuition is a lot of what pressures so many couples to actually go ahead with divorce in the Anglosphere, and it's something we're freed of in Europe. My wife and I also had a complicated birth here in France for our first child, and yet it cost us nothing. That's right, $0 other than the parking and lunch. So something that would have stressed us out like crazy in the United States or another Anglosphere country, here in France was just a minor little annoyance, and we're just happier and more secure here than we could ever be in the US. There's an irony for you, I married an Anglo girl from America when I went to France, but by being in France, she avoided becoming an Anglobitch—she and I are 100% French now. So if you want to marry your sweetheart in the US, make sure you both settle down somewhere else!

As bonus, we don't even pay more taxes here in Europe even though Americans assume that. Our healthcare costs so much less, and for that matter our family courts are much quieter and less expensive, plus with far fewer inmates there's much less need for what I did in the US as a corrections officer. So things just cost less in Europe than the Anglosphere and less taxes are needed. I actually pay less in taxes in France than what I paid while working Rhode Island in the US! It really is not just worth it, but essential to expatriate out here or to other countries outside the Anglosphere. You can have a real family and real quality of life here. With normal relations between men and women actually loving each other and enjoying each other's company.

Appendix R: Jesse <u>6 March 2018 at 02:59</u>

It's scary to even ponder this but in my humble experience, hard as is to believe, the divorce court nightmares in the US have been getting even worse in past 5 years. I myself am on the expat trail on or before 2020, have a long-term contract so split my engineering consultation between Brazil and Chile and man, have to say, from what the poor American guys around me have been going through, it won't be a moment too soon when I leave.

The cautionary tales in my case were 2 guys I never would have thought would face the nightmare of a family court in America. These are the guys who would thumb their noses at MGTOW types, I wouldn't call them white knights, it's just that they had good, loyal religious wives and their marriages seemed solid.

Until they weren't.

One guy, Mormon, engineer like myself, had his own business making good money, 4 kids and the white picket fence. The kind of family you never thought would fall apart. But damn, when the wife filed for divorce, it all went straight to hell for the poor husband. His business kept away from home all the time and the sweet loyal wife began to stray, I mean I get ti she's human, happens even to the Mormons but what I don't get, why do the divorce courts slam the poor guy so hard? I mean, he lost EVERYTHING even though he had supposedly the best lawyers west of the Rockies. His home-- gone. Lost custody of the kids. Lost one of his cars. Lost hundreds of thousands in savings he had saved up for retirement. Alimony. And OMG, the child support. Pure hell for a guy, Over $100,000 every year plus the alimony.

That's the worst part, I just don't get it, the judge in the divorce court, she looked at his business over the past 15 years, she picked one year where he had big profits, said "that's the basis for the CS assignment". Does hits judge not understand that his business isn't guaranteed to make anywhere around that kind of money every year? Does she even understand how business operates and that you simply don't know how much you'll make in a year? Probably not, since these crazy femi-nazi family court judges in the USA and Canada, are so busy studying crazy feminist theories they never actually learn anything about how people in reality make money!

This poor guy, last week he came begging to me and some of our mutual friends to borrow money, his business is doing reasonably well but not as well as that one fabulous year, so he's behind on his CS and the judge is about to toss him in prison. I mean, WTF???? This is a hard-working, prosperous, patriotic Mormon engineer and business man, salt of the earth, and his country's family courts treat him like dirt, reduce him to the humiliation of begging friends and family for extra money because even after he's already lost everything from the divorce, his CS and alimony payments are so high that even a successful business year isn't enough to cover it.

Same thing with the other guy I know, also religious, evangelical Baptist, 3 kids out of the nest. So you'd think he'd be safe, right? Nope. After 3 decades of marriage, the wife/s gossip-y friends convinced her to divorce her hubby, and even without CS, the 3 decades of marriage means the alimony is utterly brutal on top of losing his house and all his retirement savings.

And with him again it's the same thing, divorce court judges get to do this weird "imputation" thing, pull a random high number out of like, nowhere, and say to the poor man, "hey, this is what you owe every month, pay up and go to jail". No regard for, you know, reality. And again the poor guy is begging friends and family, or he goes to the US modern day debtors prison. And from the guys around here have all been saying, it's the whole Anglo-American world doing this, so Canada, UK and other Anglo-American places too.

I just don't get how Anglo family court system can be so grossly, obviously irrational and unfair, I mean being an ex-husband in an Anglo country must be pure hell. It's why once I move down to Brazil and Chile, I'm never coming back. I may move in the region a bit, maybe Argentina or Colombia, or Ecuador with all the hot "mujeres" down there. Or maybe Europe, I knew a bunch of guys who went there too, seems like yeah, it's all about sharing custody for most part but even if a mother gets custody, the family courts have the common sense to, you know, first look at what a guy actually is earning first, and only then assign CS, and it's a low number there, either percent-wise or flat amount. South America got its laws and social systems from mainland of Europe so it's the same system in both places, you get a lot less divorce, the women like to stay married but if divorce does happen, the woman is expected to work, none of this Anglo-American "easy street" bullshit from alimony plus CS subsidies. A guy holds onto his home and kids and doesn't lose what he's built up. Because, gosh, that means that capable and successful men in Europe/S.A. won't fear marriage and will be willing to have kids. Common sense, what a shocking concept!

Maybe this civil law versus common law division explains it, I don't know anything about that, I just know what I see on the ground. And that is, man, if you want to avoid total emotional and fiscal misery, whatever you do, do not get married or have young'uns in the US or the Anglo-American world. And if you are married, or already have the young'uns to take care of, for God's sake, get out now! There's like a ticking fiscal time=bomb on you because once the wifey files for divorce, ti's over for you if you're in an Anglo-American country. All those stats, about how it's a 60 percent divorce rate in the US and Canada? Remember, that's only for 30 years out of marriage, and like in the example I gave above, divorces after that are even worse with the alimony that gets imputed! I'm fortunately not married yet so I'll be able to play the field down in Brazil and Chile and even if I bring an American girl south with me, I won't have to worry about losing everything like

314

the poor guys around me. This crazy shit about professional American or Canadian guys winding up in a jail cell if the business has a bad (or even less than spectacular) year, because the CS or alimony imputed is so crazy high, they just don't do that elsewhere in the world. And if you're a white or Asian-American guy, you better watch out even more, I've seen cases where at least minority Latino or black guys can claim the family courts are being racist and shut up the crazy divorce court femi-nazi judges. But man, if you'r in the "unprotected classes" you are well and truly f***ed if you get dragged into divorce court. Expat as soon as possible. Especially if you're married or have a young-un already, like I said the clock is ticking on you, do whatever you have to, ask your boss for a transfer internationally, look for an overseas business partner, find any excuse you can to expatriate out of the Anglo-American countries because you once you walk down the aisle, or the first goung-un pops out, you have a big red target painted on your back for a family court judge to take away everything you have!

Appendix S: Disillusioned Law Professor <u>19 April 2018 at 05:13</u>

Thank you, Mr. Kshatriya, in your Blog posts last month for a quality discussion of the real world distinctions between the common law of the Anglo-Saxon world and the civil law of mainland Europe, Latin America and Asia. As a law professor and father of a divorcee, and teacher of dozens of lawyers who have gone on to wear the judge's robe, I can speak to the topic of the Anglo common-law perversions of family law and the consequent need to expatriate, from professional and personal experience, Several of my own students, current and modern directed me to the discussion of this topic on your Blog, and I have read with quite some interest how it has developed. From one of my student's remarks on recent Blog entries here, it appears you are writing a more detail-rich book on this highly relevant topic, and I thus seek to provide more rigorous information that corroborates and expands upon what you and your bloggers, apparently many attorneys themselves, have expressed.

To give a summary up-front what I will elaborate below, you are correct in that the divorce law and general family law picture in the US and Anglo world more broadly has become perilously distorted and corrupted by extreme ideology, to the point that marriage and family formation in the Anglo world in general, and America in particular, entail horrific financial and social risks that make them unviable options for any spouse with a good career, assets, children or indeed anything to lose. Family courts now are indeed quite "misandrist" and deleterious to men, and in particular to white (Caucasian) and Asian men as your Bloggers have noticed, due to something called "conflict theory" which I will explain below. But they are also quite harmful to family-oriented and professional women, and families above all, as I will also address.

I will detail why this is below, but to express it in outline form, it results from a dreadful combination of five factors which you have variously covered in previous Blog posts and comments, and which I will lay out rigorously here:

1: Anglo-Saxon (Anglo-Norman) common law and specifically, the fundamentally altered form of common law that has become dominant since the start of the 20th century due to critical philosophic and theoretic changes to its central elements, from prominent mostly American jurists in the century.
2: Conflict theory, the theoretic foundation of what you all generally recognize as political correctness, cultural marxism, critical theory and other modern sociologic thought systems that base themselves in an ideology hostile to the West and its traditionally dominant cultural and ethnic groups.
3: Shameless predatory profiteering and rent seeker behavior grossly corrupting the US/Anglo divorce and family courts, a manner of crony capitalistic perversion that has also become perversely wedded to the cultural marxist side of things and drives many of its distorting extremes.
4: Absolute failure of the legal education system, particularly for future judges, to convey the realities of income instability and "breadwinning" in the modern economy compared to the 1970's, a criticism that many of us in law school faculties have launched to reform curricula, to no avail.
5: The broader unique cultural milieu of the Anglo world which leaves it vulnerable to strange puritanic excesses and public shaming tendencies, thus "metoo" in its extreme forms. This appears to be a topic you have already covered in more detail.

Expatriation out of the Anglo world, as you have said, genuinely is the only remaining option for marriage and family, because as I will explain below, the perversion of the common law at its heart CANNOT be reformed in the short or long term given predominating orthodoxies in legal thinking and training—the common law cannot be "reformed" by legislative statute or even Constitutional amendment, is effectively unchecked by popular will or democratic constraints and in many ways transcends the

Constitution itself. You most leave and go abroad, and in my career working in global corporate law before becoming a professor, I've come to know the legal and social circumstances across many continents. Job opportunities and some cultural similarity are of course major considerations for expatriation, and here is the one bit of good news: expatriation for family formation will work almost anywhere if you move to a functioning society with a civil law system. Thus dozens of quality, advanced countries, mostly Western or South American, also in East, S.E. and parts of South Asia if you have Asian ancestry, in essence anywhere colored blue or purple (or up to a point yellow, as I'll explain) on this often cited map:

https://upload.wikimedia.org/wikipedia/commons/thumb/9/92/Map_of_the_Legal_systems_of_the_world_%28en%29.png/300px-Map_of_the_Legal_systems_of_the_world_%28en%29.png

The more intelligent, forward-thinking civil law-based family law systems are available throughout the world, and most are first-world, or very advanced yet inexpensive second world nations: continental, central and eastern Europe, that is both western Europe—ex. France, Germany, Scandinavia, Spain and Italy—and central or eastern European ex. Poland, Austria, Hungary, Russia, Ukraine, Greece and Slovakia, advanced Central and South American countries and not only Chile, Uruguay and Argentina but also large portions of Brazil, Colombia, Ecuador, Panama, Costa Rica and even Nicaragua, as well as much of eastern Asia that is Japan, Taiwan, Korea, ironically Hong Kong and Singapore despite their British history, China—which is now quite first-world yet inexpensive in its major population centers—and even much of southeast Asia, and surprisingly, parts of India and the Subcontinent where the traditional or statutory law trumps the British-imposed common law, with options depending on your industry and language ability. (I don't know about Israel specifically but if, as your Bloggers say, it has adopted the Anglo common law standard de facto, that is a tragedy and not a place a family oriented person should move to.)

Before getting into more specifics of what I mean by the "new common law" from the 20th century, which is the source of so much of the distortion and corruption that dominates US/Anglo family courts, I wanted to burst one common delusion that many young American and Canadian men have, and men in Anglo countries as a whole, as well as some successful professional and/or just family-oriented young women also in the US and Anglo world more generally, who aspire to families. It is about why you absolutely must not even contemplate marriage or family formation in the Anglo world anymore, for your own sake and even more for that of your future family. Having been reared in a rural and traditionally religious part of the United States where people married early, along with mentoring many hot shot young attorneys raking in big bucks and seeing themselves atop the world, I have encountered a great number of young men in particular who disregard our advice on the necessity of expatriation from the US and the Anglo realm generally speaking, to marry and start their families. The response I hear all the time: they claim that they and their relationships are special, they'll buck the trend of high US divorce and broken families. If you're thinking of doing this, DON'T.

What you may not understand especially if young, and which it took even seasoned and successful law profs like myself and fellow faculty decades to appreciate, is that the family law system throughout the Anglo world is thoroughly stacked against you: it is DESIGNED to ruin you and extract every last penny from you financially, and reduce you emotionally. This is a feature, as my computer-oriented colleagues at the uni would say, not a bug. Remember, even if you have the proverbial perfect marriage, perfect friendship and perfect spouse on the day of your wedding, your relationship 10 let alone 20 years later will be with a person quite a ways different from the one you walk down the aisle with.

Hopefully the two of you will still love, respect and want to be with each other, but in the event that this future unknown doesn't work out for you—and statistically, in light of Anglo divorce rates, it likely won't if we're being honest—you don't want to face ruin and the horrors of poverty and de facto slavery in an Anglo country which increasingly is the norm for a bread-winning spouse after divorce. Remember, a spouse and especially a wife in the Anglo world can file for divorce for even trivial reasons, and then make enormous claims on your finances and estate while seizing your children.

So yes, you may "buck the trend" and have a happy marriage and family in the US or another Anglo country. For a while. But every single future day of your marriage, the built-in corruption of the Anglo common law-based divorce court system will bring you closer and closer to failure, and if you have assets and earning potential both present and future to take, they will likely be taken from you. I do not exaggerate one slight bit when I say that a major proportion of the US GDP is from the booming "business" of divorce and all the assets that are seized and change hands, with wealth extracted from true earners and producers (usually husbands, in business or professional fields) and handed to profligate ex-spouses, the courts, municipalities and state funds themselves. A number of my ex-students have become divorce court judges, many others divorce attorneys, and they're among the most highly paid of the US legal profession—a Faustian bargain, as I've seen how they're corrupted by their "trade" and the damage to society it causes.

You must understand that no matter how happy and stable your marriage in any part of the Anglo world may at first appear, the often subtle cultural imperatives to divorce will ring louder in your spouse's ears, the gossip will grow louder, the vulture-like circling of divorce attorney profiteers will reach your spouse, and eventually the prospect of windfalls from the process will bring your marriage, and disaster for you, closer and closer to the brink.

You may be a very special man, and your relationship may be something very extraordinary. But what too many young men in America and the Anglo world don't appreciate, is that they are up against a system designed for their marriage to fail, and to profiteer at their expense. Precise divorce stats are debated since the prospective and retrospective studies usually cut-off at 20 to 30 years, but some of the worst divorces happen after that, and some research in the legal literature suggests it may reach somewhere in range of 55-65%, with alimony costs often crushing for that long a marriage, and child support devastating for shorter ones. The statistics are even grimmer because remember, a growing proportion of Americans, Canadians and other Anglo country citizens elect not to marry anymore, the ones who do are a self-selected sub-set who are considered "marriageable", more affluent and still believe in the institution of marriage. Yet even among that more "pro-marriage" and "selected for success" sub-set, divorce rates in Anglo countries are horrifyingly high!

The shockingly high divorce rate in the Anglo world, even in light of the significant pre-selection and self-selection of couples marrying when they, supposedly, have a higher rate of success and believe in the institution, should alarm you all the more when you think about why this is. It is a dreadful reminder, as I said before, that the Anglo common law-based family law system is DESIGNED to break your marriage and bring you to ruin, to satisfy the ideological PC extremes to which the legal profession and judges (who make the common law) are more-and-more being steered, and the lusting for profits of the divorce courts and attorneys. Out of YOUR pocket, no less. In fact, the more responsible and upstanding a citizen you are, and the more skilled, and the more you earn and save, then the better a target you'll be for the voraciously predatory nature of the US family courts, to the point you'll even face prison time if your financial fortunes change and child and/or spousal support payments become excessive. In theory divorce court judges are supposed to reduce your support burdens—in practice, more-and-more they don't, and it is true, once high-earning professionals can and are sent to American prisons after a divorce when their finances suffer an unexpected hit.

All incentives of Anglo family law and the associated Anglo culture now point in the direction of encouraging broken families, there's simply too much money to be made from divorce to discourage it, and too many ideological scores to be satisfied with it. Already we can see a polar opposite in comparison to the globe outside the Anglo world, where societies have intelligently walled off divorce as a profit-making center, removed incentives for it and—through culture, civil law and other factors—removed the ideological as well as the financial drive to promote divorce and the financial ruination that accompanies it in the Anglo world. In short you can be the perfect husband (or wife, in some cases): a high earner, good parent, helping around the house, and the chances are, it's still going to fall apart for you. Because that is what the American family law system is now designed to do to you and your family: to make it fall apart, for both ideologic and profit-driven reasons.

Such was the case with my son and his marriage. He was the proverbial "perfect husband" according to PC/NYT "new man" standards. He worked very hard on the job, earning excellent money that kept his wife and kids in comfort and even luxury. Yet he truly loved them, took good care of his family, went out to parks and restaurants, and cleaned up and did chores at home even though he was exhausted from work. His wife didn't have to work but he didn't prohibit her, encouraging her to pursue fun side jobs that she did well. His wife even feted him in "no better hubby" posts on Facebook and with her friends. Until, as many wives do, she simply got bored. He was "too good". Again, as many women do, she wanted some danger and action, and while my husband even adapted somewhat to get involved in interesting activities, there was only so much he could do with his working schedule.

Now here, again, is where the corruption and perversion of the Anglo family law system come into sharp contrast with the calmer, saner policies in the rest of the world. What happened to my son's wife isn't pleasant to talk about, but it's also very common. Just the nature of the human beast, especially married women—as even my own long-married wife will admit (I'm one of the very few lucky ones to never face separation or divorce)--to crave the new, unknown and excited. And so she began having clandestine relations with other men. When I found out, I was upset, but not angry with my daughter-in-law, as I said I've seen enough across the world to know this is simply human beings being human beings.

But outside the Anglo world, the urges would be quenched more sensibly and discreetly. Since a wife. or a husband, has no prospect of profiting from divorce, and since there is no ideology or legal structure, that is no Anglo common law, to promote and institutionalize divorce, a woman has nothing to gain from breaking up the marriage whenever she wants to "try something new".

A straying or dissatisfied wife outside the Anglo world will possibly sleep with the muscleman washing her car at times, take on a secret identity or even try an open relationship or swinging. (This is reasonably common in Europe and some portions of South America to ease relationship tension, as they are less puritanic in culture and seem able to grasp and hold to a bigger picture.) But the part that matters, is that the marriage will stay intact despite the straying, because the woman, the lawyers and the courts have no profit incentive to encourage it. And if it does happen, she will still need to take responsibility and become an earner, which fortunately, those societies also provide an assist for, in the interest of making sure everyone comes out OK. Custody, for the most part, stays a shared proposition. So whether the husband is "too perfect" (as my son supposedly was) or "far too imperfect" (which men in particular are stigmatized as in Anglo societies), divorce outside of the Anglo world happens less often and is much more humane and restrained. Particularly so in Europe (excluding Britain) and Central and South American countries that have largely been shaped by French, Spanish, Portuguese, German and Italian civil law customs and culture.

Sadly, this was not the case for my son in the United States of America, and the perversions of Anglo common law make it easy to guess what happened next. His wife did file for divorce, took more than a decade of assets he'd carefully saved, pillaged the kids' college fund, took the house, took the kids, the family van and then, despite the year to year variation in my son's earning power, reached a judgment to demand exorbitant child support— more for her than the kids—and then alimony support on top, essentially permanent. My son was, of course, devastated. And in many lean years, his mother and I had to lend him money to keep him from facing possible prison time for contempt. He was able to eventually arrange a different settlement for a lump-sum payment. After which he expatriated, first to Chile, a great country to set up in, and subsequently part of the year in Germany with his new German-Chilean wife and child.

But the lesson here is how horribly corrupted and perverted the Anglo divorce law structure has become. Despite the terrible ways my daughter-in-law hurt my son, she was never evil or malicious. She was simply weak emotionally, as unfortunately, far too many pampered wives are or become. And outside the Anglo world, she would have sowed her wild oats but stayed in the marriage. But in the Anglo world, she brought ruin to my son and her family. Above all, just because she could, and because that's what the corrupted common law-based Anglo family law system is designed to do, with profiteers in the system encouraging her every step of the way. Beyond the important cultural factors on the side, civil law countries don't have these horrible perversions of family law because the civil law makes them impossible. (For a sense of the emotional toll of Anglo divorce, here are a dozen men echoing many of the things my son said, particularly #5: "I was a resource, not a person".

www.huffingtonpost.com/2014/10/16/divorce-confessions_n_5999050.html Such is it for divorcees in the Anglo world, particularly white and Asian men with assets and a work ethic.)

Here is a metaphor, one my more mechanic-oriented other son related to me. If you get married in an Anglo country, you are metaphorically walking home every day to a home that has a loaded gun behind the front door with a trigger slightly pulled by a rubber band under gentle tension, and that would go off with accumulated pulls or a major vibration. On any given day, the chances of that gun going off and striking you are very small. But add up all the days together, and the risk becomes horrifically high that the gun will go off and you will be shot opening the door. Common sense would tell you, the solution is not to keep the loaded gun at your door, happily sighing in relief that it hasn't gone off yet or tuning out the real danger because it's small on any given day. This is a solid metaphor for the risk from marriage and family formation in the common-law US and Anglo world, small on any given day, but enormous when considered over years, and horribly devastating and bankrupting to you when it does happen. Instead, common sense says the solution would be to remove the loaded gun entirely from your front door. That is what expatriating to a civil law country, outside the Anglo world provides you. It removes the loaded gun as a threat, as I well detail below.

1: Now for the point by point, starting with a clarification on just why the Anglo common law in its post-20th century form, wreaks such havoc on families and ruins so many in crippling divorces, with far more than half of Anglo marriages falling apart.

The essence of what Mr. Kshatriya and the Blog contributors have discovered here is correct: that is that the Anglo common law system confers enormous power to the judiciary in notable contrast to civil law systems, which are governed more by statutes and broader democratic and popular will. This is what the common law, in both its pre and post-20th century forms, means at its heart: the judges' cumulative decisions and opinions create concrete, enforceable mandates of law in conjunction with, and often beyond anything contained in statutes and written constitutions. There was a time early in my career when I would have touted the advantages of the common law, at least for certain areas such as property negotiations and riparian rights (water management). But after learning and comparing the common and civil law systems, and in particular seeing how the divorce process has otherwise devastated the finances and emotional state of my once prosperous and happy son, I have come to conclude that there are certain areas where the modern form of the common law has become dangerous, family law being the most prominent.

And unfortunately as I will explain below, the dysfunction and corruption of Anglo-American common law in the divorce court context has reached dangerous proportions with no effective remedy to correct it. This, in practice, is at the foundation of why expatriation from the Anglo world has become unavoidable for marriage and family formation. As I indicated at the start, more broadly there is no realistic prospect in the short or long term of reforming the structures, cultural influences and legal decision-making patterns that have forged modern Anglo-Saxon family law. Not even a Constitutional Amendment, or any other sort of reform driven by popular impulses or collective action. Here is why.

The essence and power of the common law foundation of Anglo family law, in key regards, transcend even the U.S. Constitution itself (and its counterparts across the traditionally English-speaking nation states). You'd have to reform the basic substance and modern interpretations of the common law to achieve substantive change in the dreadful career, finance and family-wrecking dark heart of Anglo family law.

No statutory change or act transformed into a law, whether by a legislative body or a referendum, could repeal or reform it because the essence of common law resides in the collective thought and inclinations of judges, who are empowered to effectively make the law quite unlike magistrates in civil law societies and, in some areas, can operate effectively unconstrained by popular will or democratic wishes.

So where does the intellectual basis of judge-created common law come from? The answer, of course, is largely in law schools and the elite thought of the US and wider Anglo academia. Future judges in US and other Anglo family courts are schooled and molded by the elite doctrines of what is taught in law schools, including the seminars and proliferating academic publications dedicated to conflict theory, and cultural marxist and 3rd wave feminist theory in particular, part of their broader takeover of academia in the Anglo world. Thus these doctrines, regarded as extreme minority opinions and fringe ideologies to the American and wider Anglo general public are, horrifically, the intellectual core of the thinking that molds Anglo judges that have all but complete power over you and your financial survival in a divorce court. Unless you change this elite academic culture, which is now virtually impossible, you cannot change the dark heart of American family law and common law in general.

The US Constitution, along with its state and provincial counterparts in the US and wider Anglo world, is silent or flexibly interpretable enough in key areas that the common law system has great latitude, and family law is regrettably one of them. There is thus no popular brake on the common law-based family court excesses—the change can only occur at the level of elite culture and the elite training of attorneys and future judges at law schools. Thus the grim conclusion: since common law-based family law in practice is made by judges, and also in practice often supersedes statutory law, the victimized broader Anglo populace is all but powerless to correct the excesses or protect themselves. This in fact is a valuable lesson for law students and legal scholars, because it gets at the historical heart of how and why civil law diverged so sharply from common law: even before democratic government became the norm,

The forefathers of civil law in the Roman Republic recognized it was dangerous to empower a permanent and aloof elite, such as judges in courts shaped by abstract legal and societal theories, with crafting laws beyond popular scrutiny. Even though the Roman Senate was itself elitist and not much guided by the broader plebeian population, nevertheless the earliest civil law jurists understood that judges' opinions in themselves should not have legal force. Instead the deliberative bodies of a republic (or a democracy in the Greek model), which at least had the ear to the ground of popular concerns, should be the places where law was very carefully crafted. This is why civil law moderates judges' effective lawmaking power, and a natural, obvious ethical proposition of the populace—divorce is bad, it should be discouraged and not made profitable—translates so easily into family law and real legal decisions in the civil law world. And this is also why the worsening nightmare of family courts, and the predatory "business of divorce" in the US and wider Anglo world, are resistant to popular reform, and have no effective remedy. It would essentially take a complete collapse and restructuring of societal institutions, or even a Syria-like civil war that struck universities and higher educational institutions themselves, to bring about a chance in the elite bubbles that, in practice, forge Anglo common law and thus family law.

On this point, I also wanted to make a clarification regarding some confusion my students have brought up on this topic. Any L1 student starting up at a law school learns early about the principle of stare decisis, Latin for "let the decision stand", and thus some of my students have been confused by the very accurate points you and your contributors have been making even before my elaboration above. How can judges in the United States, Canada, Britain and other nations classed as "Anglo" have so much power to make arbitrary decisions, or incorporate radical Anglo-American feminist theories (which are indeed thoroughly misandrist by contrast to the rest of the West), when stare decisis supposedly requires them to follow precedent? Doesn't stare decisis mean they should follow older and long-established customs, including prior judges' rulings, that are less misandrist?

The answer is no, and Mr. Kshatriya and his contributors are indeed right that judges in divorce courts have rather excessive powers particularly in the realms of monetary imputation and purview of a spouse's finances, and that alimony and child support payments can and regularly are harshly assessed. The answer to this confusion is that the common law since the 20th century has been quite different to what it was before. Most of you (referring to my law school students) have, or soon will encounter the treatises of critical 20th-c jurists such as Frankfurter, Holmes, Brandeis, Dworkin, Fuller, Wechsler and Bickel. In a gradual process of great significance, these legal scholars (several of them Supreme Court justices) re-interpreted the very concept of common law, to make it more flexible and responsive to modern scholarship. Since then, stare decisis and precedent don't mean what they did in the 18th or 19th centuries. Although prior case law remains greatly important in guiding future decisions, the evolution of these scholars' ideas in practice has meant that judges today have a lot of latitude in setting precedent based on prevailing social theories. Their ideas became so influential that they've now come to dominate the concept of common law across the English-speaking world, not just in the United States.

I don't in any form want to blame these scholars for the latter day corruption of common law, as they did not have the modern madness of American family courts in mind, and at least in the medium-term, their thoughts on the common law did help to make it more responsive to the fluid challenges of contract law and technological advance.

Unfortunately, once the common law's previous restraints had been cut-- restraints which predate the US Constitution itself, and based on custom instead of statute-- the dangerous perversions of the Frankfurt-School (cultural marxism and ideas of "political correctness" on university campuses) and in particular, the harshly adversarial ideas of 3rd wave feminism were able to exert themselves through this "new form of common law". And it has become a horribly destructive force in the family courts of the English-speaking world. In effect, "precedent" can be almost arbitrarily set by family court judges on the basis of what are considered to be "commonly agreed upon principles" in legal elite professional circles but which, in reality, are often little more than radical feminist theories (the Anglo-Saxon versions of them) that have been arbitrarily lent prestige by their appearance in academic journals. Moreover, since so much of academia in the USA, Canada and Britain (mainland Europe and Latin America have a different university structure) has indeed been taken over by such 3rd wave feminist and cultural marxist radicals who are on the payroll as serious "scholars", result is that common law precedent in Anglo-American courts, which affects all of us, is in effect being "set by precedents" derived from the most radical, misandrist theories of these sorts of feminist academic journals.

This includes law schools, where "feminist legal interpretations" and others based in the conflict-theory approaches of the cultural marxists (not to be confused with traditional economic marxists, who often disagree quite bitterly with the "cultural" form) powerfully and concretely influence the pool of "acceptable" legal thought from which judges in actual courts draw their citations and make their decisions. It is an extremely undemocratic process that defies popular will and common sense, but this is the inherent danger with modern common law-- it allows, in effect, law and policy (which by definition in common law, are set to a large degree by judicial decisions and opinions) to be set by tiny legal elites with, often, extreme ideological biases shaped by radical-leaning Anglo feminist journals in universities and law schools. And in fact, the readers and supporters of such journals are also the ones most likely to be drawn to family law.

So in practice, US and broadly Anglo-American family courts get the worst of both of these worlds. The "flexible precedent" approach means that Anglo family court judges are able to reject traditional standards of fairness or impartiality in favor of openly misandrist and conflict theory driven lines of thought as are advanced in legal feminist journals and cultural marxist literature in general. And yet, the stare decisis tradition of common law, at least in areas that don't have a vocal ideological elite base pushing a new series of precedents (such as 3rd wave feminism), means that the worst of the old precedents do stay in place and don't adapt to the modern world. This explains the bizarre contradiction of American divorce courts, where women are considered powerful and independent and men are often presumed in advance to be deadbeats, yet at same time, women are "helpless and innocent" enough to be awarded lifetime alimony, outsize levels of child support (that all too often just support a lavish lifestyle) and where the bizarre standard of "maintaining the quality of life before divorce" is still followed.

This latter standard is an outrage for a modern country, as it encourages what's popularly known as "gold digging"-- a husband who is well-off and responsible is perversely hit much harder in divorce than a true deadbeat, since his higher earnings and potential earnings, from skill and education, make him liable to be drained of millions of dollars, yet if his earnings or business success falter in a given year, the imputation is not adjusted, and he can be sent to prison. This is an old and dangerous relic of the Anglo-Saxon legal tradition, which the rest of the world has jettisoned or never had in the first place—profiteering of any sort from divorce is strictly taboo elsewhere, and child support and alimony (if it even exists, which it largely does not elsewhere) are deliberately set very low to discourage divorce filings, to encourage d divorcing spouse to find productive work and to encourage successful and skilled spouses to marry without fear of financial calamity.

Yet the modern form of Anglo common law has installed this perverse, obsolete, contradictory practice into standard family court decision-making at the same time that Anglo-American 3rd wave feminist theories assert that those same high-earning men are reviled as deadbeats and worthless members of society, incapable of custody of kids and unworthy of respect from society or the courts. This is also why US family courts too often, in practice, are quite hostile to the well-being of actual families and regard family-oriented women with such contempt. They are merely reflecting the doctrines of 3rd wave feminist academic theories that dominate the legal journals, seminars and lectures where Anglo and especially American law students learn what are "acceptable grounds" in crafting decisions.

Adding insult to injury, in the minority of Anglo jurisdictions where family judges are bound by expressly written statutes in deciding asset division and maintenance payments (Britain in particular is notorious for this), these statutes almost without any exceptions presume fault and financial responsibility on the man's shoulders, whatever the actual circumstances. In fact I should stress here, I do not have a problem with judges using their reflection and sense of individual judgment to consider individual circumstances and special cases. I do not agree with statutory "3 strikes" laws that make punitive demands devoid of considering circumstances. But such fairness and rationality are not what modern Anglo common law instills in family court judges. The power of conflict theory and cultural marxism in Anglo legal scholarship means the weight of precedent creates an anti-family, anti-male and anti- "good man and woman" standard de facto for both statutes and case law. It is thus that the decision process for divorce cases in any Anglo country will almost always follow the perverse demands of the cultural marxist orthodoxy.

Result? The latitude of judges in common law systems, together with the conflict-theory basis of their doctrines, makes their power to impute financial obligations on financially successful spouses, particularly ex-husbands and fathers, dangerous in any real world context. Yet, as if the irony couldn't get any more bitter, even the minority of statute-driven family courts in the Anglo world are still stacked against you. In such cases, even the small potential relief of having a more reasonable family court judge, not steeped in the family-wrecking doctrines of concept theory, is almost always nullified by the statutory demands of custody assignment, child support and spousal maintenance. To contrast, judges in the civil law world do retain power to apply rationality and humane judgment on a case by case basis. Civil law does not mean judges have their hands tied, it simply means that they cannot, and thus have no incentive, to legislate from the bench. Court decisions do not become citable precedents in case law. Thus it is that legal decision-making is based on the more democratic and rational foundation of carefully considered statutory law with input from the people, as opposed to judicial elites in the Anglo world who have their legal thought shaped by the radical, irrational, misandrist and anti-Western conflict ideologies that mold them in law school.

The very fact that judges' decisions in civil law countries do not figure into the weight of precedent—with judges having no power to "make law" through case law—thus means that judges in Europe, South America, most of Asia and the rest of the civil law world are freed up to be more humane and more reasonably consider realities as they are on the ground in family law cases. By way of hard contrast, and as you have correctly realized Mr. Kshatriya, the very power that divorce court and general family court judges in the United States and Anglo common law world possess, in fact makes divorce law and family law judges a kind of priestly, undemocratic elite in the Anglo world. They need not be rational or respond to realities as they are on the ground, and their power to make law means they can indulge the radical ideologies and orthodoxies of "right thought" and political correctness in law school to create heavily misandrist and anti-family law through their written opinions. This is why the takeover of academia by the Frankfurt-School and its anti-Western, anti-family ideologies of conflict theory and cultural marxism are so dangerous. Again as you have observed, the common law of the Anglo world gives them the power to translate their radical ideologies into concrete law-making and case precedents that are doing more damage to family formation in the Anglo world than any other factor. To see why, I need to explain a bit more what conflict theory, the heart of cultural marxism, is within the family law context.

2: The cultural marxists and critical and conflict theorists know how the judicial law-making power of Anglo common law suits their purposes in the world of family law. As their goal is the weakening of the West and its institutions and families, mainly those for white American and Asian-American communities with more stable family structures that help maintain a functioning society, the Anglo common law system gives the Frankfurt-School cultural marxists a weapon to convert their radical, dangerous anti-Western ideologies into concrete practice that has terrible real world consequences. So it is little surprise that the Frankfurt-School ideologues have made such a co-ordinated effort since the 1960's to take control of law schools and the faculties and institutions of US and Anglo academia in general. By shaping what becomes "right thought" in academia and law schools, they have gained the power to decide the thinking of the "elites" in legal scholarship, just as their general hold on academia has helped to shape a mass media culture that stigmatizes white and Asian-Americans and their counterparts across and about the Anglo world. Demanding the decision-makers of these societies swamp themselves into cultural collapse with mass immigration from the 3rd world or suffer the career ruin of being tagged "racist".

The ugly twin to this effect in law schools is the cultural marxists' takeover of legal institutions and journals that have "normalized" misandry as well as hatred of families, responsible and good-earning fathers and mothers, and in general spouses who make actual good mothers and fathers, They are the ones who suffer the most in the perverse world of American and Anglo family courts, and that's no accident—our law schools, under cultural marxist influence and empowered by the judicial precedent-making of Anglo common law, have deliberately shaped elite legal thinking to reflect the anti-Western, anti-family orientation of the Frankfurt-School and the disgusting alliance of the anti-Western left with the neoliberal, family-hating, open borders and "business globalist" right (as opposed to segments on both left and right that value families, communities and tradition). Thus the agony that good parents and spouses, especially good husbands and fathers of white and Asian-American stock, routinely suffer in divorce court. They are the "enemies" in the conflict theory model of the world as put forth by the Frankfurt-School, since their family formation is the very bedrock of the US, Canada and other Anglo countries as Western societies. That is why they must be broken.

It is no exaggeration to take note that Anglo common law in the realm of family law and divorce, is the most powerful gift that cultural marxists have been handed in their drive to bring down Western societies, as it allows them to directly translate their conflict theory ideologies into actual case precedent that has the force of law across the Anglo world. Citizens of Anglo societies, especially productive family-oriented white and Asian citizens targeted as "the enemy", are punished harshly in Anglo family courts with unreasonable and financially wrecking child and spousal support imputations that in reality, are also massive wealth transfers to the predatory and disgusting family court monster itself (both the lawyers and the court and state, as I'll get into).

Thus is it that good families and men in particular in the Anglo world, are perversely forced to pay for the very state instruments and predatory financial interests as I'll get to below, that are engaged in a subtle but full scale war to make family formation too dangerous to consider in the Anglo world. A ripple effect and intentional one at that, is that good, intelligent, educated and high earning men, especially, are discouraged from starting families and drift into MGTOW. Which is understandable, except that of course it leads to a collapse in the birthrate and overall fertility of the educated, and particularly white and Asian segments of society. It also weakens the fabric of society in classic "idiocracy" fashion by discouraging the most responsible segments of society from procreating, and giving a perverse advantage to the irresponsible, to those with nothing to lose and especially, those from foreign 3rd world cultures imported to the Anglo world to displace the (mainly) educated and skilled white and Asian-American segments that are forced to subsidize their own demise.

To better understand this, pick up a biography book at some point and read about the great inventors, scientists, composers, thinkers, leaders and poets from 3 centuries ago, in the West and other parts of the world. What you will find unsurprisingly, is that they were disproportionately the products of strong families with educated and intellectually driven parents. This does not mean that such families were perfect of course, there was plenty of infidelity and even polygamy and polyandry in many of these families, parents and spouses messed up then just like today. But the combination of community and society incentives meant that people had their eye on the bigger picture, they would get past such stumbles and incentives, financial and community, were made to ensure that educated and skilled people would be encouraged to start families and raise many children.

The Frankfurt-School founders were well aware of this fact and they set out, with deliberate plan in mind, to create institutions in the West to remove incentives for educated and skilled people to start families, and to penalize them financially and in other ways, if they did. Not only does the fertility rate of the targeted communities drop as a result, but the quality of the Western societies targeted is also relentlessly worn down in a vicious cycle. The motivated, high-achieving people that do great things and help a society take pride in itself, in effect are prevented from being born. Thus making the targeted society more vulnerable to the manipulations and insidious undermining of the Frankfurt-School ideologues and less able to see the big picture of the ideologies that are damaging them.

The main ideological product of the Frankfurt-School founders' anti-Western program is what has become called conflict theory, that overlaps closely with what is popularly known as cultural marxism, political correctness, critical theory, white privilege theory, multiculturalism and the "diversity" obsession of Anglo academia and media. Including diversity officers and administrators who are paid quite handsomely for their work in shaming and weakening the fabric of their host societies while our students are buried deeper in debt from their tuition.

This is one of the advantages of becoming a professor, something I did not realize while working privately before that. To a reasonable, fair minded person, the extreme cultural marxism that results from conflict theory would appear to be simple madness, but I've been to enough campus events and lectures, and read enough journals both legal and outside the law field, to see how the theorists of the Frankfurt-School in its modern form operate. They'll try to deny there's a common ideological link to their constant rants about white guilt, white privilege and the war against the oppression of the West—such irony as the cultural marxists are the privileged elite of academia living high on their indebted students' forced "contributions". But regardless, what truly makes the Anglo world so uniquely vulnerable to the doctrines of conflict theory, is the practical law-making power through Anglo common law that's given to judges molded by the "right thought" doctrines of conflict theory in the law schools. The shame factor of the puritanic strain in Anglo society makes their job easier, as I'll get to.

To make things worse, great and sustained demographic damage is done to family formation and retention by the anti-Western cultural poison of conflict theory, which casts solid families and especially white and Asian-American families as "the enemy". There has been a lot of press on the way the birthrate in the US has been dropping sharply, but look at a graph and you'll see, the fertility for the white and Asian segments has been in a steady fall since the 1970's. Such drops are not unusual in the developed world and they happen in both Western and non-Western societies. But Anglo societies are also unique here in their vulnerability to the cheap labor demands of neoliberal economists, which like their cultural marxist counterparts in academia, undermine the heart of Anglo society by in effect, demanding it must be replaced for the sake of "economic growth", "sustaining the state" or other facile claims. This too feeds the vicious cycle of white (and Asian) demographic decline, as mass immigration from hostile 3rd world cultures compounds the financial dangers of marriage and family formation in the cultural marxism-dominated world of Anglo family law, pushing down wages and value of work, making it even harder for both skilled and unskilled workers to start families.

This is what gives apostles of cultural marxism, foreign policy neoconservatism and economic-based neoliberalism in the US Congress, such as Charles Schumer and Marco Rubio, and their counterparts such as Justin Trudeau elsewhere in the Anglo world, the excuse they need to claim they need mass Muslim and other 3rd world immigration to prop up Soc. Security since "the natives won't start families for some reason". Even though, of course, they know the true reason: their cultural marxist and globalist neoliberal circles are what created the problem, deliberately. Also take note, the same de facto law-making powers that Anglo common law

338

hands to family court judges, also applies to the judges who, by example, overturn Trump's immigration restrictions and thus force mass immigration upon the US and the rest of the Anglo world. Again immune to the public's wishes and shaped only by the elite "right thought" of US law schools and PC trends. The new-comers have larger families as they're less culturally affected by the cultural marxists' war on families in the Anglo world. And so now you can connect all the dots—Anglo common law in its family law form is the greatest cultural wrecking ball for family formation and thus any basis for a Western society in the Anglo world, opening the door for globalist politicians and judges to impose open borders and mass migration, to displace the Western population and culture in these countries.

The civil law of the rest of the world, by stripping judges of the power to make law through the elite thinking of their court opinions, gives rise to a powerful and important shield for society from the dangerous anti-Western ideologies that the Frankfurt-School has normalized in Anglo law schools, legal journals and general academia. The very different, more practical focused structuring of European and South American and Asian universities, is one factor blocking the cultural marxist ideologues from indoctrinating family law judges in the family-wrecking anti-Western doctrines that hold power in the Anglo world. But more important, the presence of the civil law barrier means that the misandrist, anti-Western "right thought" of cultural marxist ideologues in academia and the media cannot be translated into practical force of law or weight of precedent, since judicial opinions and thus case law in the civil law world do not stand as citable law to start with. From an historical perspective, we can see the foresight of the Romans who created the civil law. In removing the power of law-making from an unaccountable elite—the judges and magistrates—whose thinking can be shaped by radical ideologies instead of the democratic constraints of statutory law, the civil law places a brake on law and courts as a whole from straying into excessively ideological territory, making them more reasonable and consistent with the will and needs of the people and the families that form the bedrock of the community.

And when get back to family courts in civil law countries, we can also see why they produce decisions that are more limited, fairer, common sense and in tune with general popular understanding. It's because they are. In the civil law world—almost all of Europe, Latin America and most of Asia, as shown on the linked map above—both the judges and the makers of statutes are much more tightly bound to a body of law forged from the careful workings of generations of deliberative bodies, which are bound to the will and demands of basic fairness as voiced by the people. Extreme, conflict theory-driven elite ideologies, which so often become trendy in the bubble worlds of American and Anglo academia, are ruthlessly walled off from the legal doctrines that translate into statutes and the decision-making of magistrates. As I stated before, and even more so with the "new common law" since the 20th century, it is in practice impossible to reform the extremist ideological doctrines that shape judges' thinking and precedent-making in Anglo family courts. This is why expatriation into the civil law world is the only realistic remedy for starting a family.

I should note finally for this point, that although "conflict theory" is something of a catch all term, at its heart it represents a basic way of viewing the driving forces of society, and thus concepts of justice and fairness. It cannot be falsified or fought with evidence, and efforts to do so will lead to ostracism and loss of status and often livelihood itself. It's part of why we in the academic world, who are "red pilled" as I suppose my students like to say, still have to tiptoe when we speak up. Its very nature is also why conflict theory dangerously warps otherwise praiseworthy concepts like justice and fairness in the common law and family law in particular, and why conflict theorists and critical theorists in general have done and continue to do so much damage in the Anglo world. 3rd wave feminism, cultural Marxism, critical theory and conceptions of Britain and North America as being driven by minority races and ethnic groups, struggling against an oppressive white majority (though soon to be a minority itself in the USA and most of the Anglo world)—all of these are sub-sets of conflict theory.

It is conflict theory that helps much to explain why Anglo and especially US family courts are typically so misandrist, and why white and Asian men, as disfavored groups in the social justice hierarchy, are so hard hit. Conflict theory, originally a product of the Frankfurt-School, truly has become the dominant social doctrine of Anglo academia. And it rules law schools. Those classes that law schools feature on 3rd wave feminist theory and resisting oppression by historically dominant groups? They translate into the decision-making of the judge at your divorce court, and also of the clerks and assistants who actually write the statutes that lawmakers in legislatures pass—or think they are passing. Divorce is financially, emotionally and socially wrecking for men in general, but particularly for those in white and Asian groups, and conflict theory explains why.

There are some additional features to this, beyond the weapon of Anglo common law itself, that can help explain why the family law situation and societal structure in the Anglo world have become so hostile. One is that residents of the Anglo world are, disproportionately, in countries where the white population is descended from settlers instead of the indigenous people, in Australia and North America. This makes them especially vulnerable to the attacks of injustice levied at the heart of conflict theory, and in a bitter irony, Britain has been swept up in the same Anglo settler guilt narratives of its former colonies, which in turn translates itself into the common law. The civil law countries of Europe and the heart of Asia in particular, in addition to the protection of the civil law itself, have the advantage that the people there are native to the land, so this essential line of conflict theory has no power there. An additional irony is that, as I indicated before, not only men but countless women and families in Anglo societies are also harshly targeted, particularly from the white and Asian groups, no matter how much we try to pretend this doctrine does not exist. It absolutely does, and it's a direct outcome of the Frankfurt-School and conflict theory doctrines.

3: On the profiteering of the "business of divorce", it appears that previous contributors have mostly covered this, and I've referenced it a good deal before. But it should be stressed here, that as responsible as the corruptions and perversions of common law-based Anglo family law have become in making family formation unviable in the Anglo world, the crippling damage of Anglo family courts would not be possible without the profiteering the system allows and encourages. It is unfortunately true, that the rich profits of divorce for attorneys, courts and even government jurisdictions that effectively have shares in the divorce profits, create a perverse and dangerous system of incentives for it. It's a major part of why divorce is so common and so utterly damaging the Anglo world, in sharp contrast to civil law countries outside the Anglo world, where it is not only far less frequent, but much less damaging and simply quieter and simpler overall.

Go up and down the list of things that differentiate the world outside the Anglo countries in the realm of divorce, and you can see the societal benefit that results from making sure that circling vultures can't profit from it. Mediation is the standard approach, couples usually have a waiting or "cool-off" period, the default in custody is sharing of child-rearing, prosperous and financially successful spouses hold on to what they have saved up (not to mention their homes and cars), alimony is minimal or (in most countries) forbidden outright, child support is leashed according to strict formulas and halted at a low maximum, the "living standard during marriage" practice leading to ludicrous alimony demands in Anglo countries is mocked and rejected, gold-digging is harshly scorned and legally forbidden, millionaire and especially well-off spouses are protected from major asset loss (the "playboy principle" I believe some other contributors have called it), divorcing spouses are not allowed to profit from wealthier spouses but are given social support to land on their feet... This is all made possible because divorce cannot be a source of profit in these countries.

These features are all but universal for divorce outside the Anglo world, in otherwise radically different cultural spheres. Italy, France, Spain and the Mediterranean world, Austria and Hungary, Poland and the Czech Republic, Slovakia, the Baltics, Finland and Scandinavia, Luxembourg, Belgium, Holland, all throughout South America and central America, across eastern and southeastern Asia. Even in India, Sri Lanka and Nepal, which do have some features of common law from the period when the British administered portions of their countries, the divorce system more-and-more follows the continental civil law model. This is in measure due to the civil law itself (and customary law in places like South Asia and South America). But it's also due to the economics of divorce being such a complete contrast outside the Anglo world. They disallow profit-making in the divorce process, and this not only makes it more humane and far less of a wrecking force, but also makes it happen much less. In addition as I know has been mentioned before, correctly, you cannot overcome the predatory American and Anglo family court system by importing a spouse from overseas or "marrying religiously"—so long as you are in an Anglo country, your marriage will be chipped away at by a system that is designed to make it fail, and then you will suffer disaster when the family courts step in. Expatriation, again, is unavoidable for family formation.

4: The embarrassing failure of law schools to impart knowledge on the new economic situation in the US in particular, as a way of more intelligently determining maintenance imputations. This one likely needs little elaboration, but suffice to say, this failure is at the heart of why the United States, Canada, Britain, Australia and the Anglo world in general persist in the grotesque practice of sentencing ex-spouses to prison for contempt, unheard of outside the Anglo world. My son was at recurring risk of this despite being otherwise prosperous, as are millions of American and other Anglo men after their divorces. This is partly because of the perversions of the common law system covered before, which permits such extremes in child and spousal maintenance imputations unlike civil law systems. But it's also because judges in family courts are unacceptably ignorant of real-world modern economics and even the notion of fluctuating income.

I have been far from alone among legal faculty in calling out for curricular reform to better address courses on finances in law school, perhaps because such truly useful coursework is crowded out by all the conflict theory courses that have become the norm since Frankfurt-School disciples took over US and Anglo academia. But the terrible result is that, in practice, too many judges especially in family courts are still stuck with a dangerously outdated, 1950's view of permanent, stable jobs and steady employment, with little understanding of how uncertain income can be year to year. There is little understanding of not only the gig economy, but also the waxing and waning of business profits, contracts, extra jobs and the variations in income from one year to another. This is why imputations for alimony and child maintenance in American and other family courts are often so outrageous. The judges too often truly are ignorant of the realities of varying income and the difficulties of maintaining steady employment, will often impute wildly unrealistic expectations of annual income, and then send an ex-spouse to prison when they unavoidably fall short. Again, the strict limitations in civil law countries grant another layer of protection against this, another reason why expatriation is necessary.

5: The strange puritanic side to US and Anglo culture. I believe your contributors have covered this in detail and I confess to knowing not so much about it, but from the little I do know, I believe you have a point. My take on it, the puritanic essence of so much of Anglo culture turns sex itself into something dirty and shameful, and the currents of sin and shame then join with radical conflict theory ideologies and the perversions of Anglo common law to create an environment in which otherwise successful spouses, husbands in particular, are immediately presumed to be objects of blame, guilt and undeserved punishment. I do also believe this is behind many of the "metoo" movement excesses, which incidentally have hit many US law schools recently even when the accused are innocent. It is more evidence that the 3rd wave feminism of the Anglo world, even outside the anti-Western poisoning effects of its cultural marxism links, is especially toxic and hateful. In my travels, from eastern Asia to South America, Sweden to Russia, Germany, France, Italy, yes I've met "feminists" but they're tame and even pleasant compared to the Anglo version. The feminists there just seem to want to have the freedom to do their thing, do unusual jobs and maybe be a little more sexually flirty, you don't get the misandry and hatred of the "Western oppressors"—conflict theory again—that's the norm for feminists, and what my students like to call virtue signallers or "social justice warriors" (the SJW I believe is the acronym) in Anglo societies. But it is another part of the range of factors that make the Anglo world unviable to start families in, making expatriation unavoidable.

To finish up, I would like to be more optimistic about family formation prospects in the Anglo world, as I have been reared in it. Despite its flaws, I still find much to like in some of its legal and societal doctrines. But the worsening perversions of the common law as expressed in the corrupt, family and career-wrecking family courts are such a fundamental breakdown in such a fundamental element of society, that for now, expatriation really is essential to start a family. My wife and I have even stipulated that we will support our other children's plans to marry and start families only on the condition that they expatriate, and they are already learning the languages and taking the other preliminary steps to make it happen.

When choosing your country, whatever you do, don't be distracted by ludicrous and grossly inaccurate headlines about the supposed dangers of other first world countries in the civil law world. Your chances of suffering in a terrorist attack are less than 0.01%, and quite against all the nervous wringing about demographic change, every country in Europe is 90% or more populated by the same peoples native to their countries for centuries. (If anything that is the primary challenge with expatriation, since immigration is tightly controlled in Europe—look for ancestors and contact employers especially if you have special skills, which my daughter is currently doing.) Earn money in the US and save up if you must, but think of it as a posting abroad even if you were born here, because if you want a family, it is too dangerous to attempt one here. I hope this will change, but for the reasons I went through before, this will not happen easily with common law, and will likely require radical reform.

Another advantage of civil law countries like France, Spain, Germany, Austria, Italy, Scandinavia, Asia or South America is that you need not fear financial disaster from medical illnesses, university study (as my own US law students can regrettably attest with their horrible loans) or crime, which is much lower in Europe. You'll also have more vacation time and leave to be with your kids and families there. It's worth a reminder that especially if you are an American, still caught up in the rhetoric and battles of the Cold War, that you should be careful not to confuse the social based capitalism—also called social market based capitalism or capitalism with socialist features—with cultural marxism. They are fundamentally different phenomena in every way. As I said, even the main economic marxists like Lenin and Stalin hated the cultural marxists and considered them to be decadent slobs, and economic marxists often emphasized social cohesion and strong families and communities.

But the social based capitalism of Europe and much of Asia isn't economic marxist and certainly not communist either. It's a well

346

tested and proven system to improve educational and work opportunities as well as the health of the people, and in fact it depends on strong families and communities that rational, civil law-based family law makes possible. The enemy of family formation is not the political left or the right itself, as I made allusion to above, these terms aren't specific enough and easily confuse different things. The enemy of viable Western societies is the dangerous, convenient alliance of conflict theory-based cultural marxism with immediate term, low wage obsessed big business neoliberalism, both of which for their own reasons, want to break up strong families, make them too expensive or dangerous to form, promote 3rd wave feminism and trap a society's people in social aimlessness, as an excuse to replace them demographically with hostile groups imported through mass immigration. The opposition to this sick and dangerous anti-Western alliance isn't strictly right or left in economic terms, and it certainly isn't neoliberal libertarianism or radical capitalism, both part of the problem. It is a more mixed ideology that focuses on and supports strong families and communities, opposing mass migration that would hurt the social fabric, protecting the environment and people's health, incorporating some socialist elements but also encouraging economic competitiveness, starting businesses and capitalist motivation. In practice in Europe and Asia, this social based capitalism has now become the plank of what are being called the populistic or nationalistic parties there, some with a European or Asian regional "continent-wide" philosophy that goes beyond a single nation. But regardless, the dominant and most popular parties support strong families and rational family law, support some socialist assistance to encourage mobility of the citizens, oppose mass migration and support the fruits of reasonable capitalism, all held together by the rationality of civil law tradition.

The societies you'll expatriate to are just more humane and reasonable in general, something that then spills over into the realm of family law. My faint hope for the Anglo world is that the inevitable demographic conflicts to come, fueled by the damage done by the family courts, media and the cultural marxists who have given rise to the anti-Western ideology behind them, will finally break the back of the Frankfurt-School. Because it will take nothing less to break the power of the subversive ideologies that have taken hold in Anglo-American academia and mass media as elite thought. But this will take many years to run its course, and you don't want to wait that long to start a family and get your career going. When you put everything together, you'll have better prospects in every way for your career and family to stay together in the civil law countries, better protection against financial disasters and better conditions in every other way you can think of. So start making preparations before you've started your family, even more so if you already have one.

Appendix T: Ondati <u>02 June 2018 at 04:55</u>

David Futrelle is the typical white knight moron who thinks that he'll get a free-pass for selling out other men so that the #metoo and #timesup extremists will target them rather than him. And as the anon above said, correctly, like just about everything else about the Anglosphere these days, he and all he says is inflated hot air. Same thing with the debt-inflated false economy of the US, UK and Canada which is staying a-float only due to tens of trillions of dollars in debt instead of real production, or the impression offered by the White Knight fools that they're somehow "getting some" which they're absolutely not.

In fact having known a lot of these pathetic suck-up beta male White Knight sycophants, I can all but guarantee you they're the proverbial 40 year old virgins. Because as much as so many of these sad, pathetic Millennial and Gen-Z girls pretend to buy into the metoo witch-hunt fanaticism, deep down they want a man to actually be a man and dominate. After all the most popular literature in the past 2 decades has been the 50 Shades of Grey series, which, oh so curiously hit it's peak right amidst the #metoo extremism when it went off the rails from legitimate gripes against the Weinstein style creeps and into open false accusations against decent men (and even a few women) in authority. Even to the point that many of the 3rd-wave metoo feminists like Jessica Valenti and Emily Lindin of Teen Vogue were openly tweeting that women should make up false accusations out of thin air.

Actually on that point, one ironic thing I've been seeing about these cucked White Knights is that a disproportional number of them are very educated Jewish American and Canadian men. I say ironic because you'd think these fools would realize that the "send the crocodile to eat the other guy first" appeasement of 3rd wave feminists gives them zero protection. In fact in at least some industries like entertainment, I think up to a third of the metoo attacks have been levelled at these very Jewish white knight "male feminists" who thought they'd be safe, some guilty but many apparently innocent. The idiots fail to realize that by simply bringing up the #metoo memes with their names associated, even if they express support and try to throw other less "woke" men under-the-bus, they themselves become targets for the witch hunt since the essence of the #metoo mccarthyism is the lack of any due process for the accused.

One big example, Eric Schneiderman, the NY Attorney General who's been at the forefront of many white knights within the "mainstream" sending public kisses to the metoo accusers, before getting accused himself. The same for Robert Iger of Disney, that asshole Jeff Zucker of CNN (who's been responsible for a lot of the media pushing of #metoo) and Jeff Weiner who tried to jump on board the #metoo bandwagon and encourage mentoring, before their own Twitter followers shot them down with perceptive comments:

https://twitter.com/jeffweiner/status/960914153140494336
https://www.washingtontimes.com/news/2018/feb/7/number-of-men-uncomfortable-with-mentoring-women-h/
https://twitter.com/ariannahuff/status/960902212003221504
http://fortune.com/2018/02/06/lean-in-sheryl-sandberg/

As one of my old college profs and a business starter himself told me when we met up earlier this year, "Hire a woman, hire a lawsuit!" And this was a major Obama and Hillary Clinton supporter BTW who's come to realize that in the #metoo era, the social media lynch mobs with no due process have made all women in the workplace (at least young and attractive women) effectively toxic. He's stopped hiring women for his company and will never, ever mentor one for obvious reasons. Even the "open door" policy doesn't work, 15 years down road she could make up any bullshit accusation long after there's any contemporary information and ruin the guy so that he couldn't support his family. No man with any sense is going to take that risk anymore.

And a BTW a thanks to all those expats who were posting some weeks back I guess around the time all those expat conventions were going on. I learned a lot from them and I'm now set to become an expat from the US (and Canada, where I was born) myself. I had a nagging feeling couldn't put my finger on to, even before all the #metoo mccarthyism started stinking up the air, that the crazy 3rd-wave feminism of the Anglo countries had gotten to the point of becoming societally destructive, so that basic tasks like just getting work done, dating, let alone starting a relationship, getting married and having kids while avoiding financial catastrophe from divorce, were becoming impossible. I'd known too many fellow guys, and even young women who were rational and non-crazy, become casualties of divorce and bullshit (or generally trivial, "he didn't flirt with me the right way') sexual harassment crying-wolf accusations even before #metoo.

Reading your blog and what the expat guys were saying, made me realize it was something systemically sick with the Anglo culture and society. I started taking some intermediate French courses, I'd done beginner French in H.S. and looking at expat job forums. And then just recently I landed a nice webmaster job in Lille, a beautiful city in NE France right up next to the Belgium border near Mons, a Belgian city I'll be commuting to 3 months out of the year (where my company in France has a satellite).

Funny thing is, I could do the same basic job in the US but why would I stay here when being a man, esp. a white man is like having a damn target painted on my back every day at work or on the dating scene? In the US I'd be in fear every day that a female co-worker could accuse me any-time, for any reason of sexual harassment and wreck I career I've trained a decade for. Or that if I marry here, I'll lose my home, kid and savings in a divorce like so many men hit with alimony spousal and child-support demands from the family kangaroo courts.

IOW in the US or Canada, or anyplace in the crumbling Anglosphere, I'd be unable to safely do two of the most basic things for any responsible man-- build my career and raise a family.

France and Belgium aren't paradises but like all your expat commenters were pointing out, their workplace and family laws are actually rational, maybe on due to that civil law heritage the legal experts were saying as oppose to the common law cucking of the Anglosphere.

I don't really care, all I know is that I can have a good promising career and start a family security in France-Belgium which I can't do in the Anglosphere anywhere. I earn around the same money, even more in Lille and Mons if you can handle a bit of Dutch or German, with same taxes-- don't listen to any moron saying the US is "lower-taxes", that's BS when you look at the hidden taxes like FICA/pay-roll and local. But I also get low expense health care without having to worry about going broke if I get an appendicitis and stuck in hospital, if I have to take college courses in Lille they're cheap and affordable, no student loans. And I get 6 weeks of vacation every year! I'm entrepreneurial so like a lot of people there and in Germany, I'll be using those opportunities to kick-start my own business. Which I won't have to worry about giving up in the event of divorce, unlike far too many American and Canadian men caught up in the parasitic system of divorce here.

Appendices

Made in United States
North Haven, CT
18 July 2023

39225029R00214